Life Is a Journey, Not a Race

Life Is a Journey, Not a Race

An Invitation to Pause and Ponder

S. B. Sia

RESOURCE *Publications* · Eugene, Oregon

LIFE IS A JOURNEY, NOT A RACE
An Invitation to Pause and Ponder

Copyright © 2022 S. B. Sia. All rights reserved. Except for brief quotations in critical publications or reviews, no part of this book may be reproduced in any manner without prior written permission from the publisher. Write: Permissions, Wipf and Stock Publishers, 199 W. 8th Ave., Suite 3, Eugene, OR 97401.

Resource Publications
An Imprint of Wipf and Stock Publishers
199 W. 8th Ave., Suite 3
Eugene, OR 97401

www.wipfandstock.com

PAPERBACK ISBN: 978-1-6667-3771-4
HARDCOVER ISBN: 978-1-6667-9746-6
EBOOK ISBN: 978-1-6667-9747-3

03/14/22

*To
All those who accompanied me on my life-journey,
known or unknown to me—
my sincerest gratitude*

Contents

Introduction: As We Set Off | 1

Stage One: Getting Our Bearings
1. On Our Way | 13
2. Heading Somewhere | 31

Stage Two: Surveying the Terrain
3. Pausing to Ponder | 49
4. Charting Our Route | 63

Stage Three: Making Our Way
5. As the Water Flows | 77
6. Going Away, Getting Out, Moving On | 96

Stage Four: Staying on Track
7. Tunnels, Crossroads, Detours | 115
8. Obstacles, Hurdles or Barriers? | 135

Stage Five: Taking Stock
9. Co-Travelers: Companions or Competitors? | 157
10. The Footprints We Leave, The Tracks We Carve | 182

Journey's End: Homeward-Bound! | 200

Afterword: Glancing Back, Looking Ahead | 213
Selected Bibliography | 219

Introduction
As We Set Off

As a young university student in Ireland, I had what seemed at that time the enviable opportunity to get a summer job at the Daimler-Benz factory in Sindelfingen, Germany. A group of us had traveled there knowing that there was the usual need for temporary workers to replace the regular employees who would be going on their summer holidays. It was a real bonus for us to be able to earn some money and get some experience in the "real world" away from the demands of academic life. We had also, of course, our respective plans on how to use the money afterwards! Even the idea of shift work, the prospect of the irregular hours, or the discipline of clocking in and out did not bother us—at least, so we thought when we signed up.

    I was assigned to a small team whose work was to cover a frame with canvas and then glue it to the inner door panels for the newly-built cars. Admiring the gleaming end-of-the line Mercedes-Benz cars during the orientation tour and thinking how I would be part of its assembly gave me no small thrill. It did not matter that I would not own one so long as I could tell my friends that I had a hand in its production.

    But when I ended up in the designated area of my work I glanced with dismay at the machinery in front of my workmates and me. I began to wonder how I would last the summer months. Each of the four of us, from different nationalities, sat facing one side of a four-sided machine which regularly spun. All we had to do was to pick up the designated bolts from the containers beside us and insert them into the holes in various corners of the textile-covered door panel. The machine would then spin around to the next worker, and so on until the finished product would be removed from the machine by another worker. It was an assembly line of some sorts, but at least we had individual seats.

However, the realization that this was going to go on for seven hours each shift—in relative silence and concentration—was enough to put me off. Only the thought of having that extra cash at my disposal somehow made me still want to take up the job. What would I do with the money? That would not be a problem! I had already made some plans.

Our team was under the charge of a rather robust lady who in turn was supervised by someone higher-up with whom we had no contact. All our instructions came from that lady. She was, in fact, planted somewhere else nearby but in a rather obscure part of the factory. All we could hear were the hum of the machinery and her ringing voice. In fact, it was only when she would shout the welcome word: "*Pause!*" that we noticed her at all. The machines would then grind to a halt, and the assembly line would come to an abrupt stop.

It was a relief to us: time to stretch our legs, chat momentarily, exchange news and go outside for some fresh air. But only for a few minutes. Then it was back to the work routine until we would hear her voice again for yet another "*Pause!*" ringing in our ears. These breaks were regular enough so that the seven-hour shift did not always seem so daunting after all unless one was tired or feeling out-of-sorts for whatever reason.

Those breaks from the routine were indeed necessary. One important reason was that they refreshed and set us up to continue with the work and make our target for the day. The routine was well-paced and co-ordinated. The arrangement was no doubt work-related. It had been planned to ensure efficiency.

But after a week, I learned that there was also a personal benefit to me. As I moved away from the machine to take my break, I began to appreciate that the short pause was enabling me to gather my thoughts, too. It even helped to clear my mind. I still remember being able to see how my unwritten essays would shape up—at least in my thoughts. Those breaks also made me recall childhood memories, plan letters to family and friends, envision and organize my summer travels and so on, all of which I could continue to think about when back at work. I had this brief time on my hands, and it was up to me how to use it. Yes, those "pauses" from the routine were to my benefit in a rather unexpected way. They were an added unforeseen advantage.

Introduction

After a month, I was transferred to another *Abteilung* and to a different but related-type job. I was also given my own work-table. I was chuffed. I regarded it as a promotion! All I had to do this time was glue the tips of the textile strips to the ends of the bar to which seat-belts are fixed. There was no one to be shouting out *"Pause!"* It was up to me to create those work-breaks within the seven-hour shift. That made me feel important in my own way.

I was handed my share of the work, given instructions, but basically left to my own devices. The *Werkmeister* was, of course, on hand. In the first week of this new assignment I never completed my quota. But considering my novice status, he merely smiled and encouraged me to complete whatever I could manage every day.

But I wanted to make a good impression, so I doubled my efforts the following week. Sure enough, I had become adept at gluing those textile tips so fast that I soon made up for the previous week's loss. I was reaching my quota in a relatively short period. This was when the *Werkmeister* came to me. To my amazement and amusement he urged me to take longer breaks! He explained that they could not surpass the expected number of our products because that would have a negative impact on the total amount produced by our division. That would lead to problems with the over-all production. His advice to me was *"Langsam, langsam!"* I needed to pace myself alongside the team in that division.

He said that I could and should spend much more time getting some fresh air and taking even more frequent pauses. It was a much-appreciated suggestion. From then on I would bring my weekly *Time* magazine to work—a rather inventive way to catch up on the news around the world. I was also informed that there was a reading room in the factory, and workers could avail of it. It was a fantastic arrangement which suited my purposes. Some free personal time interspersed with regular work-time! There was even a workers' cafeteria if I needed any refreshment. I had it made—I boasted to myself.

The weekend break from work was an even better bonus during that summer stint in the factory—the opportunity to travel around the country! Strapped for cash but eager to explore with the assistance of a much-consulted map of the country, I decided to try my hand at hitchhiking. It was going to be a new experience for me. I had perused the map of

Germany, had ticked off places which I wanted to visit and checked out the youth hostel where I planned to stay overnight.

Time off from the factory would see me on the road, with my right thumb out, waiting for a generous car-driver to stop. On these trips I preferred to be on my own as I felt I would have a better chance of getting a lift. Somehow, I was very lucky and successful, much to the surprise of my friends. Perhaps it was because at that time hitchhiking was considered to be an acceptable and safe mode of traveling. Not to mention that it was free—suitable for cash-starved students like me! I got to see many places in Germany, visited various sites and broadened my experiences—all of which I considered part of my over-all education.

Once I was given a lift by a racing driver! Of course, I did not know that when I got into the front passenger seat. All I noticed was that his car was a really powerful one. He mentioned to me that he liked showing his country to students like me because they were quite appreciative of being given that opportunity. I nodded in agreement. When he turned onto the Autobahn, however, it dawned on me that the lack of a speed limit there—having been notified by my generous driver about what he did for a living—would not be to my liking. He took no risks, however. Except for what I considered excessive speed, the drive would have been regarded as rather exciting.

Fortunately, he soon exited the motorway; and when he slowed down as we entered a city, I told him that I had a change of plan—somehow that place, rather than the destination I had mentioned to him at the start, looked like one that I wanted to explore on foot after all. I pointed to my much-used map. He accepted my explanation with a mischievous grin, and I thanked him for the lift. We waved goodbye to each other—much relief on my part as he once again assumed his racing-driver role.

At another time, a new and stunning car stopped in response to my hitchhiking gesture. The driver was a nice-looking middle-aged lady. She said that she was going to where my note indicated and that she would be glad to offer me a lift. I accepted graciously and gratefully. Besides, her car was a Mercedes-Benz. She was a very careful driver in a powerful car. I mentioned my summer job to her, and she was delighted to hear about it since she put a lot of confidence in the brand and make of her car. I beamed with delight. I took a quick look at the door panel and made a mental note of how important my summer job was after all.

But it was really her driving that left a lasting impression on me as she wound her way at some speed up the hill to my destination. We got there sooner than I had expected. During the drive she chatted away and talked about which places in Germany I should visit as these were steeped in history and culture. She certainly aroused my youthful curiosity and intensified my desire to visit these places.

There was also that nice middle-aged lady in Strasbourg, France, whom I met after yet another hitching trip. I had been able—although it took a couple of lifts—to cross the German-French border into that city. I was particularly keen on visiting the cathedral since I had read a lot about it, its history and significance. As I was walking around the place, carefully noting certain spots, I approached that lady for some information. She smiled and answered my question. But she did more than that. She was particularly interested in my cultural and academic background, and we had an interesting conversation as she accompanied me around the cathedral.

Before she excused herself to leave me to my own pursuits, she said that she wanted to make my visit to her city memorable. She handed me a few notes in the French currency so that I could treat myself. She must have sensed my need for some refreshment and a meal! Given the way I felt after a long, tedious hitchhiking journey, she certainly made my visit of Strasbourg more satisfying. I still look back to that incident with much gratitude.

The most memorable experience, however, which I had thumbing my way around Germany that summer, was when I met a married couple—also in another Mercedes Benz! I had been sticking out my thumb on the roadside for an hour or two but without any success. I resigned myself to accepting that this was not one of my better days in hitchhiking since previously, it took only a few minutes' wait, such was the popularity of that mode of travel then for young students.

In fact, I was about to give up, having pocketed my map reluctantly when suddenly, this car stopped. The driver rolled down the window, asked me where I wanted to go and then offered to drive me there. It was the wife who was driving since her husband, I soon learned, was hard of hearing and did not drive. But could she drive! She was very confident as she maneuvered the car on the rather busy streets and, especially on the *Autobahnen*.

But I relaxed enough to engage in conversation with them. Fortunately, I had studied German the previous summer so conversation with her was relatively smooth. She would then translate our conversation to her husband in sign language—while driving! According to her, they had spotted me earlier that morning when they were traveling in the opposite direction and were rather surprised that I was still in the same spot when they were driving back. She informed me that she was a school-teacher while her husband worked in a factory.

As the conversation continued, I could sense their natural friendliness. I told them what I was doing that summer, and they were thrilled to know that I was taking the trouble of broadening my horizons through traveling around. To my pleasant surprise, they informed me that they would be glad to take me to my lodging—"*Wir haben Urlaub jetzt!*" they explained. How fortunate I was to have met a couple with time on their hands and time for others while they were on their holiday, I told myself. If I liked, she continued, we could stop by their house first for some coffee and cake, they suggested. Given my student circumstances, I could not pass up the opportunity and immediately accepted their kind offer. Sure enough, I appreciated their hospitality—they treated me like a truly welcome guest—and I thanked them for their generosity. I got to experience local life and meet personable people.

A couple of hours later that afternoon, when I bade goodbye to them as they left my lodging—miles from where they lived—they invited me to visit them the following Sunday. They must have sensed my dilemma of a lack of transport because they offered to pick me up and bring me back afterwards. In between those times, they promised to treat me to a nice, cooked German dinner. And they certainly did!

I couldn't believe how my day had panned out after all. The tedious wait for a lift earlier that morning resulted in a fortunate turn of events in my travel. Careful planning is important in traveling, but somehow one has also to be prepared for and respond to the unexpected. Sometimes it leads to trouble, but at other times the outcome is more than favorable. Meeting that couple was one such experience. It was also a life-long lesson about people, even complete strangers.

Several decades later, I am still in touch with them. While I was a student they used to send me parcels every Christmas, probably because they knew what it was like to be strapped for cash. Since my student days have been over now for several years that welcome generosity has become instead an exchange of visits and communications, thus maintaining our contact throughout the years.

In addition to broadening my horizons, that summer taught me to some extent that the many journeys which we undertake in various forms and complexities and the experiences which we accumulate as we move around, can make a difference to the shaping of our lives, our attitudes or our expectations.

It certainly gave me a good dose of *Wanderlust* in addition! Since then I have been doing a lot of traveling, for personal and professional reasons, and seeing the world, as it were, as well as meeting various individuals and groups of people. It is fantastic to be able to visit different countries, to interact with diverse cultures, and to learn about other values and outlooks. Through traveling, one's experiences widen and deepen.

I have also resorted to both conventional and adventurous means of transport—by air, on water and on land—having put aside my hitch-hiking days. Needless to say, not all the journeys or trips were exciting or repeatable. In fact, my travels also exposed me to much of the negative alongside the more positive side of life and society. Indeed, one does not have to go too far to realize that we live in a world that is both a pleasant and a tragic environment for our development as human beings. Traveling exposes one, even more so, to such an environment.

Those travel experiences also imparted to me valuable lessons about life itself; namely, that it can be compared to all those journeys which we undertake. Indeed, life *is* a journey in that we transition from birth to death, passing from one stage to the next, moving in one direction or another, gathering experiences as well as accumulating goods and so on.

But it is much more than that, on the other hand. The journey of life is also and ultimately *how we form* ourselves and *have an impact* on others. It is, after all, far more than just a movement from point A to point B. Admittedly, our ordinary mundane journeys, like the ones that made some impression on me that summer in Germany, can enrich and broaden our experiences; but how we and our society shape our lives is so much more than that. After all, the choices we make as well as those made for us as we live out our lives from day to day leave a much deeper imprint and add to or detract from their quality. The avenues or doors opened or closed, voluntarily or otherwise, as we make our way towards our fulfilment as human beings can determine *what kind of life* becomes ours.

While life is indeed a journey, like those we make in our daily lives, it is so much more than these. Life is a gift (English) but tragically, can also be a *Gift* (poison in Deutsch) to ourselves and to others. However, a consoling thought is that one's lot in life is not merely a given but also an opportunity. It awaits our own contribution and that of others. It is to a large extent packed with challenges. Often, it is up to us to confront and deal with them.

Life may even be described as an adventure. In our mundane travels or trips we probably have a specific destination in mind; and it is a matter of getting there. Sometimes, on the other hand, the destination itself does not matter as much as the journey itself. And that deviation during our travel can add to our enjoyment. In fact, surprises do have a way of making it more memorable. Similarly in life at times we pursue targeted goals while also accepting the unexpected ones, some of which can uplift although others can cramp us. As a whole, however, it is more prudent to have definite goals that can determine how we live out our day-to-day lives. Those can make a difference to the quality of our lives.

The expected and the unexpected contributed to the kind of summer which I had several years ago in Germany. Reaching my destination on my hitchhiking trips was my primary goal, but the detours also added to the enjoyment and the sense of adventure. Not only was I thrilled with the unplanned destinations, but I also met individuals whom I would not have met otherwise. Interacting with them was an enriching experience. The same can be said of life itself.

But, strangely enough, what left a deeper impression on me about life that summer was my rather mundane experience of working in the car factory. As is to be expected from a student regarding a summer job, the goal was to earn some money, of course. As it turned out, however, it was actually the *Pause*, the much-awaited intervals in the work-schedule, which somehow made a difference to my perspective! The real intention of the work-leader was obviously to provide a break for us from the monotony of the work-routine. The *Pause* meant our being able to get up, walk around, stretch our legs, all of which were necessary for health reasons. Moreover, a change in the routine was definitely welcome also for our productivity as a result of the short rest.

But additionally, it taught me an important lesson: namely, that "pausing"—among other considerations—is to *be free from* so that one can *be free for*. That might sound rather obvious, but the significance of pausing is that it allows you not just to have some respite but also to *re-focus*. Of course, what one does with that break makes a difference;

but this is what made it possible for me that summer to have the time to occupy my mind with matters other than the humdrum and routine of the work.

The second type of "taking a break" offered to me when I was transferred to another section of the textile division left an even more lasting impression. Again, the reason was rather utilitarian—my productivity had to be in line with the general productivity of the *Abteilung*. Just getting my workload completed in isolation from the rest of the division meant that that part of the over-all productivity would suffer. I needed to pace myself. It was important, as the *Werkmeister* helped me to appreciate, that one's own choices or activities must consider the "general context." One cannot just work for one's own targets, and one cannot simply set individual goals in isolation from the rest of the group. It was after all, teamwork.

Comparatively, since we live inter-connectedly, whether we realize it or not, whatever we do can and does make a difference to the rest of society. His advice of *"Langsam, langsam"* was intended for me to slow down in my output, but he also alerted me—unintentionally, of course—to the need and importance of "slowing down" in life and of being less individualistic in my pursuits.

Indeed, we are so anxious at times to reach our own goals, we seem to be spurred on by schedules; and we dart from one place to another. We want to be successful, and we can convince and even fool ourselves that haste is what will bring that about. We seem to think that life is a race, and we want to reach the finish line first. At times we even step on others as if they are our competitors. But in fact, we also ought to take our time as we journey on. Speed alerts flashed up on roads along the way are just as necessary on life's routes. It is important to catch our breath, so to speak. We need to pause, to look around and not just ahead.

But pausing is merely an opportunity rather than the main reason. We do need to ponder on life, too. While admittedly not everyone would have that so-called luxury or privilege, as human beings it is important nevertheless for us to make the effort to "create space in time" for such an activity. We can then, as it were, see our way around and take note of what is important.

This is because as human beings, we differ from all other living creatures in that certain considerations do bother us and require some attention from us, even if not always in a uniformly urgent or significant way. The ancient Greek thinker, Socrates, has warned us that an unexamined life is not worth living. That may be too far-fetched, in the opinion of some. But false ideas, unexamined viewpoints and misplaced values do have a way of leading us astray. Entrenched positions can impede progress. They can be so ingrained in our thoughts that they take over our conduct.

Making our way in life is not just, nor should it be, a matter of merely surviving but also about examining and pondering on certain questions which may arise out of the blue, because of our curiosity or simply owing to circumstances. Unfortunately, many of us are prevented from doing so because of conditions or our own actions or those of others. That is regrettable. But pausing on our life journey, in addition to "smelling the roses" or "stopping to look and listen" is confronting and reflecting on what our life and the lives of others are about. It is ultimately about "enabling" us all to develop our lives as truly thinking, and not just acting, beings.

The following pages in this book are an invitation to do that. We will be enlisting the assistance of some thinkers down through the years and in contemporary times, especially those who have been concerned with the kind of reflections that will help us along the way. As we do in our travels, we will also hear about incidents, experiences and examples. While there is no promise or expectation here of definite answers to questions which each of us is asking about the journey of life—at any rate, that is not possible to hand out—there is the hope that the opportunity provided in these pages will nevertheless help us to appreciate the importance and significance of coming to grips with some of the more fundamental challenges and of not losing sight of the wonderful moments in our own life-journeys.

Living is much too important for anyone to merely breeze through it, even if one should also appreciate its lighter side and go with the wind as it were. Life has its offerings to us, packed or arranged; but it also awaits our own contributions to make it more worthwhile for us and for others. How should we go about it? It seems to me that that question and the claim being made here are worth thinking about. I hope you will agree and will find this book of reflections helpful in your own life-journey. Will you join me then? This is a sincere invitation to you, the reader. I would like to share some "thoughts for food" to nourish us along the way.

Stage One

Getting Our Bearings

1

On Our Way

As we set out on our journey in life, it does not take long for us to notice that there are indeed some resemblances between living and traveling. In fact, we do not really have to think much about it. To start with, in both cases, there is a starting point and a final end. Living and traveling is what we do in-between these two stages. Furthermore, how we spend that time can make a difference to their quality. In life and in our travels, mostly it is up to us to find our way to our arrival point and to react to what we find on the route. Admittedly, there is also much that simply passes our way in the meantime and has unwelcome effects on our life or trip.

As we move along in life and in our travels we will also discover various enticements. Often these can make the journey rather pleasurable for us. But they can also be distracting and sometimes even misleading. At times we find ourselves confronted by a barrage of challenges in our path, some of which can stop us in our tracks. Sometimes these can even prevent us from going any farther. It is important, as we soon learn, to take account of these enticements and challenges and to respond to them appropriately if we want our trips and lives not only to be productive but also enriching. Not doing so can take its toll.

Often too the journey of life, like our travels, moves in various directions and may even lead to detours. They can be surprising, but they can also be frustrating. And yet in both instances, the diversions which initially seem to lead us astray sometimes end up taking us to the same destination even if those trips took longer than had been initially planned. That, too, can make a difference to their quality.

Indeed, not only are there similarities, but there is also much that we can learn from our mundane trips about our life-journey itself. Just like the tours or excursions which we join on holidays or on the trips that we make for personal or business reasons, life indeed offers a variety of attractions to whet our appetite. At the same time, it opens up a number of challenges which demand our attention and action.

But before pursuing this observation any further, it will be worth our while in this reflection to step back and look more closely at what lies in our path as we journey in life. There is a set of words that can guide us with this task. Let me quickly enumerate them first.

As we move ahead in life certain attractions *evoke* our interest and we pursue them. But life itself, even more than our ordinary travels, also presents certain situations which can *provoke* us into questioning whether it is all worth it. At the same time, although not on the same scale for each one of us, life inevitably puts at our disposal, even if not in equal measures, various resources for us to *invoke* for guidance and help. When we are able to avail of these—to *convoke* them, so to speak—life can be more meaningful or at least tolerable. Taking our cue from the first letters in the italicized words, which are different phases, we could describe our life journey as going on an E.P.I.C. trek.

We should now explore further how each of these phases—starting with *evoke*—can assist us in our reflections as we make our way around and chart our route. Shall we move on then?

Right from the beginning we certainly find ourselves in surroundings that want to be noticed. Advertisers know only too well that they need to attract the attention of consumers if they are to succeed in selling their products. Sometimes one has to admire their ingenuity and imagination in the way they try to whet our appetites. We are continually cornered and even confronted by such advertising. One sees their products and promises spread out in magazines or splashed out in flyers. Streets and highways are littered with eye-catching posters and signs.

Advertisers know that getting our attention is just the initial step. They go further by familiarizing themselves with what we are looking for or what they imagine we want. Just think of what happens when one does a search on the internet. Suddenly, one is bombarded with ads for something else, all vying for our peripheral vision. These ads have a way of diverting our attention towards them in the hope of sparking our interest in their products and even creating a desire for them.

Speakers, too, in various contexts—not just orators or demagogues—realize that they have somehow to captivate their audience if they are to succeed in communicating their message. In fact, that is a crucial factor in assessing the success of their talk. To maintain and retain the attention of their listeners throughout, they resort to spicing their message with anecdotes or changing their tones and emphases. Nowadays, accompanying Power-Point slides are a bonus to presenters or lecturers—and to their audiences.

Chefs are also known to show off not only their culinary skills but also their artistic bent by showcasing their work in such a way as to present their offering as more appetizing-looking to their diners. Their expectation is that by doing this it would lead these diners to relish their food offerings even more. Web artists, too, try to draw in our interest, with a view to our signing up with their webpage, through their colorful display of alluring offers. It is a mark of success when they can also exhibit the number of "likes" on their web-page.

Fashion designers definitely are on the look-out for what will catch the eye of consumers and buyers. They do this not only on the catwalk by parading models who display their latest set of fanciful wear but also in all the media by way of attractive and well-known celebrities to further convince potential customers. Travel agents are not to be outdone either, with tantalizing offers to exotic destinations and out-of-the-ordinary adventures. To make these even more captivating, they slash prices—and who can resist those?

In all of these examples, and there are several other cases, the main aim is to catch our eye and retain our interest. They want to "evoke" our attention.

But let us take a closer look at life itself. How does "evoke" feature in our daily routine? There was already some reference to advertising in the media, communicating of messages and luring towards gastronomic delights as well as to various other situations which call for our attention day by day. If we were to look around us and study the scene more carefully, we will also notice that there is much more that "evokes" our interest. In fact, it is easily an eye-catching environment that we live in. This is why it is so easy to be distracted from whatever it is that we should really be pursuing in life. After all, there is so much in our environment that appeals to all our senses.

One such attraction is the presence of anything that promises pleasure. Somehow, our make-up as human beings makes us vulnerable to its existence. We are naturally enticed by it even to the extent that it can be overwhelming. It is not unexpected that the ancient Greek philosopher Aristotle, who is famously known for his ambulatory strategy of teaching his students, had already warned us that pleasure is mistaken by many to be the ultimate good—not only assiduously sought after but also wholeheartedly embraced. Those who subscribed to hedonist teaching during his time did just that.[1] That would be a mistake, however, he bemoaned. And yet we cannot deny that many today would, and in the past did, disregard that rather wise counsel. In that respect, "evoking" our interest as we go on in life meets no traction, such is the pulling power of pleasure. What is pleasurable is sought after—without much initial effort on our part. That is certainly true when one walks down the streets of Las Vegas at night—as we did on our stop-over in that city during our group tour of the Grand Canyon—with all the flashing neon lights and the enticing colorful shows!

What can we learn from this environment about life and its attractions? It would seem, as has been mentioned already, that there is no difficulty in understanding how "evoking" takes place since it is constantly present as well as repeatedly enhanced. Secondly, since it is seeking out what is natural to human beings, it is a good, as Aristotle does admit. We are by nature drawn towards what is pleasurable. After all, as creatures of sense, the attraction to it is to be expected. We may differ regarding our individual tastes—there is much truth that *de gustibus non est disputandum*—but there is no denying its drawing power. The challenge, therefore, is not so much resisting it but rather dealing with it. In other words, the problem is not the "evoking" itself but responding to it. Being attracted to or distracted by what is pleasurable is part and parcel of daily

---

1. Aristotle, *Nicomachean Ethics*. He lived in the fourth century BC. He was taught by Plato. He founded the Lyceum in Athens and was known for his peripatetic method of discoursing philosophical issues with his students. This book is believed to have been edited by his nephew, Nicomachus; hence the title.

life for us as human beings. In fact, it can make life bearable and even desirable. That claim would seem to correspond with common-sense.

What is pleasurable, however, is not the only thing we go after because we are human beings. The pursuit of wealth and the acquisition of material goods also beckon to us. Again, Aristotle had observed how the accumulation of material goods becomes the goal of many. He admits, like the Chinese sage of olden times, Confucius, whose teachings have remained very influential thoughout the years, that one cannot live a truly human existence unless one has also some material possession that would bring some comfort.[2] Rightly so, the two philosophers accepted that deprivation of goods is not conducive to human living. Having some material possessions to bring comfort to oneself is good, and seeking them is natural. We are after all physical beings who need to be nourished and sustained by such goods.

The problem, however, is that some people do regard the accumulation of wealth as the sole reason for existence. Nothing else matters for them. They also crave the status in society that it brings them. It even becomes their overriding pre-occupation. Fagin in the musical *Oliver* with his imaginative handling of "the feel of money" and Topol with his entertaining song "If I were a Rich Man" in *The Fiddler on the Roof* both illustrate, in an entertaining manner, what to many is a life-long ambition. Wealth is no longer that which merely "evokes"—it is instead the goal, and sometimes its acquisition becomes the only purposeful act in life.

There is a fable which we heard while on tour in Romania. It is about the three stone statues on one of the mountains there. The story goes that three elderly women living at its foot were warned that because of an impending flood, they should pack up everything valuable and head for higher ground. They proceeded to do just that.

On their way up the mountain, however, they felt burdened by the weight of their belongings. They then decided to shed off some of their thicker clothes and throw away some of the possessions they were carrying. Higher up the mountain, however, they soon realized that the gold they had on them was a heavier burden and was preventing them from

---

2. Confucius, *Analects*. He was a Chinese philosopher, poet and politician who lived around the 6th–5th centuries BC. He was revered as a sage and has exercised considerable influence on Chinese society and many others, particularly East Asia, up to the present time.

reaching the top. It was then that a spirit appeared and warned them that they had a choice to make regarding what mattered most to them: either they unload the gold or they would freeze and thereby turn into stones. They came to a decision—they are still there, we were informed!

That story reminded us of the treasures and wealth buried with the pharaohs and other royalties of ancient Egypt. The commentary provided by our guides as we toured and admired the pyramids of Giza, the temples of Abu Simbel, the tombs of Luxor and other historical sites was an eye-opener not just to what had been accomplished in the past but also to how much the accumulation of wealth follows one to the tomb—even if it cannot be taken beyond it. Whatever can be said about their beliefs regarding the after-life and the need to provide for it, their worldly goods remained behind. Sadly, this fact of life is still not learned by many whether in the past or in the present. The acquisition of wealth is indeed a strong pull for several individuals. It is hard to part with it, too.

The same can be said about wanting to be thought of well by others. It is admittedly a natural desire. We do have an understandable inclination towards having a good reputation, and it is certainly very tempting to build one up. Such a desire also "evokes" us. After all, we live with others, and their view of us is treasured. It can be comforting and reinforcing as we go about our daily business. It is, therefore, obviously desirable to live our lives so that we would be held in high esteem in life and when we pass away. The loss of fame somehow diminishes us as Cassio in Shakespeare's play, *Othello* claims. He complained that the loss of his reputation is the loss of what is immortal in him. He has been reduced to being a beast as a result.[3]

As Aristotle had also pointed out long ago, what he terms "honor" (perhaps, reputation is a better word for it) becomes a sought-after good. However, he added immediately that it is misleading nevertheless to regard it as the most important ambition in life. While honor and fame draw us towards making them a crucial life-time goal, he maintained that we would lose out in life if that were to be the case. This is because they are so dependent on the tastes, preferences and likes of others—and these can change just as rapidly as they can build up.

---

3. Shakespeare, *Othello*, Act II, Scene III, *The Complete Works of William Shakespeare*, 993.

That sentiment is well expressed by Thomas Wyatt when he lamented in his seemingly autobiographical poem which referred to his affairs with high-born women of the court of Henry VIII that those who once had sought him out now fled from him.[4] And then there is the lot of fallen idols in various fields in life. For instance, sports stars and performing artists are applauded and booed quite rapidly as the mood of their fans changes. Crowds, Aristotle had observed—and admirers, too, one could add—are so fickle, an observation shared by Shakespeare's character Iago. He claims that reputation is an idle and most false imposition. He pointed out that it is often received undeservedly and lost unfairly.[5]

But we ought to cast a more attentive glance at the process of "evoking" itself as it applies to life. To evoke is, etymologically speaking, to "call out" or to summon. There is an assumption here that there is a natural curiosity in human beings, and that there is an initial but latent impulse in them. But it needs to be "awakened" as we journey on in life. Our own experience and an examination of human nature would attest to that observation. We noted that point in a number of examples mentioned earlier—they certainly do that to us from day-to-day. In this sense, there is nothing surprising about it.

There is another dimension, however, to "evoking" in the context of human nature and in its application to life. The examples of the lure of pleasure, wealth, and honor are merely illustrative of what draws us out as human beings. But why and how is this so?

Supposing we take a closer look at that point. There is something in us humans which somehow sets the scene for this "awakening" or "drawing out" on our part. It is actually something deeper in our make-up. In this context one could talk of our restlessness as human beings. Our uneasiness about some things, our dissatisfaction with our present plight or our longing for something else to satisfy us is not necessarily a bad sign but rather an impetus towards something else. We don't seem to be fully at ease. We always crave more, and we are on the look-out for something different. This is why we are prey to the allure of pleasure—yet there is so much more that pleasure cannot satisfy. Not even the higher

---

4. Wyatt, "They fle from me," 138–139.

5. Shakespeare, *Othello*, Act II, Scene III, *The Complete Works of William Shakespeare*, 993.

attractions of acquiring material goods or building up a solid reputation are sufficient either. We may not be clear as to what it is that is pulling us towards itself, but somehow we do not seem to be fully satisfied. That is not necessarily a complaint about this aspect of our life since that is the way we are, but rather it is a natural desire "for something more" that will take us out of ourselves. But why are we not content?

It would appear after all that "evoking" is actually an invitation. It is a pull towards something. So let us continue with our reflection on our life-journey. Let us follow it up then to see how this comes about in another phase: namely, *provoke*.

Noting such uneasiness or dissatisfaction on our part that seems to have been awakened, we must now ask: How does it happen? What "provokes" us humans into searching for more? The word itself provides a clue since to provoke is precisely that: a stirring up of the present situation, thus prodding one on. There are, of course, unfortunate examples of such provocations, like taunting or idle gossip. And we do challenge someone who is taunting us with an aggressive response of "You are provoking me!" However, the act of provoking in itself is not necessarily a negative one since it is merely a reference to the process of "moving on" which we naturally do. What is being evoked, on the assumption that it is good, can be helped or hastened by being provoked, so to speak. This situation can even be described as a precursor to something better, generating the desire to know more or to find solutions.

"Provoke" often has a negative connotation, as we have already noted briefly. But as used in the present instance, it means "to motivate, excite, stimulate, promote, or prompt" us. In life, we do encounter a number of provocative situations and problematic experiences such that we are stimulated into re-examining our situation. Sometimes we are simply startled by them, but at other times they even "rock the boat" or shake us to our foundation. Unfortunately, in life disappointments, losses, traumatic and other such experiences can affect us profoundly. There are also tragic incidents or prolonged sufferings, and they make us wonder whether there is any point in going on at all.

On the other hand, there are the more positive ones, too, such as healthy ambitions and honorable goals; and these can motivate us into achieving even more, making a difference to the lives of others, or enabling those less fortunate to change their lot in life. Why be satisfied with these achievements when we believe we can do even better?

But both of these negative and positive situations, which can provoke us, have a common basis. We human beings "grow" or "develop" as a matter of fact We move from one phase to another, and the transition is brought about by such provocative situations. To understand this point, we can borrow from (and adapt) Hegel's explanation of the developments in reality in terms of thesis, anti-thesis and synthesis. George William Friedrich Hegel, a German philosopher, has been widely associated with the dialectic explanation (thesis-antithesis-synthesis) of the workings of reality. This terminology can assist us to some extent in coming to grips with the phase "provoke" referred to here. But here it is used not in the sense of opposing the original situation as Hegel does with his term "anti-thesis" but rather in the sense that "to provoke" is merely "to call forward"—a phase that is characterized by some questioning, doubting and re-thinking. It is not necessarily in opposition to the original situation in the way the term "anti-thesis" is used to describe it.

As it applies to life more rigorously, "provoke" is probably best illustrated and intensified when one's experiences lead one to doubt whether life has any meaning at all or whether it is worth continuing with one's journey in life. This feeling was well illustrated in *First Reformed*,[6] a film about faith, sin and redemption. The main character, having survived the war and having become a minister was racked with existential angst as well as a pessimistic view of modern society. Turning to various remedies, he bears his anxiety throughout his ministry, only to be faced with a dilemma as to what would finally provide some meaning to his existence and situation. He was repeatedly "provoked" by his life and experiences. Still others may ask, with the Irish poet Patrick Kavanagh, who bent the coin of their destiny so much so that it got stuck in the slot. It is more than just a mischievous act; it makes a mockery of human living.[7] Others are seemingly crushed by the wheel of fate as it keeps spinning.

The whole experience of living can easily lead one even to deny that there is a caring Supreme Being It can make one very bitter about existing at all, especially when there is also much injustice involved, or as Rabbi Harold Kushner's book puts it, *When Bad Things Happen to Good People*.[8]

---

6. *First Reformed* is a 2017 American drama film written and directed by Paul Schrader.

7. Kavanagh, *The Great Hunger,* Penguin Modern 10, Section XII.

8. Kushner, *When Bad Things Happen to Good People.*

Both Job in the Old Testament and the poet Gerard Manley Hopkins interrogated the God they believed in about this situation, particularly if one believes—as they did—that one is just. It can make one very bitter indeed about existing at all, especially when there is also much injustice involved.[9] David Hume, a Scottish philosopher, put it very bluntly when he argued that the existence of evil is incompatible with the reality of an all-good *and* all-powerful God.[10] It is no wonder that the existence of evil in all its forms is truly provocative, irrespective of whether one believes in God or not. Some, therefore, have adopted the position that all we can offer are some explanations but hardly an adequate answer to the absurdity that one experiences about life itself. Others, sadly, abandon any belief in God and or lose all hope.

It is, sadly, a fact of life, as Jean-Paul Sartre and Albert Camus, 20th-century French philosophers, have observed, that life for some is a burden and even pointless. They seem to be weighed down by its tediousness or are suffering ennui. The Greek myth of Sisyphus illustrates that observation: punished by the gods, he continuously rolls the boulder up the hill, only to have it slide down again. Some find the whole situation to be indeed an uphill struggle. There is so much absurdity in life to the extent that it can provoke one into drawing the general conclusion that it is utterly senseless and thus makes a mockery of human living.

But let us inspect this point more carefully; that is to say, being "provoked" as a phase in our life-journey. It happens because we are also beings endowed with the ability to think, not just to feel or to sense. We are able to scrutinize the situation and voice concerns about it. Being provoked is brought about because we have the capacity to discern what is from what ought to be but is not. We are provoked only because we can question and raise more questions about the situation. Since we can compare, we can appraise alternatives.

Just like the symbol of the question mark, which curls back, as thinking beings we "re-flect" (face back, as it were) and in so doing, judge the original situation to be unacceptable. It can leave us dissatisfied, admittedly. But being provoked in this way can also make us seek

---

9. Hopkins, "Thou art indeed just, Lord," *Poems and Prose of Gerard Manley Hopkins*, 67.

10. Hume, *Dialogues Concerning Natural Religion*.

an improvement. It can be an incentive to strive for something better. In this sense dissatisfaction can lead us—and has often done so—to strive for something more. And that is a welcome progression for us as human beings and because we are human beings.

The earlier phase of "evoke" is mainly directed at our senses, something we share with other living beings. But "provoke"—especially, if it is not merely a call for a change but, more importantly, for an improvement—can be a significant move for us, simply because we are thinking beings. While we have to accept that in our journey in life there are rough spots and hurdles and even barriers along the way, being provoked by these is also a challenge. Questioning, because one is provoked, comes about because that is in our make-up. We should not be surprised, therefore, if along the way, we are constantly being provoked by life's challenges and situations. It is part and parcel of being human, so to speak.

That, however, is only one part of what being human entails. And we do need to remember that. But as humans, we are also endowed with creativity, a gift that is mostly described as free will. Being free, however, is more than just being able to make a choice; it is also having the capacity to change the situation, to make a difference to the outcome, and even to shape reality itself. Sometimes that gift is put into use only because we have been, so to speak, provoked in the first place. We have been drawn out, we have compared, and we want to bring about some improvement. If that happens, then the provocation, without denying that it could also leave one depressed, hopeless or resigned, can nevertheless be the urge to work towards an amelioration of the situation. It can therefore ignite some hope. It can incentivize us. In this scenario we are distinguishable from other living creatures.

When a more positive outcome results from the provocation we might ask how it has come about. Among other things, it is of course due to one's efforts, even if we also accept that chance or luck sometimes comes into play in some cases. This is why we noted previously that while we are *evoked* and even *provoked*, it is important in life also to move ahead to the next phase: *invoke*; that is to say, to call for strength, for assistance or for resources. We can achieve a more positive outcome when we do so.

Let us find out more about this phase in our journey in life.

While being provoked is the setting in life arising from various experiences or factors, it is not the one where we should end up. There is a move that we can make; namely, that we are being provoked towards a further phase in our lives. If indeed, we humans are on a life-journey, then we have to be "geared up" to be able to continue towards our destination. We need to be stocked up and to be strengthened. That is what to "invoke" entails in the present context. It is an act of calling on. It is about gathering and harnessing one's resources.

This is a particularly valuable phase as we go through life since in this case it is, among others, about acquiring knowledge and gathering information. In many ways, learning is traditionally regarded as drawing on the expertise of those involved in the study of the relevant subject-matter. One calls on them, as it were; and teachers impart their knowledge to us. The study of what has been learned and achieved, contained in books and other resources—today, the internet is truly a stockroom—is part and parcel of our invoking their assistance. Doing so thus broadens and deepens our grasp of the relevant topics and issues. After all, those who have preceded us and shared their findings in various ways can assist us to deal with our present inquiries. In enlisting their help, we are "invoking" them, so to speak.

To "invoke" can make us realize yet another dimension to being a human being. We humans are interdependent. As existentialist thinkers have described our existence, it is always a co-existence. We are who we are in our relatedness to others. It is more than simply living side by side or existing together with other human beings. We are primarily social beings—in a more fundamental sense regarding our dependence on one another. Ours is a *Mitexistenz* (co-existence) as some German philosophers put it.

Closer reflection will show us that we are social beings because our identity, each and every one of us, is formed and shaped by everyone else in addition to our own contribution to our formation. One might even go further and claim that it is also actualized by all of us. It might seem contrary to common sense—but is nevertheless supportable—to insist that being "we" is prior to being "I" or "you" or "he/she" or "they" inasmuch as I am only because we are. I become who I am, thanks to you, or her/him, or them. To put it in Tagalog, the Philippine national language, "*kayô kaya ako.*" (You are, therefore I am.)[11]

---

11. The Tagalog word "kaya" means (1) therefore, and (2) power or ability. I have used it here in both senses: (1) I am *because* of you; (2) You have *enabled* or

Where does this observation lead us as far as our journey of life is concerned? If to "evoke" is to lure us as beings endowed with senses and to "provoke" is to challenge us as beings gifted with thinking and acting, then to "invoke" is to recognize and capitalize on our social nature. We can observe this point in many ways. As we make our way in life, for instance, we turn to one another for various reasons. It might be for rather obvious or ordinary ones, such as for conversation or for some assistance. Or it could be for some companionship. But, in a more fundamental sense, turning to others is also "acknowledging" the other; it is recognizing the other's presence and invoking it. It is a realization that life demands our co-operation with one another, and by "calling on" others it puts that fact of life in place. Life—even if it can be wearying at times—nevertheless has also placed at our disposal our very make-up as social beings. In a stronger sense of the word—because it is rooted in our nature—we can "invoke" one another as we confront life in all its challenges.

And yet, "invoking" is more than just living out our social nature. It is also a reminder that being provoked, an earlier phase which we have already noted, requires action on our part, often a deliberate one. It is a matter of reaching out, so to speak. For some, it is an indicator that our restless nature is tugging at us towards something greater than ourselves. It is pointing towards some kind of transcendence. What is it?

We will differ as to how we would identify that "greater something" whom we're calling upon. For some, that reality is God but may also be called by other names. Augustine's words in this regard are well-known when he described our hearts as restless until they rest in God. Whatever point of view we adopt, an important consideration in this respect is that when we "invoke" we are calling into our lives whatever can empower us to adequately deal with the provocations of life. It is a plea for assistance. For those religiously-oriented, it is praying, turning to, or calling out to the Supreme Reality, whatever name we give to it. Or if one were to borrow technology-speak, it is "tuning in" or "plugging in" to that reality so that one is charged and energized to deal with life and its problems.

For others, however, our restlessness is merely the way we are, and we do not have to be going "beyond" our own resources for help. Strange as it may seen, given what has been stated previously, that is also a valid observation. Bringing in or "invoking" our inner strengths is engaging in

---

empowered me. The combination of the two meanings provides the phrase which I have introduced here: "*kayô, kaya ako,*" and can be translated as "I have become myself, thanks to you."—which is to an extent a derivative of Descartes' *cogito, ergo sum*.

an act that humans, because of their nature, are equipped to do. We have, to a certain extent, a kind of reservoir that can be tapped into regularly.

Surprisingly, this turn towards ourselves is not necessarily in contradiction to the religious viewpoint cited earlier. If anything, it complements it. The religious turn is not, despite what certain interpretations of religion claim, deriding what we can do ourselves or what we should also be doing. "Invoking" can also mean, and, in fact, literally means, calling in. In this sense, it is utilizing one's own resources. There is something in us all that some would describe as inner resources or inner strength. We are the kind of beings who can draw strength from what is deep down in us, whether we interpret that in a non-religious or religious way. What is more relevant for our considerations here is that, although named and interpreted differently, it helps us to achieve some strength to face up to life. It is worth our while to "invoke" it.

History as well as present times are full of the accounts of individuals who have been able to rise above misfortunes and tragedies. Certain individuals, like Nelson Mandela, Mahatma Gandhi, and Mother Teresa, readily come to mind as examples to concretize this observation. We admire them because they have shown that humans are capable of "rising above" the absurdity of the situation. It is a powerful example of human transcendence, of being "geared up" for the journey of life. At times, genuine victories are achieved not by stepping on one another's toes or by outrunning the others but by lifting oneself up—as human beings, we have the ability to do so.

In what way can all this discussion as we journey in life provide us with something to think about and fortify us as we amble along? Let us move on to the next phase: *convoke*. Having "invoked" whatever resources come our way or are already at our disposal, we should note that the phase referred to here as "convoking" is much more than just a "gathering" period despite what the term may imply. As used in this context it is therefore not just a matter of bundling these resources together and then putting them into use. This is because "convoking" requires even more of an input from us, unlike the other phases. In fact, it does matter a lot that on our journey in life, we ourselves are active participants. We are both the agents and the beneficiaries of this phase. While life may offer something for the taking, in this phase we have to make the effort to reach out even more so.

But for what? we may ask. This last question leads us to another aspect of "convoke" that we ought to be aware of as it applies to life. It is a more serious task. "Convoking" is searching for and pursuing that which will facilitate our appreciation of an over-all plan and not just of immediate or short-term answers. This is because, in addition to the attractive and pleasant lures which "evoke" us, life confronts us with so many obstacles and so much unpleasantness, causing an existential situation described as *Angst* or in similar terms by existential philosophers. It is such that we are then left wondering whether there is any sense at all to living. This assertion may seem too dramatic; but unfortunately, it is also realistic in some cases. There are indeed situations, noted earlier, when we are "provoked" by life's challenges, which then set us off on a serious quest for meaning. This sets the scene—although there are others—for this latter phase.

Given this situation, "convoking" in the context of a life-journey is our coming to grips with this quest. It is paying attention to our restive nature and then actively following through with our search for whatever will give it some rest. "Convoking" in this instance is truly pausing—at times in a prolonged manner—to investigate whether our lives ultimately matter and why. This is not an ordinary question at all as one will detect. But that is because any proposed answer will not be either. It is truly fundamental. That is why as we journey on in life we ought to reflect on it with some seriousness.

Viktor Frankl, Austrian psychoanalyst, holocaust survivor and author, believes that so long as a human being can find meaning, she or he can endure, and not just tolerate, any amount of hardship. His book illustrates an answer to the question of "why" that makes it possible to endure practically any "how" despite seemingly intolerable situations. In his view, humans by their very nature seek some kind of meaning to their existence.[12]

But is that question as to whether there is any meaning to our living not a merely rhetorical one? Could we not simply shrug it off? Or is it one that comes back instead to haunt us? We would want an answer to our question, surely. Or is it our lot simply to be in quest of an answer, but to be left in the dark? Is there a map to life that will not just guide us but

---

12. Frankl, *Man's Search for Meaning*.

lead us to our destination? Have we just been thrown into the world and somehow left abandoned, as some would feel about the human situation?

A particularly striking poem by Thomas Hardy certainly captures well those sentiments and puzzles. Noting that we wonder why we are on earth, he surmises that we could be the work of what he describes as "Vast Imbecility" who can build but lacks the ability to tend. We are consequently left to chance. Or we could be, he continues to muse, the product of an "Automaton" who is not aware of our pains. On the other hand, he suggests that we may be the result of "some high Plan" that remains to be understood.[13] The situation is seemingly perplexing.

Great minds have wrestled with this concern and similar questions throughout the ages, and they do provide varying answers. We will continue to "invoke" their assistance with our reflections. Meanwhile, we could note that this is where the process of educating can be a tremendous advantage. It is one to which every human being, as befits her or his nature, is entitled.

Unfortunately, many do not have the opportunity to avail of it. One hears of thousands and thousands throughout the world bereft of these educational opportunities. Others are even denied access, as Malala Yousafzai, the Pakistani activist for female education and the youngest Nobel Peace Prize laureate, has been asserting as has been noted in various media. Sadly, the lack of proper education is so disabling. With it, on the other hand, we are able to draw on the wisdom of these thinkers; or we can at least allow them to provide us with answers, some of which we may accept, others we may have to reject, and still others we should modify.

Whatever our lot is regarding being able or not to retrieve what they have to say and to be helped by it, it is a situation that continues seemingly to demand serious reflection on our part, irrespective of our lot in life. However, assuming that we do pursue this matter the answers that will ultimately satisfy our own questioning restless nature are those which we have worked out for ourselves, even if at times we do so with the aid of others. There is something peculiar about the quest for ultimate meaning; and that is, that each and every one of us has in the end to "work out" a satisfying answer. We could learn from a quote attributed to Albert Einstein, the famous German physicist who was keen to promote the sense of wonder, that the important point is not to give up questioning.

---

13. Hardy, "Nature's Questioning," *Selected Shorter Poems of Thomas Hardy*, 6–7.

And that is yet another side of the challenge of "convoking" in this case. Drawing on or "invoking" resources, such as the wisdom of others or the opportunities in life, means ultimately taking them on board so that one can set out for oneself. "Convoking" is therefore another step forward in our journey in life: it is assuming responsibility for our life and responding to it as each of us works out a map of life for oneself, having checked out whatever resources are at our disposal, that we will be liable to follow. But it is not a purely subjective design either, despite our strong input into it. It is a personal guide that has been drawn up, tested and enriched by one's co-travelers in life and the accumulated wisdom of humankind.

And here we can once more make some comparisons to our ordinary travels. We know from experience that in any journey there is usually a coming together of co-travelers, even if only to exchange anecdotes, swap stories or plan ahead. I have terrific memories of those gatherings when together with my fellow international students at language schools, we would meet during any free time we had for some *Gemütlichkeit* (pleasant camaraderie)—even if we were learning one another's mistakes in addition! It was also a welcome opportunity to acquaint our taste-buds with the delicacies of other countries, like cevapcici and paprika chicken in addition to Germany's tempting variety of wurst. That bonding made our excursions to various sites as part of the course even more enjoyable. Of course, as is true for many of us, there were obviously also those trips when we preferred to be on our own, enjoying our own company, relishing the adventures, or scribbling down the experiences. Nevertheless, not only were the trips in the company of the others more enjoyable they were also much more beneficial for various reasons.

In our journey in life, there are necessarily more serious reasons for such coming together and seeking one another's company in addition, of course, to simply enjoying companionship. The main point to note here is that the phase of "convoking" is the act of turning to, and supporting, one another as co-travelers in life—an observation to which we will return much later. In the end it is more important to take into account that as we go on that trek in life, we "convoke" or call together in our own personal and creative way, from whatever resource or company, anything that will direct us to the point of it all. It is a challenging but also rewarding phase as we proceed with our life-journey.

These phases in our journey in life as described here are meant merely to throw some light along the way rather than to provide any specific information. The answer we ultimately seek as to whether life has meaning or not and what our final destination is may be best left open here, at least for now. This does not mean that there are no answers coming from somewhere else or that ultimately it would be better to abandon searching for an answer. There are, of course, some thinkers who believe in the latter—the German philosopher Friedrich Nietzsche would most likely be one of them. And there are some who would go along with their viewpoint. Despite the difficulty, however, pondering on these phases and on our life journey as a whole—which is the point of this reflection—is a way of refreshing and vivifying us as we proceed in our search for meaning.

Doing so can enlighten us and may even pave the way for us towards other avenues in life. It may provide reasons to be encouraged by our efforts and by the support offered by available resources. We may then realize that making the effort to find meaning is somehow already to achieve some meaning. In this way we might see that *creating purposes* in life does spur on life. It can alert us that *looking at* life from another angle may provide an incentive to living our lives differently such that we can draw a more positive conclusion to living. That would make it all worthwhile.

We should proceed then to acquaint ourselves further about this situation. Let us continue with our explorations and our reflections on our journey in life. Keeping in mind what we have just learned here about the phases in our trek which has been described as E.P.I.C. (*evoke, provoke, invoke*, and *convoke*), we will turn our attention next towards finding out what can be known about where we are heading and how to get there.

It may help to show, too, that no matter where we may be starting from, *how* we make our journey in life is what matters finally. This is where pausing and pondering can be of assistance.

2

Heading Somewhere

FOR MOST PEOPLE THERE is something exciting about embarking on a journey. They would consult maps, research the areas to be visited and sights to be seen, check out the weather forecast, organize what clothes and accessories to pack, and so on. Sometimes it takes time to get everything together although for the seasoned ones that may not be the case. But the important thing is that the more prepared they are, the better are the chances, so they believe, that the journey will be fruitful and even pleasurable.

An important stage of the planning is the gathering together of information regarding one's trip and destination. Guide books have always been particularly useful in this regard. Part of the excitement even before the planned trip itself comes from reading these and similar material in the hope that the more we know beforehand, the more we will find ourselves able to cope during the trip and ready to leap into action, so to speak, when we get there. These days, we have also the added resource of the internet cluttered with websites of various spots and a choice of travel advisors, all rivalling one another. As one dutifully turns to these sources for information, one cannot help but feel that this attention to detail will definitely enhance the enjoyment of the entire journey.

In addition to thinking about what one will experience and see along the way and at one's planned destination, there is also the active imagining of what could turn up unexpectedly. Indeed, at times one's imagination goes wild, thereby adding to the excitement. Even the journey itself can become enjoyable. In fact, in some instances the unplanned and unforeseen may make the trip definitely more unforgettable. A couple of those unexpected developments in my hitchhiking days that summer in Germany would certainly fit the bill. Surprises, especially the pleasant ones, have a way of making such journeys truly worthwhile. Tolkien, the acclaimed writer and academic, put it more dramatically when he wrote that those who wander are not always lost.[1] One could add that they may even end up in a so-called wonderland!

At the same time, however, despite all the preparation and advance information one can understandably feel some apprehension that there could be a glitch in one's planning of a trip. An unforeseen disaster could occur. Seasoned travelers would, of course, include that possibility. Accordingly, they take out insurance plans to cover them in case of necessity. In this way they try to forestall anything that could ruin the journey. Sometimes they hatch up a plan B. Yet even for them, as indeed one hears in the news now and then or in the stories of the unfortunate ones, mishaps do happen; and their well-laid out plans will turn out to be a misadventure after all. Everything will be ruined.

It would be easier, of course, if one could simply put that experience aside; but certain situations have a way of lingering on after the trip. And it is not simply a matter of "putting it all down to experience" therefore. In fact, in such cases, one would even have regrets that one had gone on the trip in the first place. Indeed, going on a trip can at times have its costs. And the traveler has to pay the price, unfortunately.

Now if life itself is a journey, it is certainly a life-long one! It starts the moment we are born and lasts until we depart from this world. If we are in luck, we may experience—like with the many shorter journeys we undertake—exciting moments and events. They give us reasons to celebrate. We may succeed, for instance, in achieving goals, no matter how small they are. And they make our journey in life more significant. There may even be accomplishments attained, marking the advances made as we travel on.

---

1. This line, reminding us that there is more to what appears otherwise, is adopted and adapted from Tolkien, *The Fellowship of the Ring*, the first of three volumes of his *The Lord of the Rings*.

As we progress in life we realize that, just like going on any trip, it pays to plan in advance and to be prepared. Indeed, such planning and preparation can make a difference as to how we actually view and carry out our journey in life. We can thereby look back to the past with satisfaction and move confidently towards the future. As a result the present becomes more meaningful, too.

But like our mundane trips, the journey of life, regrettably, is not always smooth sailing or turbulence-free. In fact, for some it is anything but. One must admit that going through life seems, after all, like being on a bumpy road, on a rough sea or in stormy weather. There are so many obstacles, hurdles and setbacks. Life's burdens can indeed weigh us down. That is truly an unwelcome part of living.

At the same time, however, one lesson we can learn about life from our ordinary travels is the importance of also knowing when to "unburden" ourselves, when possible, or "off-load" unnecessary or over-weighty luggage. Sometimes we go through life carrying so much "baggage" on ourselves. We are therefore unable to see our way around or to negotiate properly through life's routes. We feel the drudgery of life instead with no one to blame but ourselves.

Each one of us has had, in fact, a share or two—and for some, even many more—of the bitter side of living. For others, because of their various experiences, getting on with life translates rather into an attitude of indifference so much so that it is really simply a matter of putting up with it rather than relishing it. Living, for a number of us, regrettably, is accompanied by these troubling emotions. It is a daunting situation that cannot be ignored and one that many individuals find themselves stuck in. Life can at times be troubling and troublesome—and truly provocative.

If indeed life is a journey that results in both pleasant and unpleasant experiences, sometimes overwhelmingly so, how can we face up to this challenge? When we are caught up in the maelstrom of life, what can we think about that would dispel these negative feelings and comfort us? On the other hand, if we are experiencing life to the full, are there ways of enabling us to be grateful but also to be realistic? Furthermore, what useful information can we pass on to other life-travelers so that for them the journey in life becomes more meaningful? These are fundamental questions that we ought to ponder on. In our more ordinary trips guide books appear regularly with offers of advice. Today, some internet sites, like Trip Advisor, have tried to meet a similar need for travelers or holiday-makers. Are there such resources for our life-journey? To whom should we turn?

Such questions, and many others like them, are worth addressing and considering simply because they could make a difference as to how we view and live our lives. Admittedly, for some it seems to be sufficient to move on from day to day. Somehow the routine of the day and the fullness of their schedule are enough to get them engaged with life. Others spend their lives chasing one goal after another, and their achievements may truly give them sufficient boost to continue in life. Somehow, we admire these successful individuals. We even seek guidance from, or follow the example of, those who seem to lead what appears to be a fulfilled life. Following in their footsteps does assist us sometimes in our own journey in life.

At the same time, however, we soon learn that identifying any object or any goal in life or emulating others will not necessarily bring us satisfaction due to our differences and preferences as individual beings. Or as the characters in William Thackeray's novel *Vanity Fair* discover, they were after all chasing after what is not worth having.[2] Moreover, as Aristotle pointed out, one should distinguish between "the ends" and the "final end" but only the latter leading to one's fulfilment as a rational being. He strongly encourages us to see these "ends" as merely transitory sources of pleasure or momentary phases of enjoyment.

Now and then we may even wonder whether there is "more to life" than what passes as "moments of satisfaction." Ecclesiastes describes the feeling well: "Seeing there be many things that increase vanity, what is man the better? For who knoweth what is good for man in this life, all the days of his vain life which he spendeth as a shadow?"[3] These questions in different guises and at intermittent times prod us on to pursue the matter more steadily in the hope of finding a more satisfactory and satisfying answer. They "provoke" us. In one way or another they make us pause so as to ponder.

The experience of life of some people is such, unfortunately, that they would even begrudge anyone who talks to them of its meaningfulness. The French philosopher Jean Paul Sartre's famous work, *Nausea*, a philosophical novel which is a commentary on the human situation,

---

2. *Vanity Fair* is a satirical novel commenting on early nineteenth-century English society. It was first published as a 19-volume monthly serial and has been made into a film and serialized on television.

3. Eccl 6:11–12.

expresses that sentiment dramatically. Even the title of that book is a reminder of how life can be most unpleasant indeed. The semi-documentary Lebanese film of 2018 *Capernaum*,[4] graphically portrays the chaos experienced by the young Zain as he makes his way in life amidst the poverty and depression of his surroundings. In one dramatic scene he voiced what must be the sentiment felt by many in similar circumstances: he resented being brought into life by his seemingly hardened parents. His environment is poignantly reminiscent of the slum quarters of hundreds of impoverished Filipinos in Tondo, Philippines, and of the *favela*-dwellers in Sao Paolo, Brazil, eking out some kind of living. It is certainly not a human being's lot to be envied. One wonders how in such circumstances one can truly talk of life as being meaningful.

One suspects that lurking behind the differing perspectives on life and the variations in satisfaction is the more deep-seated need that we as human beings feel: for something that *connects* the various pieces in life together, something that will provide some sense to it *as a whole*. Is there such a thing?

Writing about this human experience, Harold S. Kushner, the Jewish writer focuses on and discusses this need of ours for more.[5] What is this "more" that we are seeking? Is there much more to life than just chasing after items of satisfaction? Or is life simply a matter of surviving, which unfortunately seems to be the plight of some individuals? These are provocative questions. They do demand some attention from us.

Wise men have constantly been preoccupied in dealing with this general feeling and craving that humans seem to experience. Sages throughout history have offered advice to their followers, which at times did succeed in enabling them to live a fuller life. Even today gurus in different guises, who teach various strategies, are still fashionable and are sought after. It seems to indicate, however, that ultimately what we do require in life are not just pieces of advice, necessary though they may be, but an over-all scheme of things. As human beings, we seem to be on the look-out for some general plan that we could follow. There is something in us that makes us somewhat restless and somehow unsatisfied if we are not getting the "full picture" altogether. It appears that we are on the

---

4. This film was directed by Nadine Labaki and produced by Khaled Mousar.
5. Kushner, *When all you have ever wanted is not enough*.

lookout—even if we are not always fully aware of it—for an over-all plan to life or a road-map to living.

To better appreciate this point, let us consider momentarily this need of ours for a general picture or a comprehensive plan to living by examining various aspects in our regular routine. Perhaps it will also help us further if we do so. For instance, those of us who are involved in administration welcome an agenda for meetings or a general plan of action to inform us of what lies ahead and to ensure a more organized set of directives. Institutions also take pride in articulating and communicating their vision while spelling out their mission as this allows others to get an over-all view of their status and activities.

We know, too, from assembling jigsaw puzzles, that as we put our finger on an individual piece, it is in the hope that it will fit in because it is only when the total picture comes into view that we feel some sense of achievement. We appreciate summaries, even if they do not and should not replace the detailed narrative, not just because of lack of time on our part but also because they can be effective in putting us "in the picture" more readily, so to speak.

In all of these examples, we can observe the difference between the specific strategies being implemented in particular cases and the fundamental principles which are supposed to inform these, and can thereby assess those strategies in the light of the principles. In short, we usually do give ourselves scope in our daily lives for what is general in addition to what is practical or specific.

From these rather mundane observations and comparisons we should be in a position to appreciate the importance of what is general, including how it can also illumine what is particular. In fact, as the American philosopher Charles Hartshorne puts it, the problem is not the process of generalizing since we as humans are prone to doing it—the examples above illustrate that—but rather the kind of generalization that we are engaged in. Correctly identifying this human tendency, he alerts us to our need for general guidance in life.[6] Such a need, one could add, is not

---

6. Charles Hartshorne was a contemporary American philosopher. Among his many writings is *Creative Synthesis and Philosophic Method* where he puts forward and

merely an interest in the details; it also involves, and more urgently so, a search for an over-all picture, as it were.

The human tendency which Hartshorne identifies can be illustrated in our looking out for a map of life to guide us. These days, it would probably mean more to some people if one referred to a *sat-nav* or an *app*! Because of our make-up as human beings, we really seem to be in need, and in search, of the larger picture of life. It is no wonder that we often ask whether there is any sense to life at all or if there is an over-all scheme of things that would tie the bits and pieces together.

To understand that part of our make-up, we could indeed learn from our experiences in traveling and in other areas of life. As we had noted earlier, travel maps can greatly assist in our trips inasmuch as they provide not just significant details but even more importantly they open up for us a total view of our itinerary. Such information greatly helps with the planning. The details are crucial, as was pointed out, but so is an over-all view.

Similarly, as we undertake our journey in life, we are in search of—even if not always in such an explicit way—a guide to life; that is to say, a map in life. Our fundamental question about life then turns into a quest for some guidance. We want, so it seems, to get somewhere. And a map would be invaluable for making it there. But how is one to imagine this so-called map of life? How can we come across it—if there is one? It is important first of all to be clearer about these questions before going any further with our inquiries.

In this case it may help us to compare the situation to the way we make a distinction between a *text* and its *context*. Let us "invoke" its assistance with our query at the moment. After all, consulting a map is like reading certain texts, which can, in the view of some people, be meaningful when read in the light of the context in which the texts had been written. That is why we hear often that someone's remarks whether verbal or written should not be taken out of context. Or sometimes one insists that there is "more" to what is in one's mind compared to what is, in fact, being verbalized. Indeed, to understand a text and its meaning, it is important to know the context of the sentences. In fact, a sentence that has been lifted

---

develops his metaphysics. It grounds all his insights into reality which he develops in his other books and journal articles.

from the paragraph or the section (or even a wider context like a chapter) does not always convey as full a sense as it is meant to.

Moreover, awareness of the general theme of the whole text itself as well as of the background (including that of the writer), connotations, varying interpretations, culture and so on can heighten and deepen the reader's sensitivities to such an extent that the reader can confront not only the explicit but also the implicit meaning of the text and of the words which make up the text. It does involve paying closer attention to the general picture or context of whatever it is we are trying to understand. To borrow and adapt the British mathematician, scientist and philosopher Alfred North Whitehead's terminology, it does mean checking out the "wood" in the midst of the "trees" more circumspectly.[7]

Arguably, the same claim can be made regarding our need for a map of life's journey. It may come in handy as we head somewhere. This is because the quest for meaning can be greatly enhanced by taking life's context into account since it is not simply a matter of examining the specific phases that life offers but also of interpreting the meaning of those and eventually appreciating them. Just as the general context can shed some light on the individual literary entries so can an over-all map of life somewhat enlighten us about our daily lives and activities and even motivate us. A life-map, like the context of what has been written or said, refers to some kind of a unifying vision. The felt need for one is recognition of its significance in our daily activities.

But we will have to probe further into our use of the concept of context here if we are to tackle other fundamental questions in this regard, such as: How does one arrive at such a general picture or a map of life in the first instance? What can we learn about our quest and in our quest? Where does one start?

Strangely, it is in our everyday lives. The search for a so-called map of life takes place primarily in our day-to-day activity. Or some would call it the "concreteness of life" as we pre-occupy ourselves with our daily activities. These specific life-situations do serve somewhat as pointers because it is through them that we become somehow aware of a larger picture; namely, the feeling that there must be more to life than what

---

7. Alfred North Whitehead, *The Aims of Education*. Whitehead was a twentieth-century British mathematician, scientist and philosopher, who taught in both the U.K. and the U.S.A. He is widely known for his influential book, *Process and Reality*, and is regarded as a truly original thinker whose insights into reality have made a difference to how one views and interprets it.

we are actually going through. In fact, we can only recognize them as specific because there seems to be a broader background—even if we are not always conscious of it—against which they are set. Our quest for a map of life, often felt rather than deliberated, is based on and grounded in the day-to-day experiences, that is to say, as we live our lives and carry on with our daily routine.

There is something about human nature that is not fully satisfied with mere instances, selected examples, particular situations or individual activities. Our human desire for some continuity, comprehensiveness, and unity in our understanding of life itself, and in our attempts to make sense of it, is what drives us on this quest for a more general vision or a life-map. This is reminiscent of what we noted in our previous reflection regarding our nature as human beings.

Whitehead's analogy of "seeing the wood by means of the trees" can be helpful here once again. It is the trees that we initially encounter; but it is also they, which help us to become aware of the wood. In seeing the wood, we have gone beyond merely noticing the trees. Furthermore, we may even see them in a different light because we observe them this time against the backdrop of the wood.

Similarly, the larger picture or the vision that is opened up by the various life-situations can enlighten us when we look again at the specific situations, including those that have set us off initially on our search for a map of life. Yes, indeed, a context or a life-map can help us re-orient ourselves by taking a fresh look at those life-situations, past and present.

But there is something even more fundamental that we need to consider here if we are to benefit from a life-map; namely, the question of what facilitates us to read it so that we can be helped by it. After all, we also have to possess some relevant know-how if it is to serve our purposes. This means that we require a certain skill or training that will equip us for this task. We have to develop some kind of "literacy" in this regard.

We know from our schooling how important literacy is, that is to say, the ability to read and comprehend, for us to be able to understand and to advance in our learning. In schools and elsewhere we develop such reading capabilities to sharpen our comprehension. For some of us that literacy is developed even further the more we get similar and further experiences following the time spent in school.

We can say the same thing about the possibility and use of a life-map. We do need to be able to read, interpret and follow it. There is no point in having it otherwise. It is important and even necessary for us to be "literate"—in a rather extended sense. In this way, we are in a better position to read the map of life, to navigate our way, and to comprehend the context of life.

In the present consideration that kind of literacy takes the form of reflecting on life and its challenges. We need to pause and ponder. Doing so is a way of responding to the "provocative" dimension of life. That may be rather strange and even unconvincing at first; but for us because we are human beings, and not just living creatures, periods of reflection have much to contribute in casting some light on life's significance.

This is because the process of reflection helps to nurture and develop an outlook in life, one that can make a difference as we venture out in life. To make use once again of Whitehead's imagery, it can help position us to "see the wood" while we "look at the trees" that comprise it. It can be helpful and consoling at times to know that, despite it all, "there is a wood and not just the individual trees" and that there is more to life than what we are presently experiencing. Such "wood" in the form of a map of life, read with much thought, can reassure us during dark nights, giving us hope even if not immediate solace.

The process of reflection can open up vistas, and not just opportunities, so that we can view life in a certain way, making a notable difference as to how we cope with it. To adopt and adapt the Jewish writer Martin Buber's depiction of his philosophical thinking, reflecting for him is "opening the window" so that we can look at life from a certain view.[8] Much earlier, Plato had made a similar point with his very well-known analogy of the cave. His phrase of leading the prisoners out of the cave into the sunlight is particularly appropriate to describe such thinking. It contributes to the way we look at life and thereby how we understand and meet its challenges in a certain way. It is "literacy" in the wider, and more fundamental, sense.

---

8. Buber, "Replies to my Critics," *The Philosophy of Martin Buber*, 693. Martin Buber (1878–1965) was an Austrian Jewish and Israeli philosopher. He is best known for his philosophy of dialogue (which makes the distinction between I–Thou and the I–It relationships), a form of existentialism. He has been quite influential in many fields, particularly insofar as his insights have a bearing on many areas.

But in what way does reflection or "pausing and pondering" play its part in enabling us to "read and understand" this larger picture of life, so to speak? As was pointed out previously, literacy is the skill to unscramble what has been scribbled down. Not being able to read letters or signs can be irritating and even frustrating.

Just imagine going to various places and feeling lost because one cannot make out what the street signs mean, simply because one is unfamiliar with the script. It can be perplexing and even irritating, as we discovered when looking at a map of Marrakesh and seeing that all the directions were in Arabic script! But what is even more frustrating is the realization that those are, in fact, intended to direct you somewhere!

Yet picture the relief experienced when one can indeed read them— even if one cannot understand them fully, something that I appreciated while we were on tour in Greece and on an exploration in Japan. It is at least the first step. Understanding them, of course, is the more crucial one if these letters are to confirm a location or to direct one somewhere. Literacy in this instance is essential in making any progress in heading in the right direction and arriving at one's destination.

The same can be said about the journey in life; and thinking, yes, thinking, can come to our aid with this task. Reflecting about life is, in fact, finding and understanding our way around life. In the first instance, it can help us to locate our place; that is to say, the important sense of feeling a certain belongingness in life. This may sound like a preposterous claim, given the numbers of isolated, lost or dissatisfied people who can claim that too much thinking led them astray. For this reason one cannot merely brush aside that point of view.

However, to object to too much thinking is really to misunderstand what it *offers*, rather than guarantees. If one realizes that what reflection does is to prod us on, to look further, to seek for more, and therefore not merely to accept one's lot or fortune, then perhaps it is a more realistic expectation. It is really about "opening one's eyes" rather than promising success or specific outcomes.

That may, of course, still result in mere dissatisfaction or unhappiness. But that is not really what it is meant to do. Instead, "opening one's eyes" in this instance is more like unlocking doors, rather than simply staring outside. It is meant to stir up our human restlessness to seek out so-called distant shores. It is a journey that each and every one of us has to undertake for ourselves. It is like literacy itself and what it offers us:

the ability to read, but it is up to us to put that into practice. In short, it is meant to *enable* or *empower* us rather than to crown us.

This expanded usage of literacy in the context of enabling us to read and understand our life-map takes us to an even more fundamental consideration, one that is rooted in our nature as human beings. How?

Let us delve into this claim with some vigor. As we go about our daily activities, we soon realize that we are curious by nature, and consequently we inquire about so many things. Even in our early stage of life we *ask* questions and are unsettled when we do not know what is happening. Most of us would be familiar with how youngsters can inundate us with their questions! It is no wonder that social media have become extremely popular, and they certainly feed into our desire to know what is happening almost minute by minute. In many respects, we are like other creatures, moved by instincts and desires. But we differ from them because we can and do inquire. For this reason, we ask *what* the situation is. In following through with our enquiry we aim to get *information*.

However, we humans distinguish ourselves further because we also wonder about the *how* of things. That question stimulates us into imagining possibilities, assembling data, and even inventing things. The results can be staggering. That is why sometimes a human being is described as *homo faber*, a maker of things. She or he can even be said to create and not just replicate. In reality, human beings, because of their inventiveness, add to what is already there. Pursuing the question of *how* leads them to *knowledge and more knowledge.*

There is one specific question that truly makes us human beings even more distinctive; namely, the question of *why?* It is provocative. It is a question that probes further because it goes beyond mere observation or insight. It is a question that can be unsettling because it digs deeper into what underlies the situation. It seeks the reason, and not just the cause of things, of events or even of existence itself.

The German philosopher Martin Heidegger put his finger on this fact when he pointed out that humans differ from every other creature because only they ever wonder why they exist.[9] Of course, this does not

---

9. Martin Heidegger was a contemporary German philosopher, best known for his 1927 magnum opus, *Being and Time*, which is a key document of existentialism. It has made a considerable impact on later philosophy and on other fields.

mean that every *why*—which even a child raises—is always asked in such a profound way. Nor are we also at all times in search of rather profound answers. Rather, the question *why*?, even when raised in a rather perfunctory or non-deliberate way as when one is choosing between alternatives and looking for a reason for the choice, is indicative of some thinking and even deliberating rather than merely acting. It is the question that philosophers have identified as heading towards *wisdom*, and not just information or even knowledge.

But first a short diversion before proceeding with that claim. Let me share with you what transpired between my nephew and me when we were out for a stroll one day. Regular walks along the river bank had become part of our routine, especially at week-ends. It was a popular spot for such leisurely pursuits, and we were fortunate to be close to what nature had to offer.

Aware of my responsibilities to "direct his mind"—in a manner of speaking—to what lies behind our searches for answers, every time he asked me a question, rather than merely provide a direct answer, I would reply with another question. The idea was to provoke and challenge his thinking. I thought it was an exemplary way of instancing Socrates' didactic strategy, and I took some pride in reaping some intermittent success.

As usual, on this occasion this question-and-question (as an alternative to the question-and-answer) strategy continued for a while. Now and then I would check on how he was re-acting and was encouraged by the way his facial expressions would indicate that we seemed to be making progress. Of course, that brought some satisfaction to me. So we carried on with this exercise as we walked farther.

After a while, he came up with another remark—yet another question which I had assumed would bring him up further down the road towards wisdom.

"Can we have a break?" he looked up at me quizzically.

"Why?" I replied spontaneously. I have a high record for using that interrogative.

This time he faced me in disbelief.

"I am only seven years old!"

It was a quick retort to a provocative situation. And with those words, he raised both arms in desperation while checking for my reaction.

Then he stopped momentarily. It seems that this time he was taking control and providing his interpretation of our "pause and ponder" session! He wanted to pursue wisdom, it seems, but at his own pace.

I should have learned from our last walk. At that time he had suggested that I should slow down since, as he explained, for every step I took, he had to take two to catch up with me! He then chatted about school. I listened. Good compromise—I consoled myself: at least, it is about learning!

Several years later he is older—and is now much taller than me. The walking situation has been reversed!

How does this episode lead us back to the quest for a life-map, which is really our preoccupation here? So far, we have been likening the journey of life to our mundane trips and our need for a life-map in the way we use travel maps. But now we can note a difference because it seems that this need for a life-map is due to our being able to ask the question: *why* are we here? Or as Heidegger would more dramatically put it: why have we been thrown into existence? Unlike a travel map that can merely provide an answer to the question of *where* we are specifically and *how* we can reach our destination, our need for a life-map is indicative of the human desire to confront *why* we are on a life-journey. It is much more than just a question of where we are or even of where we are heading. It is a consideration that has profound consequences for how we carry on with our journey in life.

If indeed the question of "the why" of our existence is of such importance, then we do have to give it greater attention. This why *reflecting* on it, rather than simply asking about it, does matter. It is a time in our rather crowded schedules that merits some "deliberate space" on our side. This is why it is more than just creating a gap in our schedules. In fact, it is an activity that is much more than just doing something since it also requires some thoughtful deliberation on our part.

Returning to our previous consideration of texts, we should now be in a position to appreciate why the task of interpreting a text—as is well illustrated in literature—is much more than merely providing one's own understanding of it. While this can be and often is done, one nonetheless risks arriving at merely subjective conclusions. This can be avoided—although not always successfully—by reference to external sources. This is also the case with our quest for a map in life. It is important therefore that our individual efforts should also avail of the collective wisdom of humankind and the extensive experiences of others. After all, if it is true that the quest for meaning in life is a common human activity, then there is something that we can learn from one another. We can and should "invoke" one another's assistance.

How should we go about looking for it? And how are we to be guided by it? As we have already noted and will do so even more later, we would do well in the first instance to turn to one another. The experiences that we ourselves acquire can be compounded by those gathered as we interact with one another. The journey of life as a whole is a social activity even if it is also true that sometimes, we do have to embark on it in isolation for a number of reasons; for instance, with some quiet moments when we wish to be left alone. But those moments can help us to appreciate even better how much we need and benefit one another. This is because human beings are social creatures, as we have already remarked, and generally thrive best in the company of others.

This is not to deny that there are aspects of living in society which are detrimental to one's own development. One has only to look around, check one's experience and listen to the news. But there is some truth nevertheless in the observation that one becomes what one is because of the kind of society that one belongs to and because of how one interacts with members of one's society. For this reason, it is imperative that we work for the betterment of society as a whole. In doing so, we also improve our own individual lot. That outlook in life is acquired and tested in society.

This observation brings us back to the comparison of life with the journeys we undertake. As had been mentioned previously, most travelers, even if not everyone, appreciate traveling in the company of others. Not only is there more safety and more fun, there is also the element of sharing with and of learning from one another. It can make all the difference to the type and quality of the journey. Similarly, as we go through life, there is the realization that we are not alone as we face up to whatever life presents to us. There is that feeling that we are "all in this together." We learn from an early age that we develop our own selves as we interact with others and take into account the experiences of others, past and present, positive and negative. We soon realize that we also contribute to that pool of experiences, both positively and negatively.

This is an appropriate opportunity to gather our thoughts before we proceed any further with our reflection. Just like traveling, living is heading somewhere. Again, as on a tour and on an exploration, we need a map to guide us along the way. But it is also important that we put ourselves in a position to make use of it properly: to read it, to interpret it and to follow it. Otherwise, we will go astray. We need to make a serious effort: finding anything involves searching for it. In doing so, it also helps to realize that we have company and resources. Turning to these and "invoking" their assistance can facilitate our journey in life towards some destination.

How should we go about this task? Let us find out next.

Stage Two

Surveying the Terrain

3

Pausing to Ponder

WE HAVE BEEN DESCRIBING life as a journey. We have noted that with most of the journeys we undertake, particularly in an unfamiliar territory, we find the assistance of a travel map welcome as it provides important information on our location as well as some direction towards our destination. Accordingly, we have wondered whether there is such a thing as a life-map to guide us. Furthermore, we have taken account of the fact that being able to read the map intelligently is important if it is to be a useful guide for us. In like manner, our life-journey would be facilitated if in the first place there were a such a map at our disposal.

But even if there were, we would need also to be able to "read, interpret and follow" it if it is to serve a useful purpose. In this respect I had suggested in the previous reflection that just as we develop literacy to make out and understand written texts and maps, we also need a similar skill, in a certain sense, to benefit from any life-map. I had indicated then that thinking things through is the human skill that we need to put into practice in these circumstances. It is particularly important because in this regard we are faced with the question of not just where we are, which a travel map can answer, but why we are here at all, which is a fundamental human concern. That expanded interpretation of literacy involves the matter of "pausing so as to ponder" on our part. But the question still remains: how should we understand and put that suggestion into use?

We could start by thinking about the life-map, that is to say, the general picture of life and its purpose, as life's message to us. What does it have to say to us? What is involved then for our present consideration is how we can position ourselves so that we can receive it in the first place and then, of course, be able to read it. Obviously, there is a difference here between that task and merely reading a travel map in the way we consult the latter for information.

To assist us with this matter, let us first of all note what is involved in sending and receiving messages generally.

Some of our experiences in daily life can be of help in this regard. So why don't we examine those with that consideration in mind? For instance, isn't it quite thrilling when we receive a message to which we have been looking forward? In addition, how it comes can also generate some excitement. It used to be in the form of a letter, a telegram or a note. Certain envelopes had a way of letting us know what kind of message awaited opening. If it was a letter, especially if it had been handwritten, we would take a good look at the handwriting and sometimes comment on how beautiful it was—or otherwise!

There was a time in much earlier days in some rural areas in Ireland, when the arrival of the postman, then the traditional bearer of more formal messages, would also signal a few minutes of chat, even if it was only a comment on the weather or a grumble about the politicians. It was a form of social interaction brought about by the delivery of a letter or two. Sometimes a message would also come in the form of a simple note passed on by hand; but it would still be a sight that would elicit a smile, particularly if it came from someone we fancied. Many of us can recall childhood days—or a tryst between lovers—when we received such notes and the warm feeling that they evoked in us.

Nowadays, we get a message as a text, an e-mail, a Tweet or a posting on Facebook or through other social media. But no matter in what form it comes, often we look forward to it. Instead of waiting for the postal delivery, it is more common for us now to turn on our mobiles, computers, or laptops first thing in the morning to check whether any such message has been uploaded during the night. And when it has—and it happens to be what we have been waiting for—there is terrific rejoicing. Added to that joy of receiving the message is the awareness that not only had the sender remembered us but had also taken the trouble of transmitting a message. Sometimes a text message or an e-mail even has an emoticon or an emoji attached to it, and that definitely lets us know the mood of the sender.

Sending a message, too, can be a pleasant experience. In the good old days—although still true for some individuals today—writing a short note to accompany a card was a joyful occasion. Words would be carefully chosen because we would want the receiver to know exactly what we are sharing with him or her. For some, greeting friends in this way has been replaced in these technological times by the sending of e-cards, some of which are truly entertaining and at times thought-provoking.

There are other kinds of messages, of course; and their content can make us sad, furious, annoyed, and so on. Unfortunately, we do inevitably get such unsettling messages. Certain letters from financial institutions or specific individuals can be alarming because of the contents of those letters. A lawyer's message can likewise be most unwelcome. And then there are those envelopes bearing the return addresses which immediately alert us to the dreaded contents. These are not messages that make our day if one were to be truthful about it. There is the natural temptation to put them aside to be opened or read another day or even to tear them up.

There is, regrettably, also the bad news that needs to be passed on to us, such as the death of a loved one, the unsuccessful job application or the rejection slip of a publisher. Such messages presage a dreadful situation that has to be dealt with, sometimes urgently. Some messages left on answering machines or the Voicemail of our more sophisticated gadgets likewise disturb us. We would rather not have such messages, and deleting these does not always ensure relief. And presently there has been the growing menace of bullying messages appearing on social media, and their content can be devastating. Getting such messages is also most unwelcome.

There are messages which are truly difficult to write, too. Trying to break bad news to others or writing a letter of complaint is onerous. Often we postpone doing it. Now the trend is immediately to turn to social media. Good or bad, many seem to upload messages even if others will be hurt. One often hears anecdotes of how lives have been ruined, all because someone, for whatever reason, had posted a negative message or comment about someone else for the entire world to see and hear. This can be particularly troubling for adolescents. To be fair, there are also messages sent that way that seem to bring some comfort—and even much-appreciated action. Indeed, the messages we get in life are varied, and our experiences in this regard differ.

But there is another kind of message that results in a different experience. It can be baffling and even disorienting when the message itself is incomplete. It is bad enough when there are problems with the transmission or communication of the message—we can always blame technology for that—but when everything has gone smoothly only to find an incomplete message, we can be left uneasy. Of course, sometimes we can make out what is being said. The context can be helpful in this respect. Or if we know the sender, his or her mood or attitude, we could hazard a guess as to what is being said. Nevertheless, an incomplete message makes us wonder what the sender really wanted to say.

There are messages indeed where the meaning is ambiguous. It can happen, especially with text messages, because we tend to send shortened, unpunctuated or simplified ones since it makes them easier and less costly to transmit. Normally, there is no problem; and we can make out the meaning. But sometimes the ambiguity is due to the wrong or misplaced punctuation. It can even change the meaning of a sentence. Certain messages convey a different or even a misleading sense just because they have not been punctuated properly. It can be frustrating for most of us when messages are misleading simply because the proper punctuation marks have not been inserted. The meaning changes completely when the seemingly insignificant comma, for instance, is in a different place.[1]

What can we learn from all these situations? How do they compare with life's message itself in our search for a life-map? If indeed we wonder whether life holds any meaning—and as has been claimed previously, don't we ask that question in different ways now and then?—then suppose we compare life and its fundamental message to these written messages that come our way from one day to the next.

It is not as far-fetched a suggestion as it may seem at first. After all, we often, even in ordinary conversation, compare life to a book. Don't we at times refer to various stages in life as like the chapters in our book

---

1. Carey, *Mind the Stop*.

of life? So in the present context, our search for a life-map would be like leafing through it.

There are two points worth noting about this analogy. First, this book of life contains some blank pages for us to write on. If one were to be dramatic enough, one could say that life has been thrust upon us since we did not have much choice about coming into this life yet we are expected to add content to it. There was one line in a Woody Allen film—I seem to recall it many years later, but rather vaguely—where the main character claims that no one ever asked him whether he wanted to be born. It is reminiscent of what the German philosopher Martin Heidegger claimed about the human plight as equivalent to having been thrown into existence and then seemingly abandoned. If we are honest with ourselves, we do feel like that at times. So despite our not having been consulted about being born we discover that we have nonetheless landed in something called life and are now forced to get on with it.

Secondly, life is like a book that nevertheless has retained some scribbling which is not of our making; that is to say, we have somehow inherited something from the past. Like a book that has been opened for us rather than completely authored by us, we can ask—and at times do so—whether the scribbled pages of our book of life contain any meaningful message for us. In fact, we even wonder—and some even ponder seriously—whether life as a whole makes much sense. What is the message that life hands to us? More importantly, what is it saying to me personally?

Yes, the messages we get about life and from life can be ambiguous. At times and for some, fortunately, the experiences provided by life are wonderful, thrilling, and worthwhile. To them, the message of life speaks volumes. We even describe some individuals as "bubbling with life" and their enthusiasm in their respective lives can be catching. There are also various individuals who have seriously taken on the challenge of adopting a life-style that appears fulfilling to them. They seem to be driven on by a number of goals which they had set for themselves and which they are determined to pursue. While admiring them, we often find ourselves wishing we were in the same situation, such is their enthusiasm about what life has to offer.

For others, in contrast, there is more of a sense of acceptance or relief for whatever life has to offer or to say to them, no matter how small it is. There is resignation or even contentment, even if unexpressed. Life does not have to be on the fantastic scale for them to be convinced of its meaningfulness. Small pleasures somehow suffice. The detours and distractions of their journey of life are acceptable or, at least, tolerable.

Life, regrettably, can also be tough on many of us, even brutal at times. As we move about in life, we meet obstacles, face trials, and endure hardships. Some of these are trivial, but others are truly more burdensome and enduring. But we are still able to carry on despite, as we would say, being marred by life in one way or another. Even an apparently fulfilling kind of life can be dotted by events and experiences which simply do not bring any sense of satisfaction.

For some it is even worse, far worse. Life seems to be saying that their time in this world is not for enjoyment or pleasure at all. It is therefore nothing new to hear that for some individuals, being born is indeed a curse. It is as if having been brought into this world, they are being punished even if they themselves had not been around to commit any crime. But again at times and for some, life presents itself as a testing-ground for a future that will somehow eradicate all its miseries and misfortunes. Our desires for some kind of fulfilment, one hopes, lie in the distant future, even if not for our present existence.

Given this disparity and unevenness in the way that life treats us with its baffling messages, what can one say about life itself? Indeed, life apparently deals out its stack of cards arbitrarily and even unfairly. We are left puzzled. Why do some appear to prosper while others fail, and fail miserably, as they live out their time in this world? Why is there a yawning gap between the lives of a few and those of the rest of us? How does one make sense of the drudgery that is experienced as well as the contentment that more often surfaces? Is there any significance at all to life? And if so, how does that apply in our particular situations? These are important questions which need to be faced up to and addressed as we attempt to read life's message that had been drawn up and laid opened up for us.

Now here is where the comparison with scribbled messages or texts comes in for our inspection. We can "invoke" grammar for some tutorial on this lesson. If punctuation marks can make a difference in the meaning that we get from these messages then it may be worth our while asking whether something that we do as we carry on with our daily lives can also bring out anything meaningful for us to appreciate.

We noted how commas in messages, such as texts or other written communications, can clarify meanings or even change them. Without their assistance, the message is rather garbled or even misleading. The insertion of that small mark can make an important difference as to how one ought to understand or interpret the message. Commas are crucial pauses in reading a message, and they have to be inserted in the right places for proper comprehension by the reader. If life's message can be likened to the messages which we receive and send in our day-to-day lives, what can we learn from this? Could so-called *comma-moments* or pauses in our life-journey be of use in discovering the meaning of life? We will have to confront those questions in the hope of generating some answers.

But supposing we halt for a moment. This may even seem like backtracking on our journey, but the difficulty with providing an immediate answer here is its complexity. We do need to proceed with caution. Any answer laid out will not meet with universal agreement because we differ, due to our individuality, as to what makes life meaningful for each and everyone.

The ancient Greek philosopher Aristotle—we will recall—had already alerted us to this problem, pointing out that our search for what would fulfil our desires in life will result in different answers. Generally, he said, what people want in life are "goods": virtue, honor, wealth and pleasure. But in the end this is not truly what will satisfy humans. He insisted, in contrast, that it is happiness that we all are looking for. Many would side with him on that. When people are asked about what matters most to them, their ready reply is often that it is, indeed, happiness, rather than material goods.

But Aristotle's version of what happiness is would hardly meet with total agreement either. This is because he associated it with a certain understanding of what it means to be human; namely, rationality. It is, according to this thinker, what differentiates us from every other living being, a conclusion that many would not go along with. Whatever about wanting to be happy, they would not equate it with being totally "rational"; that is not, they would say, what they really desire in life. It is much too abstract or lofty in their opinion.

It is no wonder that some would even doubt whether dealing with this question is worth the bother. The search for what will make our lives meaningful is a waste of time since what will work for one will not work for another. After all, we are individuals. Moreover, it is too specific. How can one know what someone else wants in life? Such views are a recognition that the search for meaning in life is a complex and even an arduous task.

What makes it complex is not just that answers may differ as has already been said but that—strange, as it may seem—it is only when we, in fact, make the effort to find out, that we can be better situated to answer whether life is meaningful or not. This observation may sound rather perplexing, too; but we ought to note that a necessary step towards finding such an important answer—and here the lesson about the comma can throw some light—is to *actively position ourselves* to read the message in the same way that there are preparatory stages that we go through to make it possible for us to read, edit and interpret messages. It is arduous because we have to put some effort into it. We need to take it on with some seriousness.

And to help us do that, it is crucial to take "pauses in life" from time to time. It is important to create some intervals in the midst of the routine as well as in the hustle and bustle of daily life. Just as we need space in our physical surroundings in order to move around, we require some temporal gaps in our schedules. Like the commas in a sentence, therefore, it seems to be important that we take a break in life to group our activities together, assess them, and see how they fit in within the overall scheme of things in the way that commas, as punctuation marks, can make sentences more intelligible. It is important to pace ourselves. We need to have what I learned to appreciate during my summer job in the German car factory: *Pause!*

In this instance we can draw on what we learn from school regarding the importance of proper punctuation marks. We had noted that point earlier regarding the difference that correct punctuation makes to the meaning of the sentence. In our life-journey, prompted by grammar for reading and comprehension, we should avail of what I like to call "comma-moments" as we move on. Only by taking that step can we be better positioned to find out whether life makes sense or not. Commas inserted in a sentence can mark an important difference in the meaning of a sentence. The same can be claimed about comma-moments in our life-journey.

How? In a straightforward sense, comma-moments in life are really like the other breaks that we need to take in our lives. These make us pause, even take a step back, look around, before moving on. For instance, during any physical activity, our bodies soon get weary and let us know that we need to slow down or even take some rest. When we recover, we can then proceed with whatever activity we were engaged in. Those intervals help us to catch our breath, but they also allow us to build up some strength so as to continue.

We are also familiar with the importance of taking time off as we go about our regular schedules. Inundated with so many concerns, we sometimes have to dart from one place to another or shuttle between one task and another. At times like these we welcome breaks from having to be dealing with all those concerns and tasks. And, as is well known, breaks do have a way of making us cope better and even continue with more vigor.

Then again there are times when such breaks signal a change in direction in our lives—a different job, assignment or even an activity—which can spell the difference between merely plodding on or struggling and moving on confidently. They can energize us into doing something more interesting. For the fortunate few, taking a break means that they can look forward to lengthier interruptions in their timetable, such as going on a holiday or a trip. The change of pace or scenery can bring about significant and welcome results. For the rest of us, even momentary pauses in one form or another, available to practically everyone in our otherwise everyday routine, can be a real breather. These breaks can truly be welcome opportunities and are good for body and soul—the *Pause* during my summer holiday job as a student was a most enlightening break!

Comma-moments are in the same category as these breaks—but with a difference. They are not intended just to refresh our bodies or to re-direct our activities or to uplift our spirits. They are none of these and yet they are all of them! This is because taking a comma-moment involves our whole selves. It is not just having a restful stop or a bringing about of a necessary re-orientation. They are designated as indeed comma-moments because in inserting them into our lives, we bring our entire selves, as it were, into the task. It is, if one were to phrase it in everyday language, involving "our mind, body and soul" or a "recharge"—if one wants to resort to technological-speak. This is because comma moments are "moments"; that is, to say, they are invigorating, significant or momentous.

The connotation of the word "moment"—momentous—is that it is more than just a happening or an activity. Instead, it is one that means something to us. Achieving victory, for instance, is more than just overcoming a foe or a rival; it is also reaching a successful outcome. The giving of an award is not just the handing over of a trophy, a certificate or a medal; it is even more so a recognition of merit or success. Celebrating a jubilee is more than simply marking a stage in one's life or the passage of time. It is an eventful celebration. All these show that these times or moments have a certain significance which makes them stand out. They are certainly not just ordinary breaks in our routines or schedules. In a similar way, comma-moments are more than our attempts to take a pause in life since with comma-moments we engage in them for an important reason. It is to be *free from* in order to be *free for*—yet another lesson that takes me back to my summer job at the car factory in Sindelfingen, Germany.

Because with a comma-moment there is deliberate action on our part, it can also be likened to the pauses by orators to heighten awareness of content, to allow time to assimilate material, to encourage anticipation of what is to come, to maintain interest, and even to catch a breath! We can notice that strategy being put into practice by great speakers. The comma-moment allows us to do all of these—about life.

Sometimes, too, when we are reading aloud a piece of writing to others, particularly if it is rather dense or weighty, we stop for a few seconds so as to let its meaning sink in. We take a pause, just momentarily so that our audience can consider what we have just read more deliberately. Taking a comma-moment can be likened to such a move, except that with such a pause, there is the likelihood that we are also doing it for the sake of our listeners. The significance of what is being read can be missed by them if we simply gloss it over. Halting our reading in this way can have the effect of highlighting a point, a claim, or even just the choice of words.

The difference in the case of a comma-moment, however, is that such a pause to read life's message is more for our own sake. It lets us reflect and assess the significance for ourselves even if, admittedly, such a move will also have an effect on others. But that would be more of a welcome consequence rather than the main intention.

An interesting twist in our highly digital society is the observation that the digital age has awakened people to the importance of the human need for seemingly "doing nothing"! Seemingly, there is an App to achieve this. For our purposes here we can interpret this so-called awakening to mean the realization to "pause between the digital activities to reflect on life itself." As one will readily observe, there is a lot of "switching on" and "staying connected" because of the ready accessibility of gadgets that it will help to be reminded to "disconnect" from these so as "to be re-connected" to life itself.

Tracing our way back to the grammatical lesson noted earlier where appropriate commas can be useful so as to decipher the meaning of a sentence or a text, we can see its connection with reading life's message. Appropriate pauses—which create an atmosphere of reflection—do enable us to review our life, establish balance, maintain priorities and sharpen a focus. These comma-moments can aid us in making sense of the seemingly endless series of activities that we are engaged in or the various pursuits that we are trying to follow. They occur when we take the time to see how the particulars are to be understood in the context of the general, or when we take a moment to view the details as they come together in the light of the overall scheme of things.

The comma-moments being described here allow us to see connections, small enough (like the symbol of the comma) so that we can continue with everyday life but important enough to leave an impression on us. Comma-moments are inserted not just as breathers (although they can be useful in that way, too), but because they serve the important function of providing sense just as the proper punctuation mark does in a sentence. Moreover, as we see the sense of the various groupings, they can open up the bigger picture. It seems that as we take—and make—the time to insert these comma moments into our lives, we provide ourselves with a greater opportunity to see not just the sense of the various happenings in our lives but even more importantly, the sense of it all—an important target.

As we highlight the role of comma-moments in life, we may also find it instructive to examine the actual mark of the comma itself. The comma, unlike the period (or full stop), is a dot that curls downwards towards the left. It does more than just bring out the meaning of the sentence. It connects, as it were, with the past—the group of words that have been separated by the comma. It then throws some light on the next words and how they relate to the preceding ones. In life, too, we need to be made aware that the question of where we are heading is partly answered by considering where we have come from. One could add—resorting to techno-speak as another way of explaining the point—that it is not clearing the board as such but making room in the memory bank so as to receive more informative data.

To help us appreciate further the status and import of comma-moments in our lives, it may also be instructive if we were to make use of the Greek distinction between *kronos* and *kairos*. The first refers to time as it passes by in a rather linear way. It measures it in terms of seconds, minutes, hours, days, and so on. This is what watches, clocks and other time-pieces do. They are chronometers. Irrespective of what we do, *kronos* ticks away. *Kairos*, on the other hand, is a special time. It does not just happen. It also brings with it blessings, enlightenment, joy and other gifts. That is why it is such a special occasion—singularly so. It is a "now moment" indeed.

A comma-moment is a similarly positive experience, too. Like *kairos*, it is not simply an interval in the passage of time. These are truly momentous events. However, unlike *kronos*, a comma-moment needs to be made to happen rather than simply happens. We have to bring it about—we have to "convoke" it as was explained earlier. We punctuate a sentence with a comma to make sense of the group of words; in a similar way, we need to insert the comma-moments into our routine in life. It is about deliberately creating, as it were, *space in time* to make room for what is truly significant to break through what is merely temporal.

In a word, a comma-moment is a *reflective* moment. Religious circles have always encouraged some form of meditation for their followers. In one of his Wednesday audiences in Rome the Pope, making the distinction between what he calls "true rest" from "false rest" encouraged the faithful to opt for the former. He observes that society today provides even more of the so-called false rests with all its leisure attractions while what is needed for our proper development are opportunities to rest in order to nourish ourselves spiritually. In another context he reminds us that we need, as he put it, is to make room for silence so as to hear the sound of love. Once again, he urged his listeners during his Sunday address at the Vatican when he returned from his operation, to call a "halt" to our continuous pursuit of activities and to give ourselves time to reflect.[2]

Buddhism is well known for its encouragement of various activities to bring about its goal: enlightenment. While there are differences from what Buddhism prescribes to its followers, comma-moments as described here are important steps, rather than exercises, towards finding some kind of life-map to guide us on our journey. The current interest in mindfulness and in Taoism's *wu wei* invites comparisons, too. However,

---

2. Pope Francis, *Vatican News*, September 5, 2018.

unlike mindfulness which is focused solely on the present to the exclusion of the past and the future, a comma-moment enables us to appreciate the past and work for the future. These reflective moments are not achieved by shunning life in society either to achieve quietude, as Taoism teaches, but by placing a comma-moment in its proper context as we go about our daily schedules.

The comma-moment being described here is not necessarily linked to any religious belief or affiliation. Instead, it refers to human nature itself. Our human nature requires these reflective pauses irrespective of any religious affiliations or none. It is closer to, but not the equivalent of, what some philosophers refer to as *Augenblick*: when one grasps time in such a way that there is a unity of past, present and future. It is a moment of *vision,* rather than of negation. As a result, the division in the timescale acquires its significance: the present time, the past time, and the future time. The comma-moment is also in some way like how Kierkegaard interprets "the moment" when time and eternity seemingly touch each other.[3] Comma-moments make room for us to do that, even if only momentarily.

Comma-moments can also be the opportunity to re-charge oneself. Just as travel vehicles require re-fuelling or re-charging so do we ourselves. The source of that powering for human beings differs in the same way that vehicles may take gasoline, diesel, or nowadays, electricity. But wherever that power comes from, it is important that we re-connect. For some who are religious believers, it is a personal God or some transcendent power to whom they pray or make some offering. For others, it comes from within them as they seek to energize themselves by probing into their inner resources. And there are various strategies or techniques to do so.

But here the main thing to consider is that as we *pause in our journey in life so as to ponder,* we could also avail of the occasion to reconnect. We have to be silent so we can listen. We have to "plug in" so that we can be re-charged.

---

3. Søren Kierkegaard was a nineteenth-century Danish theologian, philosopher, poet, social critic, and religious author who is widely considered to be the first existentialist philosopher. Among his best known works are *Fear and Trembling* and *Either/Or*.

It is useful to be constantly alerted, as we preoccupy ourselves with the important and necessary tasks of life, that life is a journey, not a race. Just as when we go on our road trips, we ought to heed speed alerts in life. We hear a lot about work/life balance and the importance of slowing down and prioritizing. We do need to take comma-moments in our stride. In this way, we can have the opportunity to envision the larger picture, read the map of life, or to see "the wood." Somehow, as we move forward we may find some direction in that way. It may lead to our destination and help us find fulfilment.

One will probably think of the image of a snail and its slow movements to describe the journey of life depicted here. That would seem to be rather unhelpful given the pace of our lives today. But it seems that the worm, as it unearths the richness of the soil and brings it to the surface thereby promoting the growth of plants and flowers, captures better many of the claims made here regarding how one can face up to the challenges of life.

In this reflection, taking our cue from the use of the proper punctuation marks in reading texts we have examined a lesson for life and about life. In particular, we have reflected on the significance of the comma, and how its extended usage on life's journey can aid in our attempts to read the meaning of its message. Rather than deal directly, however, with the question as to whether life has meaning or not or what gives meaning to us—which are important issues indeed—here we have looked at a related concern. We have focused instead on the importance of *positioning* ourselves to help us to "read" life's message. It has been suggested that we must make room for comma-moments in our life to be able to read what life is saying to us and to listen, as it were, to the rhythm of the universe, of which we are a part.

But what is it? We will continue with our reflections in a short while. Meanwhile, we need to pause. And we must also ponder.

4

Charting Our Route

AS WE WANDER THROUGH life, we do wonder at times whether the route we are following has already been laid out for us and even whether the entire territory has in fact been mapped out from the beginning. Somehow, we have reasons to believe that we are not as free as some would want us to be, that the circumstances of our birth do restrict or even block any progress which seems to favor others instead.

It can be annoying, and even frustrating, especially if no matter how much we try we do not seem to "win the favor of the gods," in a manner of speaking. We have been given our lot in life, as it were, by them or by whoever is in charge. We will recall that that seems to have been the plight of slaves, members of the lowest caste, as well as of those who find themselves in our times—including many of us—repeatedly pulled back no matter how much they attempt to get out of their dire situation. That bleak reality is still with us and regrettably appears to be the lot of several.

And yet, there are other times and occasions, too, when we become convinced that, indeed, we can succeed in anything that we do so long as we put our minds to it and give it our best shot. There are seemingly no barriers to block our path. We are free, so we believe, to plan and live out our lives. We are the masters of our fate. No one has been given the right to trample on us.

Accordingly, a common exhortation to us is that so long as we put our minds and hearts into whatever we want, we will achieve it. Freedom is a cherished possession and is worth fighting for. Libertarians would definitely hold this point of view. So do those who believe that one can be anything one wants to be in life and should not be restricted by anyone else.

But then again, there are occasions when we are led to conclude that everything is really a matter of luck. What one does makes no difference. There is no planning in the over-all scheme of things. If good fortune is on our side, then we can expect and get positive returns from life. On the other hand, if we are unlucky, then we will experience the bitter side of life; and we simply must learn to put up with it.

Some would also attribute mishaps as being "in the wrong place at the wrong time." It would seem to be due to luck but of the negative kind. When the details of the fate of the Kurdish family who recently perished in a car accident in Ireland became known, many felt that somehow circumstances had gone against them this time. The father had just submitted his PhD thesis to the university and, with his wife and very young daughter, was driving home after looking for new accommodation in the town where he had just secured employment in his field. He had had to change the day of their trip. That seemed to have been an unlucky twist of events since it resulted in the fatal crash when another driver, on the wrong side of the motorway, hit their car and killed all of them as well as the errant driver. It was a heart-breaking episode, and many felt at a loss to explain their situation properly.

The so-called presence of luck was definitely evident in the way a nurse, who had almost missed her bus, rescued the driver of that bus in Dublin. He had a heart attack while driving the bus in a busy city-center street. She was able to apply her skills there and then and so saved his life. The lucky streak was also evident in the way the 105th Greek passenger who already had his boarding pass had failed to join the ill-fated airplane from Ethiopia on its way to Kenya because of some mistiming on his part. His initial frustration turned into immeasurable relief. It would seem to have been a matter of being "in the right place at the right time" in both situations.

Such situations pose challenging questions. Is it entirely simple luck, good or bad? Is it ultimately a matter of a casting of lots? Why do our specific routes in life differ and our experiences vary, sometimes with no apparent reason? Why do some prosper and others perish as we tread on life's paths? Are we pre-determined, or are we free? This set of questions can be unsettling to anyone who observes the differences in the circumstances and lives of individuals and of peoples and who reflects on what life opens up for each of us to follow. Somehow justice or fairness—or good planning—does not appear to be much in evidence.

It has certainly been the subject of much debate among thinkers down through the centuries. There are some who would claim that life has been determined indeed right from the start, and we are simply deluded if we think that we have any kind of freedom. Life is simply a matter of stepping onto the paths already laid out for us.

But there are others who would disagree, arguing instead that we are truly free and this aspect of our nature distances us from all other creatures. Any restrictions imposed on us come from the outside; that is why we should fight against these because they block our full development as human beings.

Then there is the third group who would maintain that it is all a matter of chance—sometimes, we win, at other times, we lose. It all comes down to how the dice is cast. The best attitude to take vis-a-vis life is, therefore, one of indifference: we simply put up with it and get on with whatever comes our way, the attitude seemingly adopted by Thomas Hardy in some of his poems.[1]

There seems to be some truth in each of these perspectives and arguments since our varied experiences in life would indeed appear to illustrate and confirm each of them. For this reason as we go on our journey in life and as we reflect on our experiences, the task of charting our route in life becomes even more problematic. To what extent are we indeed navigators or drivers or pilots? Should we simply accept our lot in life, both good and bad? Can we genuinely hope for improvement and work towards achieving it; or have our lives been mapped out already from the start, and it is all in vain to make any alterations? If there is indeed a lifemap, does reading it simply entail tracing it out and following it, or does it involve some additional planning or even a few diversions on our part?

Let us see if we can pursue these concerns further in this reflection.

There is a philosophical perspective that reconciles to some extent these differences of standpoints and may help to resolve some of the apparent difficulties that we have come across. Let us "invoke" its assistance. It is

---

1. Hardy, *Selected Shorter Poems of Thomas Hardy*.

based on the insights and ideas of the contemporary American philosopher named Charles Hartshorne although there are traces of this way of thinking going back to ancient philosophy both in the east and in the west.

It accepts that both the determinist and the liberal points of view have some credibility since we do experience that there is an aspect of reality that is simply a given; that is to say, nothing we do can change it. On the other hand, according to this philosophical viewpoint, there is still some amount of openness in reality that awaits our part in shaping it. That means that it is not fully determined either. There is genuine, and not merely imagined, freedom. What is even more intriguing about Hartshorne's philosophical standpoint is that it also accepts that luck is a reality, that there are some happenings which are truly due to luck: sometimes the result is good, at other times it is bad. It has come about seemingly for no reason, except that it took place in the way it did, and the result is welcome or unwelcome.

In case we are tempted to think that this way of thinking does not make much sense or that that it is incredible or even contradictory, it is actually based on contemporary physics rather than on Newtonian physics. The latter somehow has had a significant influence on the way we portray how reality works. It has led us to believe that anything that happens must have a cause and that we can predict exactly the kind of effect that would ensue if we have accurate knowledge of all the causes. It is the kind of thinking that leads us to argue that there would be complete predictability about nature if only we knew accurately and exactly the nature of all the causes. Our scientific outlook today—and consequent success in this area—has been greatly influenced by this way of thinking. It is determinist in nature and is opposed to the completely libertarian point of view held by those who champion total freedom and even a rather chaotic world.

Basing his observation of the workings of reality on contemporary physics, Hartshorne offers his alternative description and explanation of how reality turns out as *creative synthesis*.[2] The term "synthesis" describes the coming together in the present of what has previously existed. In that respect, whatever is happening now can be referred back—but only partially and in different degrees—to whatever has contributed to

---

2. Hartshorne has developed this philosophical concept in many of his writings. The most systematic and extensive treatment of it is in his book, *Creative Synthesis and Philosophic Method*.

its coming to be. In other words, these are the causes which have brought about the present effect.

In this sense, it is correct to maintain that present effects are the result of the activities of past causes and that the nature and quality of the effect is traceable to the kind of causes which have produced it. Accordingly, there is some truth in the determinist perspective and argumentation after all. There is a certain amount indeed of predictability, although in varying degrees, for that reason.

On the other hand, it is inaccurate to maintain, as absolute determinism does, that it is possible to predict to the last detail what kind of effect would result just by identifying accurately all the causes. The ambivalence is not necessarily due to ignorance on our part. Rather, the synthesis or the coming-together of all the causes that has resulted in a specific effect is "creative"; that is to say, there is a certain amount of unpredictability or indeterminateness, not because of our ignorance but rather because that is the nature of reality itself.

Hartshorne holds that there is always a certain amount of freshness or novelty in every event or happening. For this reason, causality is never completely predictable. Our inability to foresee exactly what or how something is going to happen is rooted in the way reality operates, rather than in our inability to predict or know the future.

This aspect of causality is what is one-sidedly upheld by indeterminism and by those who oppose any semblance of control in their defence of freedom. There is indeed a certain amount of unpredictability in nature; however, not in the way that that school of thought describes it since it generalizes it completely.

Luck also has its place in Hartshorne's way of thinking; and its so-called reality is incorporated in his description of the workings of reality. Since the synthesis, i.e. effect, is creative or fresh, no one can ever explain or track it fully to previously existing causes (which in turn are the results of a previous synthesis). The actual result, although largely dependent on those causes, is nevertheless, outside its total control. The result may be beneficial or damaging, but it is not and cannot be totally determined. It is simply how reality operates. It is a matter of luck although we can limit it as much as possible. We can maximize the positive outcome, but we cannot totally control it either.

In short, we are both the agents insofar as we can make things happen, but we are the recipients too of whatever has happened both because others made it happen but also—and this is where luck comes in—because that simply is the way it has turned out. There is no other explanation, in Hartshorne's view.

Is this simply yet another grand theory constructed by philosophers? Insofar as it is rooted in contemporary physics, however, the answer would appear to be negative, or at least is worth investigating with some realism. Is it defensible? We could always check it out and see whether that way of thinking does justice to our various experiences in life. We would need to have not just counterarguments but also empirical evidence. It is important that such abstract thinking be based on concrete reality if it is to be of any use to us here.

The question that is more relevant here, however, is whether it will help with our reflections on how we chart our route in life. In what way can it be said that daily life and the decisions we make are indeed planned but still open, caused but also free? How can it help us understand and appreciate that we are indebted to what has happened in the past but which nonetheless is still awaiting our own stamp on it? Will the explanation of creative synthesis as pervading the whole of reality help us to realize that our own journey in life may have been regulated by whatever has already happened but which is not fully designed until we ourselves make our own specific contribution? Can it, in fact, serve as our lifemap to guide us? Are we merely stepping onto footsteps implanted on the route we are following or do we carve our own trails in life? These questions are pertinent here inasmuch as we would want it to empower rather than just acquaint us with our way around as we travel on life's routes. We would want the explanation not only to be credible but also to be well-grounded.

At the outset we ought to note that the concept of creative synthesis is a description, rather than a prescription, of how reality operates. As such, it merely maps out the territory instead of showing the way itself. That is another task. In this sense, therefore, here we are merely exploring the possibility of its functioning like a travel map, which still has to be read properly. Having noted that, however, we would still want to find out whether it does help us to understand many aspects of life just as a travel map also designates the routes that we can take depending on where we wish to go.

Let us initiate our inquiry with the concept of *synthesis* for the simple reason that, as was already explained, it is about what we have inherited from the past. Accordingly, the present, not just ours but the whole of reality, has been brought about by past occurrences, which have caused its existence. It is "the given" in life; or as Martin Heidegger describes it, its "facticity." Insofar as it has already happened, it cannot, Hartshorne would argue, be undone. And we do owe much to it therefore. The past then is always an integral component of the present.

To put it more concretely, there is already some paving, as it were, that has been laid on the path that we are taking now. It is set, and there is nothing we can do to change it. Hence, the past is eternal, forever incorporated into reality. Despite the fact that sometimes we want to forget the past—and that might be possible given the limitations of human memory—its reality persists nevertheless because it is incorporated into the present. As Hartshorne would put it, the past is eternal and it cannot be undone at all. Even if we or anyone else forget about it, it continues to exist although not exactly as it has occurred inasmuch as it has been assumed into another reality. To put it more colloquially, what is done is done, what has happened has happened.

Creative synthesis as a life-map can point out to us that there are matters and situations which are truly outside of our or anyone's control. In charting our route in life, therefore, we have to acknowledge that there is therefore a certain determinateness or a given such that we can only be at the receiving end, as it were. Synthesis as a way of describing life's trails shows us the "what" of reality. Because we owe much to the past, including the immediate past, we can be grateful for, resentful of or indifferent to it. But we cannot cancel it out. The question therefore is to inquire as to the kind of attitude we ought to have towards it.

So is it merely a matter of accepting it? Yes, as far as it goes; that is to say, insofar as it is forever etched into reality just like footprints left in cement. For this reason, sometimes we are indeed favored if what becomes our own present reality is positive, giving us reason to be appreciative and grateful. Several individuals and many groups of people throughout the world feel that way, sometimes because of their home, cultural or religious upbringing. Or at other times, we find ourselves reaping the positive results of what has occurred in life or in nature. For these we ought to be grateful.

Unfortunately, it could also be the case that what becomes our lot is bad and even damaging. How past occurrences or activities find their way into our terrain is sometimes beyond our control. They are blots on the landscape. They are cemented into our pathways. At times, we are taken advantage of by others, who may block our way. In some cases it is like traveling through a dark tunnel whose exit seems to be far, far away. We cannot see the light of day.

In this case, it would be understandable that some do curse their misfortune and feel resentful. It would appear that they have been abandoned in the tunnel or had a breakdown with no rescue in sight. Or it looks like they are stuck in the potholes of life's paths and are made to wallow in the mire thrown at them by whatever has happened in the past. The Stoics of ancient Greece admonished their followers to adopt an attitude of seeming indifference to life and whatever it hurls at them. That would not suit everyone, however. It is a regrettable and an unfortunate situation.

But there is an important lesson, nonetheless, that we can derive from this "synthesis" of the workings of reality. It is the realization that whatever we ourselves do—to anticipate the discussion on the "creative" aspect of the process of creative synthesis—is contributing to the kind of reality that emerges. We may not be a in position to demolish the past, but we can reconstruct it, as it were. That means that you and I, inasmuch as we too are causes, so to speak, have truly a hand in shaping the kind of individual that we become, the kind of environment that emerges, the nature of society that is formed, and the shape of world that we are living in and will leave behind. The idea of creative synthesis also alerts us to the fact that we do not only receive what has transpired in the past, but we are also agents who form whatever becomes the past. In other words, we too are causes and not merely recipients of the past.

This realization should help us to consider and value whatever we are leaving behind because it is what it is also precisely because of our own contribution to it. It should make us more cautious about and sensitive to our legacy for those who after us will be affected by what we are doing now. It should open our eyes to the tracks we are laying for those succeeding us.

A very good and contemporary illustration of this observation is the growing realization that the danger of climate change, an effect, is traceable to what all of us, as well as each of us, have done and continue to do. The concept of synthesis describes rather graphically how everything that happens becomes part and parcel of what is happening and will continue to happen. It affects each and every one of us and all of nature, a point worth considering seriously.

"Synthesis" or the coming together of various acts, activities or event can give us reasons to be grateful for what has transpired in the past, careful about what we are doing in the present, and responsible for what will shape the future. In this sense, while the concept itself is descriptive, it also alerts us to possible attitudes that we can *adopt* rather than just accept.

To understand this point better, we ought to set our sights at the other aspect of reality, i.e. *creative*, and examine it more thoroughly. It provides much more clearly a certain direction that we can take in the way we live out our lives. In this sense, if we take the concept of creative synthesis on board as a life-map, we will find that it functions much more than travel maps do inasmuch as it does have a prescriptive side to it after all. It can indicate not just where to go but also *how* and *why* we should take a particular route. It all comes down to what we contribute as "creative" agents to the syntheses in the world. We can take some direction from this philosophical and scientific description of the workings or reality regarding the challenge of how to live our lives. But the inevitable question is how?

We should pursue this reflection then. But first, we ought to note how the aspect of "creativity" in creative synthesis is comparable to, but also contrasts with, what many of us understand by the concept of freedom. The two are not exactly the same, therefore.

We have already heard that philosophers and others generally have underlined freedom as that which distinguishes us humans from other living creatures. We are agents, and not merely recipients. We can choose and not just deliberate. We can refuse as well as accept. It is this side to our human nature and this ability in human beings that stand out when defenders of indeterminism argue that we are the authors of our lives or captains of our souls. It is also what many of us would fight to defend since to take it away or to obstruct it is tantamount to dehumanizing us.

"Creativity" as understood in Hartshorne's concept of creative synthesis may be like, but is to some extent different from, freedom as has just been explained. This is because creativity is an aspect, rather than the entirety, of what constitutes human reality whereas freedom, in conjunction with rationality, is interpreted as defining human beings.

Moreover, creativity, like synthesis, is universal rather than exclusive to humans; that is to say, it is true of all of reality and not just of humankind. In other words, it is an extension of what is generally and traditionally regarded as belonging exclusively to human beings whenever the claim is made that only human beings are really free. It would also be more accurate to say that in Hartshorne's philosophical thinking there is a human form of creativity—which still distinguishes us considerably from all other creatures both living and non-living. But creativity is not the sole prerogative of humans. In short, creativity is universal; that is to say, every instance of reality is creative.

How does human creativity, as used in the concept of creative synthesis, provide us with some guidance as to how to lead our lives? We will recall that it was already mentioned that it alerts us to the difference that we can and do make because of the way in which we have added to the "syntheses" in the world. The sum total of reality, i.e. all the syntheses, is different *due to* our contributions; that is to say, because of how we have exercised our causality. It is better or worse *because* of what we have done. This situation should be some kind of an alert, a warning as well as an encouragement to us, it was suggested previously.

Following up on this point, our examination of the "creative" side to creative synthesis puts the spotlight even more on the way we exercise it. We are used to insisting that as free beings, we should be allowed to act as we please. We even couch it as a human right with a number of corollaries, like freedom of speech. Any attempt to silence it or even just restrict it is regarded as trampling on what empowers us to live our lives as human beings. There is much truth in all of this, and indeed we would do well in society to speak of and defend our rights as human beings, including freedom of speech.

But what is often ignored is that human freedom is not so much what is at stake, but rather the *exercise* of that freedom. Freedom of speech, for instance, is not simply a matter of utilizing it because that is our right. It is rather an action that has consequences on those over whom it is put into use. In fact, it is not an isolated action that we can simply turn on—there is no such thing—because it imposes certain consequences on those who are at the receiving end. Freedom of speech is not just about the agent but also about the receivers, i.e. the listeners or the hearers. In other words, it is always a social act and not just an isolated individual one. It is to be regretted that the fundamental human right of free speech is very much misused and abused because it is misunderstood.

Now it seems that this issue—which is very much a hot one these days because of the ubiquity of social media and the seemingly urgent need felt by some to upload anything and everything or to speak out without much thought—and the observation made above is better brought out by the concept of creative synthesis as it applies to human beings. Being creative—and in this instance, resorting to our rightly prized if at times misused freedom of speech—is merely one aspect, the other being the synthesis aspect. Our exercise of our creativity in this instance, and all instances, has always an effect on all the others. Whether we like it or not, it does have restrictions, not because it degrades us human beings if that were limited but simply because that is the nature of the exercise of creativity, or human freedom if you like.

Freedom of speech is not an absolute right even if it is a unique one. It has consequences and repercussions, both good and bad, and we do have to take that situation into account. We need to consider not just the activation but also the reception of that right. It is not just about *speaking* but also about *hearing* what is being said or communicated. In this context, it is not simply about one's creativity but also about the resultant synthesis.

The concept of creative synthesis can also have a role as we make our way in life insofar as it provides some grounds for hope. That may look like a huge claim, given all the despair, desolation, and suffering in the world. It would hardly be of any consolation to be admonished that things will improve when clearly there are more reasons, seemingly, to conclude that the opposite is true. One has only to tune in to any media or to observe what is and has been happening in one's neighborhood or throughout the world. There would seem to be more reasons for pessimism.

Nevertheless, if creative synthesis is not just a philosophical concept but is rooted in the way reality operates, as we are informed by contemporary physics, then there is a certain amount of indeterminateness throughout that may allow us to hope for a better outcome. What this means, as was outlined earlier, is that there is always a certain amount of freshness, of innovation, of unpredictability such that the situation, before it becomes a past event, can be shaped by whatever is being done now so that it does not become a mere duplicate of what has happened. There is a certain amount of openness, no matter how minimal it is, about reality in general and about life in particular.

Despite the commonly heard assertion, history does not actually repeat itself if by that is meant that whatever has happened will inevitably occur again as it has done previously. It would be accurate, of course, to insist that we should learn from history to avoid making the same mistakes. But more importantly, what the concept of creative synthesis can teach us in this instance is the importance of ensuring that the present, i.e. as we actualize the future, is lived in such a way that it makes a more positive addition to what becomes the past. The past is the outcome of how we exercised our creativity. While it is not always possible to keep that point in mind, given the nature of human beings generally, it does and should challenge us to act much more positively and significantly—to take care of the kind of footprints we leave behind, so to speak. A well-known quote attributed to Albert Einstein provides a helpful reminder; namely, that we should learn from the past, live in the present but hope for the future.

It will be worth our while to take note of this point once again. The kind of past that emerges is due to what we are doing in the present. There is a basis for hope because the nature of the past, as shown by creative synthesis, is that it is never merely a repetition of what has happened but only if we take into serious account—and respond accordingly—that we also have a hand in shaping it. To borrow a line from the Irish poet Seamus Heaney's poem, but going further than he pens it: history and hope *can always* rhyme, simply because we can make it so.[3]

As we ponder on life, "provoked" by its various challenges, we can "invoke" this philosophical thinking about creative synthesis. It shows us that there is a certain amount of inevitability but also a certain amount of unpredictability in the whole of reality. As we chart our route in life then we should learn to accept what *is* but at the same time work towards transforming it into what it *should* be while being prepared that it *may* not be as planned.

Let us now check on how creative synthesis, despite its seemingly abstract explanation, can help us with the task of charting our route in our life-journey and of facing up to what confronts us along the way. It will serve as our map to guide us in our reflections as we steer through what lies ahead of us; that is to say, as we "convoke" our thoughts regarding some of life's challenges.

---

3. Heaney, *The Cure at Troy*, line 18.

Stage Three

Making Our Way

5

As the Water Flows

AS ANY TRAVELER WOULD know, water is an essential commodity to bring on any kind of trip. Not only is it a refreshing drink as one wanders from place to place; but it also replenishes what the body loses, especially in hot tropical climes. Even just its sight can be very much welcome to a weary traveler—one does not have to be in a desert for that to happen! Water can also be handy for washing away tiredness, physical as well as mental. It soothes and it cleanses. After an arduous trek, a wash, a bath or a shower definitely is invigorating. "Wash your hands!" was common advice during the pandemic, drawing our attention to the sanitizing value of water.

Water is also believed to cleanse one spiritually and to have salvific value. It certainly features in all religions; and its use has been incorporated into their rituals, practices and celebrations, such as christenings or immersions. Believers bathe in rivers and other such bodies of water, regarded as sacred, to purify themselves. In this respect, one will readily think of pilgrimage sites like the Ganges River in India, the Jordan River in the Middle East or the Lourdes wells in France.

Because of the water's healing properties spa towns all over Europe are certainly popular to this day. People down through the years have come to appreciate the therapeutic value of soaking in these waters. The ancient Romans had duplicated the wholesome benefits of languishing in such warm water channeling those into their public baths. One can still see what remains of these constructs in a number of Roman-occupied territories, a certain draw for historically-informed and culturally-minded tourists.

Water entertains us, too. In fact, it is one of many priceless forms of keeping us amused and delighted. Just think of fountains, like the popular Trevi Fountain in Rome, where one tosses a coin in the hope of returning. As one travels around the world, one will come across even more attractive and imaginative fountains which delight the visitors and locals alike. Many of us will also recall our childhood days when splashing about in the puddles on the road or jumping in and out of any body of water, no matter how small, would provide hours of delight.

There are, of course, the more conventional swimming pools and various natural bodies of water offering the possibility of an enjoyable time taking a dip or simply relishing the flow of the water against our skin. More sophisticated ways that water spoils us would be water-skiing. Such facilities are an attraction, especially when one is on a holiday. Nowadays there is, of course, surfing, especially if the weather makes it more challenging as well. Information about storms that create giant waves is sure to be uploaded on social media and gets the immediate and delighted response of courageous surfers.

Rain watering the landscape may be a spoiler for some tourists, especially if it also hides the view, as well as for hikers and other road-users who have to tread on the mud. It is nonetheless crucial for breaking down the hardness of nature so that life can once again sprout. In such a situation I call to mind the adage: *ut vivat, crescat et floreat*! which I learned at school, and it helps to dispel or at least lessen any disappointment on my part. There will be growth, and it will help us all, I console myself.

There is something, too, about seeing a body of water, be it part of the natural landscape or the product of someone's creativeness, which captures one's imagination and admiration. That can be uplifting. No wonder, it features in many a travel plan or tour.

Waterfalls are a sure attraction to visitors from near and far. The cascading water accompanied by its roaring sounds will most certainly be included in the itineraries of many trippers. One example would be the world-famous Niagara Falls of Canada. How it dominates the scenery!

Its roar and might are definitely a force to be reckoned with. It certainly fascinates and impresses the millions who flock to it every year and in all seasons. Victoria Falls, a waterfall on the Zambezi River in southern Africa, is another formidable sight. It is located on the border between Zambia and Zimbabwe and is considered to be one of the world's largest waterfalls because of its breadth, stretching across one's horizon. Although on a comparatively smaller scale, Pagsanjan Falls in Laguna, Philippines, has its own attraction in the way the rush of water drops into the river below towards the adventurers waiting in their bamboo rafts. It is exciting even just to watch the entire spectacle.

But quieter waters also appeal to many a traveler. It is re-invigorating to gaze at the serenity and calmness of a lake and its surroundings. Somehow it makes one take it all in, so to speak, and at the same time be taken in by it. Lakes are a favourite spot for relaxing and unwinding. That is certainly the experience of visitors to Lake Bled, a scenic lake in Slovenia surrounded by mountains and forest and featuring an island with a historic church, and to Taal Lake, with the picturesque Taal Volcano at the centre, in the Philippines. I remember with nostalgia the many hours my classmates and I spent stretched out in front of Walchensee in Germany, admiring the water surrounded by the alpine forests of Bavaria—hoping at the same time that the lessons of the day would somehow sink in without much effort on our part!

On the other hand, a fast-moving river, especially when one can hear its churning sounds, can also be uplifting and leaves one wanting to be carried away by its current, no matter to where it flows. Rivers present a challenge for explorers, both the uninitiated and the experienced. There is something about their twists and turns that can make one want to "go with the flow" and at the same time experience the thrill. Somehow one gets that feeling too on a river cruise while taking in the sights as well along the banks. That is certainly true on the Danube and the Rhine in Europe as well as the Chao Phraya River in Bangkok. No wonder, such an experience is popular with tourists.

Then again, there is always the open sea, which beckons to anyone who is ambitious enough to look towards the horizon and to wonder what lies beyond. Somehow it presents a picture of limitless possibilities. It makes one wander much further and even considerably farther in search of distant shores. Indeed, many voyagers did that in the past and led to the discovery of new lands. Or it could inspire one as it did the poet Henry Wadsworth Longfellow with a pulsating longing for "the secret of the sea and the heart of the great ocean" as he portrayed it graphically.[1] It is an impulse that is definitely felt by many, especially the adventurous.

In one's travels, such bodies of water in the landscape do not only catch the eye while providing an escape from life's ponderous burdens and turmoil but they can also be a source of imaginative and thought-provoking moments. In a certain sense they can even be said to serve up some kind of "refreshment for the mind" in that they help us probe deeper into the pitfalls, meet the challenges as well as relish the joys of life.

As we resume our reflections on life-journeys, we should turn to this source. The label "fountain of wisdom"[2] is relevant as well as inviting in this instance. A good example is the Fountain Arethuse, to which the poet John Milton appealed for inspiration.[3] Likewise, Alexander Pope while warning about shallow knowledge urged us to drink deep instead from the Pierian spring as the ancient nymphs did to re-invigorate themselves.[4] It symbolizes the fundamental human search for meaning.[5] Traveling through Ireland, one comes across several lakes and rivers. Cavan, one of that country's counties, is reputed to have a lake for each day of the year. There is certainly a body of water at every turn of the road no matter where one is going. Since these lake are believed to have been filled from the Otherworld, bathing in them or drinking their water is said to bestow healing, inspiration, wisdom and knowledge. Throughout history such an association of water with these gifts to humans is quite widespread in various countries, no matter which part of the world.

Not surprisingly, like many a traveler and stroller down through the ages many individuals have not just cast their glances at but also applied their minds to these bodies of water. After all, it does seem that water nourishes both body and soul, so to speak. In this respect it can be said to offer some lessons that we can learn about life's journey, too. Accordingly, they can provide much that we can ponder on as we continue here to make our way in life. We would do well indeed to draw on that reservoir of insights and their restorative powers.

1. Longfellow, "The Secret of the Sea."
2. Sia and Sia, *That Elusive Fountain of Wisdom*.
3. Milton, "Lycidas," *The English Parnassus*, 132–135.
4. Pope, "An Essay on Criticism," *The English Parnassus*, 199–214.
5. Sia and Sia, *This Deep Pierian Spring*.

Plato famously teaches in his *Dialogues* that it is our duty to search for the truth or at least to follow the best possible doctrine and the hardest to disprove.[6] He seems to have heeded that teaching in his own method of philosophizing. He then provides a rather picturesque advice to treat this doctrine as one rides a raft over the waters of life. He too seems to detect, although in a fleeting manner, some connection between thoughts and water. If that is so, then we should "invoke" such thinking as we move on with our exploration of life and its challenges, this time by casting a glance at how water in various scenarios flows.

But before going off any farther on that route, we will switch our attention first to a few selected poets who have reflected on how water serves as a setting for some thoughts about life. At the same time they provide refreshing insights which could be of benefit to us as we turn our minds to our life journey.

William Wordsworth, a popular English poet, transports us to the lakeside. He composed a very well-known poem titled "I Wandered Lonely as a Cloud"[7] which schoolchildren learn at school. It is particularly appealing not just to that group of learners but also to so many others because it makes one appreciative of what nature presents to us. In spring the sight of these golden flowers heralding the coming of that special season when somehow nature comes alive again is invigorating. One thinks of a rebirth, a renewal—and an opportune time.

Associated with the Lake District in England, this influential poet settled there after some years of wandering. He had been born and raised on its fringes and returned there for some kind of poetic retirement and became closely associated with that district. He had a particular vision of the landscape: leave nature with its naturalness. Seeing an organic relationship between the natural world and human beings, he strongly encouraged it in his literary works. The lakes which form that popular spot are surrounded by flowers and greenery and have lent their name to the place.

---

6. Plato is a highly regarded thinker of the Classical period of ancient Greek history. He founded the Academy in Athens and is well known for his *Dialogues*. He has been a pivotal influence on Western thought.

7. Wordsworth, "I Wandered Lonely as a Cloud," *British and American Poets*, 401.

His poem about the daffodils that he had spotted in his wanderings is illustrative not just of the closeness of humans to nature but also of the effect that such a sight has on their feelings and thoughts. The daffodils were growing beside the lake and stretched along the margin of the bay. Comparing them—"thousands and thousands of them"—to the stars on the Milky Way, Wordsworth wrote of the pleasurable feelings and thoughts that they continue to bring to him. Visitors to that part of England come away with a similar affection for and memories of nature's offerings.

From a different view, Matthew Arnold, another well-known British poet, provides a rather graphic description of Dover Beach, which is separated by a channel of water from France in a poem with that title.[8] He notes how calm the sea was that night, at full tide and lit by the moon. Darkness falls on the French coast after its gleam has faded. The cliffs of England are still visible because of the moonlight, the bay is tranquil, and the night-air is sweet.

He describes the sounds as "the grating roar of pebbles" as the waves play with them in a rather childlike manner. But to him the sound is "the eternal note of sadness" which he likens to what Sophocles had heard in the Aegean Sea. Sophocles was a 5th-century BC Greek playwright who wrote tragedies on fate and the will of the gods. While it was the "turbid ebb and flow of human misery" for the Greek, to Arnold it was the washing away of faith, which he now hears as a sad, long roar withdrawing from the scene. Against such a background, this poet still holds out for true love even if the world, which appears to be a land of dreams, has no certitude, no peace or succor.

We find ourselves in this world, so this poet imagines, as in a darkening shore being swept over by struggle, flight and ignorance. The seashore and its surroundings certainly provided Arnold with much to reflect on regarding the world he was living in. It seems that in a certain sense, the beach and the water reflected an image of Arnold's society. It certainly provoked him into noting the challenges confronting him and fellow "beachgoers" in their walk through life.

For some, on the other hand, the movement of the sea itself as it edges its way towards the shore can be likened to how life unfolds in so many other ways. Although the sea-water keeps moving towards the shore, periodically it recedes, builds itself up into a wave, and then returns with greater strength, splashing on the rocks. It seems that the movement of

---

8. Arnold, "Dover Beach," *The Penguin Book of English Verse*, 344–345.

drawing back helps it to go forward. It provides it with more force. Somehow it renews itself as it makes another attempt to forge its way ahead.

There is something indeed that we can learn from the sea and its movements when faced with life's challenges; namely, that at times "drawbacks" are merely temporary and may even provide the incentive to push ahead again. It can remind us that life may seem to be a series of beginnings, like the constant ebbing away of the sea and returning to the shore. We could take heart from watching the waves and the sea. In this important sense the sight of the sea can stimulate our thoughts, as it did for Arnold, and can revitalize us.

For the Irish poet, Patrick Kavanagh, it was the water in the canal instead and the wish to be commemorated that prompted him to write a few lines of poetry.[9] He wanted to be entertained by the flow of canal water: "so stilly greeny at the heart of summer" where there is a lock that "niagarously roars" for those who sit in silence in mid-July. With such surroundings, he muses, no one would resort to speaking in prose.

He observes that there will be a swan gliding along, a light peering though "the eyes" of bridges, and a barge bringing "mythologies" from distant places. In such a setting, a canal-seat rather than a tomb like those erected for heroes, would help a passerby to remember him. Kavanagh expresses the human wish to be remembered—a universal one—but selects a particular watery setting that is closer to his heart.

Indeed, when one stops by the Grand Canal in Dublin and lingers along the banks, one can feel what this poet expresses: closeness to nature. Somehow, water has a way of bridging the gap between us. Water renews and revives that closeness with the natural world. It is comforting then to realize that one's aloneness is not loneliness after all. For this reason, strolling along not just canals but also rivers, streams, beaches and other bodies of water is a popular pastime. They are also the scene for much reflecting.

These poets have provided us with some kind of setting for our reflections on water. Moreover, they do illustrate in their poetry how bodies of water can provoke certain feelings and inspire deep thoughts. Others, on the other hand, have edged more towards forging a link between water

---

9. Kavanagh, "Lines Written on a Seat," *Chief Modern Poets of Britain and America*, Vol. I: Poets of Britain, 332.

and some aspects of life. We could head towards them now and, as it were, take a few more sips from a pool of their inspired writings.

The Scottish poet, Thomas Campbell, for one, provides in his poem "The River of Life"[10] an insight into the connectivity of water with human life. He compares the stages of life to the movements of the river, describing youth as "the gladsome current" flowing in it. To the young mind, the passage of time, in Campbell's view, seems to be that much longer and each stage is somewhat of a wait. But as old age sets in, the poet asks why we seem to feel its fast movement more. Yet he wonders why anyone would want to slow down time then, especially if our friends have already departed from us, one by one.

The last stanza in his poem sums up those sentiments. According to this poet heaven provides us with fading strength as the years pass by fleetingly to replace our gradually losing the strength and sweetness of youth. For this observer of nature's rivers, these copy the way life itself moves on, like the river, churning at the start and then slowing down stage by stage.

One will immediately associate such a description of growing up and fading away with a passage in one of Shakespeare's plays, *As You Like It*. He describes living as the seven ages, each with identifiable traits. What distinguishes one age from the other is particularly revealing in terms of their personal characteristics and of their likes, dislikes and preferences. There is a noticeable difference as one moves from the exuberance and passion of youth to the diminishing strength of old age.[11] Like the river there is gradual slowing down as it makes its way forward. Somehow, the flow of water in it is similar to the pace of life.

Directing our gaze to a side of life that we should think about is American poet, novelist, and short-story writer, Sylvia Plath, with her poem "Crossing the Water."[12] She is a poet who has drawn on her life-experiences and has written several poems to articulate them through her references to water. Living near the sea seems to have stimulated her into articulating her insights into and feelings about life in several poems with references to water.

The first lines of this poem alert us to the darkness overshadowing someone who is crossing the water—seemingly the way this writer

---

10. Campbell, "The River of Life."

11. Shakespeare, *As You Like It*, Act II, Scene VII, *Complete Works of William Shakespeare*, 218–219.

12. Plath, "Crossing the Water."

envisions a journey in life. She notes that although there is some light for the boat it seems to be unhurried, struggling to shine through the thick leaves of the water-flowers. These appear to be slowing down the rower, and the crossing seems perilous enough. Somehow the cold is prevailing; and darkness is blanketing everything, even the fish in the water.

But then in the last few lines of the poem Plath lifts our eyes to the stars which appear among the lilies in so dramatic a manner as to seemingly blind and even reduce us to silence. Plath, comparing our life journey to crossing the water, shows that there is a dark and sad side to living, but somewhere and somehow some light struggles to get through—a common theme in many of her poems. The miseries and misfortunes in life can become dissipated, even if not entirely.

Another American poet and writer, James W. Foley, shares an insight in his poem "Drop a Pebble in the Water"[13] into how even a tiny pebble dropped into water can also teach us about human living. As we know, if we let a single pebble fall in the water, there will be a single splash which soon disappears. But possibly unknown to us, there are several more ripples which keep circling and spreading and even flow out to the sea without our being aware of it. They become the waves which somehow disturb something larger and mightier than the pebble. Similarly, an unkind or careless word, though gone, lingers on and keeps spreading from its source. Its ripples could cause a "mighty wave of tears" and disturb a life that had been happier before then.

Of some comfort, the poet reassures us, is that the same disturbance could happen in life with a word of cheer and kindness from us. We may forget it, but its happy effects continue to flow and grow. The poet's words are particularly comforting as he reassures us that gladness spreads and joy circles around. Even one word of kindness, which we utter, has a way of being spread around for miles and miles. There are indeed lessons about living that we can draw from the water—at the drop of a pebble. We can derive some satisfaction that any good deed of ours will extend somehow to reach someone's "shores" somewhere.

This poem and its insights into life make me recall another American poet's work, "The Arrow and the Song"[14] which we learned in school. Henry Wadsworth Longfellow mentions his shooting an arrow into the air, not knowing where it would land given the swiftness of its flight.

---

13. Foley, "Drop a Pebble in the Water."
14. Longfellow, "The Arrow and the Song."

Similarly, the speaker "breathes a song into the air" again not knowing where on earth it fell. It was long afterwards, that he found the unbroken arrow in an oak and the entire song in the heart of a friend. It is a good reminder of how our actions have a way of ending up somewhere, hopefully bringing about good.

Another side to living is described in a poem titled "It's a Long Way"[15] by American poet and literary critic William Stanley Braithwaite. He refers to the sea-winds as duplicating what living is about. Comparing his dreams in life to the sea-winds which blow over the sea-plains, he realizes that there is a long way to go before his heart's dream would come true. Meanwhile, he realizes that we have to work and love to the best of our ability while we let our hope keep us on the go. But he sounds optimistic: it may be a long way the sea-winds blow, but he knows that there is a shore out there where his dreams will eventually land.

Indeed, the sea-shore brings to our attention that not only is there a boundary to the ground we are treading right now—with all its toll on us in daily life—but there is another shore somewhere else to which we can direct our hopes and expectations. It may be at some distance and there may be a lengthy wait, but we have the reality of hope to buoy us up as we keep going in life. Seemingly, there is no reason to discontinue with our dreams.

Indeed, as a young kid in the Philippines I always dreamt of crossing the sea to those distant shores. A favorite pastime of my friends and mine, as we lay on the beach after much frolicking and throwing sand at one another in-between taking dips in the sea, was to throw pebbles across the Pacific Ocean, hoping in our rather naïve and imaginative thinking that somehow or somewhere they would facilitate our reaching those distant shores.

Of course, they almost always fell short of our expectations—the pebbles would hit spots which were very visible to us—but we consoled ourselves that there was no harm in dreaming dreams. The gusts of wind were not on our side either. In fact, they would often blow back mockingly in our direction what we had hurled towards the open sea. But once or twice, a more accommodating current of air would take up what had been flung towards it and carry it much, much further than we could see, very much, we told ourselves, like that arrow in Henry Wadsworth

---

15. Braithwaite, "It's a Long Way."

Longfellow's poem that we had learned in school, that was shot into the air and landing one did not know where!

We would converse endlessly about practically everything, but especially about what we wanted to be or do when we grew up. We had no idea how we would go about it, but that did not stop us from dreaming. Later in life, we followed different routes—and ended up in distant shores, both literally and figuratively. But we never forgot those boyhood times spent on the sea-shore, peering into the vast body of sea-water in front of us, wondering and imagining what lay ahead of us.[16]

We have taken, as it were, a few sips from the literary offerings of some poets about the presence and flow of water in lakes, rivers, seas and oceans. But now we ought to imbibe more. We have also been engaged in some initial reflecting on how water makes inroads into our lives. From watching the waters along the literary route that we have been traveling the question for us now is: what further lessons can we take in as we make our way in life? In line with Plato's remarks noted earlier, we could pursue that question a bit farther by turning in the direction of the thoughts of a couple of philosophers.

Let us check out the ancient Chinese thinker Lao Tzu first since Taoism, which has been closely associated with him, has always appreciated the connection between the nature of water and living.[17] In his view, there is much we can learn about life by likening ourselves to water. He taught that there is nothing under heaven which is softer and more yielding than water and yet nothing compares with it for confronting the solid. Water teaches us, according to him, that the weak can overcome the strong, and the supple can topple down the stiff. Indeed, water gets around rather than subdues what lies in front of it. And in this way, it is more successful with its distinctive action—what flows overpowers what is stuck down.

Behind Lao Tzu's paradoxical assertions, which can sometimes be rather challenging to unpack, there are some profound truths according to his disciples. Like the saying attributed to him that we should listen to the sound of one hand clapping, they literally can stop us in our tracks.

---

16. Sia and Sia, *Those Distant Shores*.

17. Lao Tzu was an ancient Chinese thinker, regarded as the founder of Taoism, and the reputed author of the *Tao te Ching*. He is highly influential not only in Chinese society but also elsewhere. His teachings encourage a particular way of living.

They make us wonder and then ponder. Is there a deeper meaning? Indeed, when we look at the nature of water and its character, it will be worth our while examining attentively what he teaches about it and its relevance to living. Let us try then to find out more.

Lao Tzu exhorts his followers to make their hearts like a lake, with a calm, still surface, and great depths of kindness. Indeed, a peaceful lake on a windless day or with only some gentle ripples because of a breeze has such a calming effect, and one can immediately notice it on a person's well-being, as we have noted earlier. But if we are to examine such a scenario further we will come to see that the welcome gentleness of the surface, despite appearances, does not obscure the depths of the lake itself. We will discover that there is more than what merely catches the eye. Likewise, as Lao Tzu points out, we should come to appreciate what is beneath every human being. There is a hidden depth that needs to come to the surface, and may do so with our respect and co-operation. Later on we will be focusing more on this observation as it has been developed by another ancient Chinese philosopher, Mencius.[18] We can linger on then with a view to uncovering this insight into human nature.

In the meantime, there is something we can learn from the nature of water, too. This is why Lao Tzu encourages us to imitate water. He points out that water is accommodating to what it encounters yet it maintains its own nature. It re-shapes itself but holds on to what it essentially is. It changes its form but not its essence. Its integrity is not sacrificed but is, in fact, developed as it interacts with others. Again, this is a teaching that Mencius sets out for his followers and which later on will engage our attention further as we venture into other challenges in life, particularly as we relate to others.

But it is not just what water is that this Chinese thinker alerts us to but what it actually does that invites imitation by us: it enables, it supports and it maintains life. It transports us and our goods. It allows us to reach various destinations. Without water, it can be said that with respect to life there would be no "is" but no "can" either. It is water that nourishes and helps us all to survive. It does not discriminate. It seems that in this sense, one could indeed maintain, as Lao Tzu pointed out, that water instructs us further on how we are to live and support ourselves and others as we travel along life's highways and byways. This is an observation and claim to which we will return a little later, too.

18. Mencius was a Chinese philosopher (372–289 BC). Regarded as the "second Sage" after Confucius himself, he developed the insights and teachings of Confucius.

For another ancient philosopher, the Greek Heraclitus this time, it is the flow of water that serves up an insight into what is fundamental about reality. Heraclitus is well-known for his reference to the river when commenting on reality—and therefore on life itself.[19] He maintains that no one ever steps into the same river twice for two reasons: it is not the same river and he/she is not the same person. This is because everything changes. In fact, according to him, there is nothing permanent and everything is changing. Heraclitus maintained, in contrast to another Greek philosopher, Parmenides, that this means that becoming, rather than being, is the more fundamental reality and thus change rather than stability is the ultimate way of describing what reality is.

This may sound like an "up-in-the-air" kind of debate that metaphysicians are accused of engaging in. While it may have that appearance indeed, it is an important debate nevertheless about what reality is and how we are to understand it ultimately. However, we do not have to detain ourselves examining their argumentation in this instance, but it does have some practical implications for living. Whatever about the debate itself, the issue that deserves our closer attention in the present context is what lesson we can learn about life—if indeed, like the river, it is ever-moving. Our interest will have to be limited into looking at how the nature of a river provides some food for thought as we journey on.

Heraclitus' reference to the flowing river is particularly appropriate when one considers that its current is what pushes it forward. That observation on his part stimulates us into wondering what does that for us in our own life-journey. We may well ask what carries us all along as we travel in life. Earlier, we noted that in life what Aristotle refers to as "goods" that humans crave for "evoke" our interest. In that case, the question for us here is: what is it that preoccupies our attention, what motivates us and what do we value the most as we sail along on life's channels? As we make our way in this reflective journey, it is a question that will keep surfacing. For the moment we will merely take note of it here.

These two philosophers have paved a way for us in a twofold manner: they have not only opened up a line of inquiry, but they have also provided

---

19. Heraclitus was an ancient Greek philosopher (6th-5th BC). In contrast to Parmenides who championed being and static reality, he regarded change and becoming as ultimate. For him, everything flows or is in flux.

the foundation for it as is the case with much of philosophical thinking which engages in fundamental issues, such as the ones we are pursuing here. Let us investigate further.

But first, a few observations about water as a reminder of what we have already come across earlier. As is commonly known and is rather obvious, the natural state of water is movement. It does so in different ways: it seeps, it dribbles, it spouts, it runs, it drains, it spurts and so forth. We have even various ways of describing its manner of flow: it oozes, it trickles, it drizzles, it gushes, it pours, it cascades and so on. Irrespective of how its action is described, the reality is the same: it flows. Lao Tzu makes use of that observed fact to show us how we should live our lives. Heraclitus for his part capitalizes on its movement to depict the whole of reality. Some of the poets, too, who shared their sentiments about the water in our surroundings picture it as indeed flowing.

What can we learn about life from the way water flows? There is a corollary to Heraclitus's observation that it is not the same river because it is constantly flowing. It has power, therefore. One could add to his observation that its power means that it also needs to be harnessed or channeled. Flowing water can be forceful—we see this everywhere. Heraclitus may not have referred to this situation, but as we reflect on water and how it flows we realize that we can channel its power to improve life.

As we noted earlier, too, water nourishes and sustains. But now we can add, taking our cue from Lao Tzu and the poets, that we can also capitalize on its movements, exemplified by the river, to enrich the quality of life itself. It can transport us, too. Its own movement, helped by ours, makes it possible for us also to move around. Water is truly an ally. All around us—dams, canals, water-mills, the sophisticated as well as the simple constructions and contraptions—we can observe that one of nature's offerings facilitates progress and improvement on our way of life.

The movement of water, to which Heraclitus drew our attention, alerts us, additionally, to the destructive side to it. Unfortunately, one cannot ignore the damage to life, property and the environment: flooding, drowning, storm surges, ruination of crops and other fluvial tragedies. It is extremely regrettable since it causes much hardship and heartbreak. This is an undeniable fact of life and of the behavior of water. We ought not to minimize the regrettable effects on everyone and everything because of this reality. The tragic experience of those affected by super-typhoon Haiyan/Yolanda and the consequent sea-surges and by the tsunamis in Japan, India and other countries bordering the sea, as well as of those in similar tragedies throughout the world, is a testimony to this fact of life.

As we have learned earlier, there is much that is tragic in life. And yet one may wonder at times who the true culprit in particular cases is since human negligence is also a contributory factor. This fact of life and of water is a powerful reminder that we do need to play our part towards making sure that harmful consequences are avoided as much as is possible. Caution, as well as care, is called for. Some catastrophes result because of the way we humans have behaved and continue to act.

Where is this observation about water and the way it flows leading us? To answer that, we will need to retrieve what we had learned about creative synthesis and how it may serve as a life-map for our life journey. We will recall that in the whole of reality there is a given—the product of what has transpired and is therefore now outside of our control—but also a freshness as it develops further because of what all of reality, including us, contribute to its further development. In short, we *receive* but we also *provide*.

This observation about the flow of water suggests that we need to be realistic but, more importantly, creative in our dealings with all of nature, including water that surrounds us. We need to *co-operate* with what nature puts at our disposal rather than try to *dominate* it. We are served best when we take not only our concerns but also our responsibilities seriously. As Lao Tzu and many others have pointed out, we need to *walk alongside nature, not step over it*. Instead we often like, regrettably, to control, subjugate or at least tame it.

But we have to realize that we are part of a much larger universe, populated by us but inhabited by many more. These are significant considerations if we are to reach the important goals in life. Earlier the poet James W. Foley opened our eyes to the ever-widening circles created by our actions, with both destructive and constructive consequences. In this instance Heraclitus' observation about water and our experience of its movements should make us not only pause, but more importantly, ponder—and then respond responsibly.

There is something else, however, that we could add here—drawing on what has been explained previously as *creative synthesis*—as we turn to the presence of water in nature. Unlike the air all around us, water even as it flows is "bounded" in various ways; for example, lakes and ponds with their surroundings, rivers and streams with their banks, and oceans and seas with their shores.

This may seem rather obvious and not worth our while following through, especially if our interest is in how it can provide some material for reflection. But, in fact, this reality directs our gaze to the way nature sets limits (the so-called "synthesis") to the flow of water. There may be movement within the water, an observation shared with us by Heraclitus but also by the others. But if we take a second look, we will notice that the flow of water in these bodies is somewhat confined, even if not entirely. We do not readily attend to this fact because usually we are very much taken up with the beauty and charm of these natural boundaries, as we have heard from the poets William Wordsworth and Mathew Arnold, for instance. But there is much more to such "boundaries" than meets the eye. They can, in fact, convey some kind of a message for us, too, to take with us as we venture forth on this reflective trip.

At the same time, nevertheless, there is an "openness" that we also find in nature's bodies of water as shown in the ripples of the lake, the churning of the river—and more significantly, the spaciousness of the sea. These are all reminders that there is much more that is left for us to explore. If anything, they hold out a promise of adventure. There is some amount of fluidity all around us, and it is rather inviting. The poets here sensitized us to that fact. In life—as it is in all of reality, including these bodies of water—much awaits our input or imprint. What we ourselves do (the "creative" aspect) adds to what is there or what has been inherited. Not only that, but we should realize also that it is a fresh addition—our input—to what is already there.

With that in mind, let us pursue this observation of the "boundaries" and the "openness" in nature's bodies of water further. Firstly, these so-called boundaries of water can show us that there is a "given" in all of reality, as was pointed out with the concept of creative synthesis to which we had turned earlier in our search for a life-map. Simply put, they are "there" and we find them all around us. This means that these borders are nature's way of ordering and restricting the movement of the water within them. At the same time, because they are there, they are an integral part of the landscape which nature places in front of us.

Secondly, I would like to think, too, that the "openness" we find in nature's bodies of water as manifested in the ripples of the lake, the churning of the river—and more significantly, the spaciousness of the sea—are reminders that there is also much, much more that is left for us to explore. There is some amount of fluidity surrounding us, and it is rather enticing. In life—as it is in all of reality, including these bodies of water—much awaits our input or imprint. As we had already noted, what we ourselves do adds to what is there or what has been inherited. Not only that, but it is a fresh addition to what is already there and has the potential to contribute positively or negatively.

What lesson for living can we derive from this natural arrangement? Let me elaborate on this point a bit more. In life, what is a "given" is both a gift and a curse as had been pointed out earlier in this reflective journey that we are undertaking here. This means that it may bring joy but can also bear hardships and is therefore not always welcome. What finds its way into our life and even becomes part of it can be wholesome or enriching but can also be ruinous and depressing. This is why there is so much happiness as well as tragedy in the world. Such ambivalence about nature's offerings leads us to pursue the question of life's meaning, the loss of it and the right frame of mind to cope with it.

So how do the so-called boundaries of nature's water help us in this instance? We learned from Lao Tzu that water, exemplified by the lake, shows us the importance of calmness in life. So firstly, life requires from us a certain disposition but also a particular response. I would suggest then, among others, one of *active acceptance* of what life deals to us. Both of these terms are significant here. This may sound rather surprising, and even patronizing; but it is a bit of realism rather than of defeatism. Hence, it should not be equated with simply a surrender to whatever it is that comes our way. To anticipate a later discussion on this matter, it is rather *yielding* to what is inevitable. As Lao Tzu points out, the two actions do not amount to the same thing.

Meanwhile, suppose we take another look at this suggestion from another angle. As was noted earlier, reality is "the coming together" of everything that has taken place and everything that is. The present situation stems from the past and is constituted by it. All the previous events or happenings determine to some extent what constitutes what is presently. Regarding this aspect of reality, therefore, it already is, no matter what we want or do at the moment. The *acceptance* of this reality is a *recognition* of this state-of-affairs.

At the same time, as we have learned from the concept of creative synthesis there is much creativity in reality, including ours. Consequently, it is an active one. By that is meant that there are some additional factors in the process which we are contributing. Lao Tzu's advice about imitating the movements of water is far from suggesting that we remain passive. Instead, while being realistic at the same time, we are also being challenged to be much more *imaginative* in our dealings and *active* in our response. This is what creativity on our part entails.

Heraclitus cites the movement of the river, but we could add in the context of our use of the concept of creative synthesis that it reminds us of the "creative" side of reality. Nothing, we had learned previously, is fully determined. There is always an aspect that is undetermined and hence unpredictable. Just like the bodies of water in nature, there is an openness about and in life itself.

In life we do encounter both what gives us pleasure and pain. We experience joy and sadness. Going through life, we can be left contented or we can be displeased. We receive rewards and undergo trials. We have reasons to be grateful in addition to be resentful. Moreover, we think we are liberated but sometimes also feel restricted. At times, as in a journey, despite some enjoyment and thrills here and there, we become so exhausted or dispirited that we want to give up.

However, we do need to keep *moving on* just as water continues to flow in various ways, no matter what it encounters in its way. Water runs over various surfaces and different types of terrain: the smooth and the rough, the drenched as well as the parched, the straight and even the curved, and several others. There is much that we can learn from this scenario as the poets and philosophers in their wisdom have shared with us.

To draw on Heraclitus' observation about the river, we move with, or are towed by, life's "current" as it flows. But should we always swim with the current? That is an important consideration. Our swimming instructor taught us as kids that for safety reasons we should always do so, especially if there is any danger of drowning. Fighting the current not only weakens us, but it also makes a foe of the water. Instead, we should align ourselves with the bank or shore and gradually edge ourselves towards it. It was a lesson that has been truly beneficial.

But does that apply to living as well? Do we have always to go with the flow? Should we not at times stand up or oppose the current of thought or the dominant way of life instead? What if certain standards or principles, particularly moral ones, are at stake? Ought we not rather uphold those? We will need to examine this point further at a later stage. After all, we are empowered by our "creativity"—as Hartshorne puts it—and we should put it to good use. To borrow from the poet Sylvia Plath, our life journey is about "crossing the water" despite seemingly insurmountable barriers or even misleading routes along the way. And as William Stanley Braithwaite points out, somewhere "there is a shore" awaiting us. What kind of shore we will have to wait and see. That is a motivating factor surely.

Let us find out more about what is entailed in all of these as we resume our reflections in the following pages.

6

Going Away, Getting Out, Moving On

So far, in our reflections on our life-journey we have been making our way around with the help of the concept of creative synthesis as a map to guide us. We made use of Heraclitus' observation about the river and likened life to it: always moving, constantly changing, and gathering experience. Our hope here has been that this comparison of life to travel—and to the flow of water—will promote an attitude of openness and a search for purpose on our part while accepting the givenness that is part and parcel of living.

It is now time to make other inroads and venture even further by looking at certain aspects of our travel. Once again, we hope to find similarities between our ordinary travels and our life-journey. In fact, many philosophers regard travel as a helpful metaphor for life inasmuch as it encourages a certain way of existing in our world. This is yet another example of how the way we think influences the way we behave.

As we have learned, Gabriel Marcel, the French existentialist philosopher, uses precisely that term to refer to human nature: *homo viator*.[1] Despite the instability we experience, we are buoyed up by hope as we embark on our life journey. Others compare life to a pilgrimage, as indeed many religions teach their followers. Human life is regarded

---

1. Marcel, *Homo Viator*. Gabriel Marcel, who died in 1973, was a French philosopher, playwright, and music critic. He has been generally regarded as a leading Christian existentialist who described and reflected on the modern individual struggling in a technologically dehumanizing society.

as being in transit: we are moving towards a certain destination. It is up to us—or to those who are in charge—to determine the purpose of that journey by how we live our lives. Such descriptions connote or demand a certain way of living.

Along similar lines, Mark Twain, the famous American writer, provides a rather thought-provoking angle. He regarded travel as being fatal to prejudice, bigotry and narrow-mindedness.[2] Somehow, it does have a way of broadening one's horizons, literally and intellectually. One could add that it also helps with character-building, a concern that we will follow up later when we turn once again to Mencius' and Buber's insights. George Santayana, the philosopher who straddled two countries, Spain and America, claims that travel is, in fact, the key to intelligence. Instead of our being encompassed by mere feelings, in his view, travel opens our eyes and mind. The turn from the familiar to the unfamiliar makes us wiser. According to Santayana, it keeps the mind nimble, kills prejudice, and fosters humor.[3]

If we are to go along with these writers and traditions, travel and life are certainly interconnected in so many ways. Somehow we would be hard-pressed to disagree, particularly if we have been lucky enough to do much traveling ourselves. In Europe the Erasmus Programme, and in the United States the Fulbright Exchange Program seem to have taken that link on board in that these combine study with traveling, especially for younger students. In this regard, as we have been learning all along and will address once more later on, education does play an important role in enlightening us about life itself. To have the opportunity to travel as well is definitely a bonus to one's development.

As we examine further what it is that we should keep in mind as we travel on life's routes—and recalling our previous reflections at the same time—we could ask: Is it all a question of "going away" or "getting out" or "moving on"? Each of these indicates a specific intent. Moreover, as we proceed here with our deliberations we will also find out how these

---

2. Mark Twain's real name was Samuel Langhorne Clemens (November 30, 1835–April 21, 1910). He was known for his wit as well as for his writings, among others, on the adventures of Tom Sawyer and Huckleberry Finn. The quote in the text is one of those ascribed to him. He regarded travel as an eye-opener to important aspects of life.

3. George Santayana, whose real name was Jorge Agustín Nicolás Ruiz de Santayana y Borrás (1863–1952) was a philosopher, essayist, poet and novelist. His *The Life of Reason* is regarded as the first extended discussion of pragmatism, a school of thought closely associated with American philosophy.

terms designate somewhat the nature of our travel as well as provide a particular understanding of life itself.

For most of us, traveling is equivalent to simply *going away*, irrespective of purpose or manner. The Chinese philosopher Lao Tzu, whose remarks and observations have been helpful to us with our earlier reflections, pointed out that one travels best who has no fixed plans and who is not too intent on arriving. That observation may sound rather strange; but as travel aficionados can vouch, being in transit, whether by land, air or water is itself an experience. Moreover, a change of scenery, a different atmosphere or a new location does wonders for one's psychological make-up and mood. Indeed, travel itself is simply part of daily life and, generally speaking, fits in with our human outlook.

Travel could be undertaken, of course, for a specific purpose: some further enjoyment, because of our professional duties, due to business connections or for some other reasons. It could be that one simply wants a break, and going somewhere else provides that. Travel can also be an adventure; and to be able to visit other places, especially exotic destinations, can be thrilling. Most of these are pleasant experiences, and we usually return with fond memories and stories to share. Professional, business or official travel is undertaken to meet the requirements of the job. Its nature and end-result are dependent on the outcome of one's performance. The important thing in this regard is to reach one's destination so that one accomplishes what one has in mind. There are, of course, those trips which are undertaken because of emergencies. And depending on the kind of emergency, our reaction will vary. But whatever it is, it is primarily to deal with the urgent situation at one's destination.

Holiday time, especially during the summer months, has become the equivalent of "*going away*" to a planned destination or even anywhere. In Europe, roads are so clogged up with traffic due to multitudes of vacationers wanting to reach their holiday destinations that one wonders whether it is all worth it. And yet, most of them, dreaming of the wonderful time ahead of them, will readily agree. Mainland China, as well as places which have a number of Chinese residents, can expect the exodus of thousands and thousands of their citizens during their lunar New Year celebrations to spend time with families sometimes several kilometers away. Thanksgiving in the USA is not just about the turkey dinner with one's family, it is also about packed cars and full-up planes for a few days before and after the day itself. Traveling at Christmas time, for most countries in the world, can be unnerving because of the crowds that rush to avail of all means of transport. In all of these times, it is a matter of managing to "go away" indeed.

The thrill of simply "going away" revives what I experienced about the reality of that German word, *Wanderlust*. It is the equivalent of what is known in jest as "having itchy feet"—a description which many a traveler would accept. As a young student, the idea of being able to simply get on a train in Germany, show off one's Inter-rail ticket to the inspector, hop off at some unplanned stop merely because it aroused my curiosity, then get back on the train for—somewhere else—was truly an enriching experience. At other times, I would open a map of Europe and then decide that another European city would be worth the adventure: Budapest, Prague, or Paris, perhaps?

It was a stage in my life-journey when both age and circumstances favored such travel. It was also the occasion, when stranded at the border between Austria and Hungary and having to spend the night at the train station, I experienced what Confucius said that all we need is "a bent arm for a pillow" for sleeping! Fortunately, an empty bench kept me off the cold cement floor. It may not have been the most comfortable sleeping experience, but it was a tale to share—and to exaggerate in the re-telling!

A similar experience took place in the USA when Amtrak, by way of compensating for the extraordinary delay in the train journey to Washington state, sent me and the other passengers a voucher—valid for any of their train routes in the USA. This was too good a chance to go just about anywhere in the country, I told myself. It was indeed one of those "get-away" breaks that I thought would be fun, too. So instead of hassling myself with all the choices opened up for me, I simply packed, headed for Los Angeles Union Station, the main railway station in Los Angeles, California, and boarded the first train about to depart that morning. I found myself heading for—the deserts of Arizona! A fantastic experience, as it turned out, because I had finally the chance to acquaint myself with the culture of the Native Americans, something I had been hoping to do. The souvenirs and artwork I brought back with me in my backpack are happy reminders of that trip that was made on impulse.

It may sound strange at first, but a phrase that one is likely to hear regarding travel and life is: "I do need to *get away*—soon!" It seems as if for both of these not only is time of the essence but the trip is meant to be more of an escape rather than simply a break. This could come across as pitiful and even lamentable, yet one can easily imagine perfectly that it is an understandable outburst. After all, there are certain situations in both contexts when we urgently require getting away from them. We have had those experiences in our lives!

But the kind of travel which leads to the outburst cited above is quite different. Of course, it could be uttered in jest, and that is all there is to it. After all, it is quite a common expression. When one is pressed on all sides with work or commitments, and one seemingly has no time to spare, that expression easily slips out of one's month. Or if one has to dart from one location to another endlessly, then indeed one feels like escaping from that routine.

Nevertheless, when one actually means what those words express it is a different matter altogether. In this case wanting desperately to travel in this circumstance comes about not so much because one wishes to see places, visit certain sights or link up with friends somewhere else or to deal with whatever is the reason for going on the trip. It is not so much that one is, in fact, looking forward to what lies ahead as wanting simply to leave behind an unacceptable situation. Somehow one gives the impression of having been cooped in for whatever reason and wanting desperately to be free. Indeed, it would seem as if in such a case the destination does not have to be specified; what is more important is that one manages to get out. In some circumstances, regretfully, escaping is probably a more fitting description.

This feeling of wanting to get away seems to be the recent experience of many because of the COVID 19 pandemic which has been gripping practically the entire world, with no end in sight. It has resulted in a situation where indeed very many have felt like "escaping to somewhere fast" just to leave the situation behind. To make matters worse, there is no place to travel to, however. Governments of various nations have had to impose tight lockdowns on their communities in the hope of stemming the advance of the fast-moving virus. Individuals, families, and communities, while accepting the need for the strategy adopted by public officials on the advice of the scientific community and medical staff have

Going Away, Getting Out, Moving On

all felt that, as weeks became months and another lockdown had to be imposed, there was a need to "break away"—no matter to where because the limitation of movement had personal, economic and psychological repercussions. Travel was definitely out of the equation, and even contacts with others were limited.

There has been much concern about the economic impact that travel restrictions have been having on society. Indeed, the situation has brought again another financial crisis as businesses close down or cut back. The damage will regrettably be felt for several years. But equally, the psychological burden weighing on people has been getting heavier, particularly among those who live on their own as well those over a certain age. But no matter what the individual circumstances are, one cannot but feel that there is a certain restlessness, not just because those restrictions have become protracted but because they do go against the very nature of human beings.

It does indicate that "wanting to get away" is not simply a feeling even if in some circumstances, like the present situation with the pandemic, it probably is. Because we have a restless nature, it is ingrained in each and every one of us to want to be able to break away from whatever keeps us back, and to venture forth. It is closely associated with our free nature, but is a variation from merely having the ability to choose. It is more a matter of being able to move away instead of having to stay put. When we are confined in whatever form, then we are robbed of what is natural in us.

A comparable yet different travel experience for those fleeing from or displaced by persecution, wars, disasters and other calamities both natural and human-made is focused more on what awaits them. Migration for varied reasons, for instance, has been a fact of life throughout history. Today, unfortunately, we hear, watch and read about the sad plight of individuals and families of those who walk barefoot and cross perilous seas and hostile territories seeking an improvement in their lives,. It is much more than a getting out of the dire situation, however. It is searching for better living conditions.

"*Moving on*"—the kind of travel involved here is not simply a question of a change of location but more significantly a matter of an improvement in what life offers. As human beings it is natural for us to seek something "better" somewhere else. That phrase carries that important connotation. As it applies therefore to the kind of migration resulting from such tragic circumstances, it implies more than simply a departure from dreadful conditions. More importantly, it is in the hope of an arrival at more congenial circumstances and welcoming locations.

This kind of "moving on" is part and parcel of our nature as human beings. We are in search of something better—it pulls us, as it were. We are restless, so to speak, and we want to risk everything. This means that given such circumstances described earlier which force people to migrate, it is not just understandable but even more so, imperative that they do so. It is degrading when human lives are subject to these conditions. We owe it to ourselves to seek an improvement in our lives. And we all have the responsibility to make that possible for everyone.

There is, however, another comparison between travel and life in the sense of "moving on" that also deserves our attention here. There are those who choose to "leave behind" everything in search of something "better" than the present plight. "Moving on" as far as they are concerned, means renouncing everything. For some of us, that would be a rather drastic move, but the motivation behind it deserves our attention.

For certain groups, like the Taoists, it involves withdrawing completely from society. This is because life in society is regarded as a distraction and if one wants to achieve peace and harmony, one can do so only by heading towards a life of complete isolation so as to seek union with nature. It is not a simple exercise as it involves both thought and action. We certainly got that impression—a lasting one—when we visited the Taoist temple in Taipei, Taiwan.

Others do live a similarly strict life but in communities, like the Trappist and Carthusian monks, Carmelite and Benedictine nuns, and members of various religious organisations, both male and female, in other religious traditions. Silence, work and prayer are certainly the order of the day. For them life is a religious journey towards its source. "Moving on" seemingly is a moving within. That point definitely comes across when one spends time with them even at some distance, especially when they are at prayer, an experience that made an impact on us during a week-long visit with the nuns at St. Bede's Monastery in Petersham, Massachusetts, USA.

For some, on the other hand, the search for peace and tranquillity is achieved on the mountain top. It looks as if it involves a "moving up" literally and symbolically. Indeed, a climb to mountain tops has always been associated with traveling to them so as to be close to the source of life. Pilgrimages to such places as Croagh Patrick in County Mayo in Ireland, are very arduous but popular. Yet for the pilgrims to this mountain, it is a rewarding journey in the footsteps of the country's patron saint, St. Patrick. It is one that annually attracts thousands, irrespective of the weather, some even going barefoot. One hears of the peace and tranquillity that they achieve in so doing.

Still others, in fact, build their monasteries where they spend their entire lives at the very summit of the mountain. That is certainly true of the religious communities atop Mount Athos, a mountain and peninsula in north-eastern Greece and an important center of Eastern Orthodox monasticism. It has a very long tradition, having been inhabited as far back as ancient times. The more than 2,000 monks from Greece and other Eastern Orthodox countries like Romania, Moldova, Georgia, Bulgaria, Serbia and Russia are known to live an ascetic life in isolation from the rest of the world.

The tour we joined to visit the Eastern Orthodox monasteries in Meteora in central Greece was definitely and literally a breathtaking experience. We were struck by how they had managed to construct these in the first place. Sitting atop the rock formation, these monasteries are built on huge natural pillars and rounded boulders which resemble a hill. They certainly dominate the scene, and it was difficult for us to look anywhere else so imposing is the view.

The place certainly deserved its name since it means "lofty" or "elevated"—and it was! Our guide informed us that the earlier monks used removable ladders or windlass to gain access to the top! Fortunately for us, now there are steps carved into the rock which we proceeded to take slowly and hesitantly. We did see the rope ladder that is used to haul goods to the monastery today. We heard that of the six monasteries still in use, the Holy Monastery of St. Stephen and the Holy Monastery of Roussanou are inhabited by nuns. Monks dwell in the others. In 2015 the total monastic population of these Meteora monasteries was 56: 15 monks in four monasteries and 41 nuns in the other two.

It seems as if for these religious communities in Mt. Athos and Meteora, life is a completely spiritual journey, one which took them to the summit and away from ordinary living. "Moving on" for them was an uphill journey in more ways than one but which they seemed nonetheless to have found most fulfilling! For the visitors, the peaceful walk around their truly awe-inspiring place following the arduous climb up provides a sample of what an inspiring journey can be like. It was worth the effort.

Let us catch our breath here, as it were, so as to gather together our reflections on the link between travel and life in the present context. We have been focusing on what is involved and wondering whether it is a matter of *going away, getting out,* or *moving on.* Each of these shows a different aspect of our life-journey. But is it, as the phrases which we have just looked into imply, simply a matter of "departing" or "exiting" or "continuing"?

It may seem odd, but it seems to me that it is none of these and yet it is all of them! There is a sense in which as we travel in life, we are leaving behind certain experiences, we are getting out of particular circumstances, but more importantly, we are searching continuously for some form of improvement. It is really whichever of these movements dominates and characterizes our life-journey that truly matters. But if we care about finding meaning and purpose, hopefully we are more intent on *moving on* in life. After all, it is a matter of importance, rather than merely one of choice.

But perhaps we should be clearer as to what is involved in identifying our life-journey with the process of "moving on" rather than with the other two movements cited. After all, it can be understood in a number of ways. Moreover, we had noted how it is exemplified in different ways by various groupings. In this respect, philosophy can possibly come to our aid given its claim that progress can be achieved in our thinking when we leave out or critique wrong or misleading interpretations of a word, phrase or idea.

Ludwig Wittgenstein, a 20th century Austrian-British philosopher who is strongly associated with Anglo-Saxon analytic philosophy, was well-known for his insistence on clarity in our thinking by debunking systems of thought which, in his view, are based on unclear premises. Thomas Aquinas too, medieval Italian philosopher and theologian, developed a logical pathway whereby he would discuss first what he considered to be falsehoods prior to focusing on what he regarded as the truth. He exemplified in his prodigious output that logical thinking involves eliminating incorrect options to what is being proposed in addition to pursuing the right one.[4]

We could take the advice of these thinkers here since to be able to know what something is, it does make some sense to indicate to some extent what it is not. I like to think that this suggestion can be likened to clearing the footpath initially of debris, leaves, or rubbish so that we can make our way forward more readily. Without these barring our path, we could also pick out the right road and thereby avoid ending up in cul-de-sacs. Such a strategy in thinking opens the way for us also to see more readily what is correct or true.

We could start then by clarifying that "moving on" as used here to describe our journey in life is *not* the same as "moving ahead" either. Admittedly, at times these two phrases amount to the same thing. They both point to a forward movement. They also indicate a positive choice that is under consideration or being made. Nevertheless, as used here to describe our journey in life, there is an important difference: not so much in the activity itself but the context in which it is being carried out.

"Moving ahead" somehow implies that life is a race and that one needs to outdo the others or outshine the rest. But it should not be. It is not about stepping on one another either to get in front. We are not in competition with one another as far as our journey in life is concerned, even if we do have to admit that in certain contexts such rivalry is healthy and should be promoted. As we "move on" in life, we do not have to, nor should we, leave everyone else behind on the understanding that only then can we succeed. That is a false move, despite its popularity.

"Moving on" in the present context is *not* about asking others "to move over" either. Again it has to be admitted that there are circumstances when it would not just be acceptable but even necessary to insist that those in the way should move over. Obstacles blocking one's journey in life, including individuals or groups or circumstances, should be "moved over" or removed in certain cases. When it is a matter of anyone or anything unjustifiably blocking one's path, then one ought to take direct action so as to be able to proceed on one's journey in life. In contrast, "moving on" is directed at oneself in this context. It is about continuing and pursuing one's forward-looking move. It is concerned with what lies ahead and motivating oneself towards it. More importantly, it implies—in

4. Both Wittgenstein and Aquinas, in addition to their philosophical insights and teachings, have exercised considerable influence on the pursuit of logical thinking: Wittgenstein with linguistic analysis and Aquinas with the *via negativa.*

the way it is being used—accompanying, rather than outrunning, one another as we trek on in life. We will have the chance to return to this topic at a later stage in our reflections.

As has already been mentioned on a number of occasions, we cannot discard the past simply because whatever has taken place persists. It becomes part of the present. So "moving on" is not about denying whatever has happened but rather about surpassing it, as it were. Good or bad, since it becomes part of our present and will continue on to the future, often we have to make use of our creativity so that it results in what is good, useful or acceptable. In this way, it becomes beneficial for the future. Again, we will, as we continue with our reflections, hear more about this point.

As it applies to our journey in life "moving on" can also be clarified further if we follow through our earlier reflection on life viewed in the way water flows. As we will recall, there is something in the movement of the water, particularly Heraclitus's river, that exemplifies for us that living is about "moving on" as well. But there is something else that we could bring up here as we turn our attention once again to the presence of water around us; namely, the danger that stagnant water poses. It can be murky, it can be dirty, and it can be dangerous. Health officials, particularly in tropical countries, have rightly been warning the populace that such a body of water can be a breeding-ground for malaria-carrying mosquitoes. A similar warning has also been issued about water that is left in open containers. That, too, is the habitat of mosquitoes that spread dengue.

Life that does not "move on" can be compared to stagnant water. It is not so much the physical movement—although that too is crucial for healthy living—but more importantly, the attitude that we adopt in life. As the water flows, so should life. As humans, we are meant to do the same because we have the capacity. It is important to make use of whatever resources are at our disposal to "move on." There is some wisdom in the saying that the best way to show appreciation of something is to put it into good use. We can do that as we journey in life. Just as important is that we also support, rather than compete with, one another. All these observations, which we will take up again later on, are entailed by the phrase "moving on" used in comparable contexts.

Meanwhile, there is something that we can learn from those who do take seriously the challenge of "moving on" in various forms as exemplified by groups referred to previously. There is an underlying belief in all of them that life *beckons* to us: while we need to continuously glance back, there are more reasons to look forward. Often we do have to exert more effort to find those—as we have been noting along the way in these reflections. To adapt what the Dalai Lama says about our quest for happiness and the need for us to exert an effort to achieve it[5]—those reasons for moving on do not come pre-packed. We have to continue assembling them ourselves, so to speak. In short, we have to *motivate ourselves*. Only then will we have some success.

And yet there is a sense, strange as it may seem at first, in which "moving on" can and should include *retracing our steps*. This is not the same, however, as merely returning or turning back to where we had started although that move can at times be helpful, too. It is not an about-turn, a retreat or backtracking therefore. Neither is it a matter of giving up because the going is arduous or challenging. "Retracing our steps" as associated with moving on, implies a more deliberate and careful maneuver on our part. It entails stopping, searching and deliberating. More importantly, it connotes *learning* from the earlier stage of moving forward so that one would be in a better position to progress or *make amends* in order to bring about an improvement in the situation.

One of the strategies taught to us in our hiking days as youngsters involved being able to retrace our steps whenever we discovered that we had lost our way. Instead of continuing on in the same direction, we were instructed to firstly come to a halt and then to look around. We were then prompted to check back on our previous itinerary. Since we had been warned to mark out certain spots or identify specific landmarks as we trod along, it would be a matter of merely recalling those. It would also aid our memory, we were assured, if we associated those with something that we were more familiar with, in addition to utilizing our compass.

But as we were to realize once we had understood what was involved, it was not simply turning back on the same route. It was therefore much more than just moving in the opposite direction back to our starting point. As we retraced our steps, we were reminded to examine again those spots which we had earlier marked out. The whole idea, as it turned out, was for us to note where and why we had gone astray and thereby

---

5. The Dalai Lama uses this phrase "the art of happiness" as the title of some of his books and sermons.

be able to get our bearings. That would then provide some guidance on how or if we could proceed further and make any necessary corrections.

I came to appreciate this practical strategy on a number of occasions since I had to resort to it when we travelled to unfamiliar territories or ventured into new locations in our travels in various countries. In fact, I discovered that it can facilitate one's exploration and even provide some kind of confidence to venture farther. After all, there seems to be a way out if one gets lost, one tries to reassure oneself. But, of course, it was crucial to heed the advice of taking the precautions cited above. Otherwise, one lands in a real quandary—as had happened to us on a couple of occasions!

That practical advice became even more helpful, however, when I discovered later on that it can also be a lesson for our life-journey. That was not too evident at first. But when I came across the Danish philosopher, Søren Kierkegaard, and his insights into how we should live our lives. I could somehow see some connection. His oft-repeated observation that while life must be lived forwards, we can understand it only backwards, I interpret to mean that as we "move on" in life, we will make some advance—strange as it may appear—if we also retrace our steps in a reflective manner, very much like what we had been taught during our hiking days.

Indeed, as we go about our everyday routine or engage in some extraordinary tasks, sometimes it is important indeed to halt and look back not so much to simply recall the past—which in itself would be commendable—but rather to *re-orient* ourselves. While we are on our journey in life sometimes we accomplish something worthwhile or we make positive contributions. They do not have to be particularly spectacular to stand out as landmarks for us. But that is certainly marking progress. During those moments when we need to "re-orient" ourselves, these achievements can then provide some consolation and hope that all is not entirely lost even if not everything is going according to plan. Just as familiar spots that we had singled out as we move on and coming to our rescue when we retrace our steps in our ordinary travels, as we had been trained, these can come to our assistance in our re-orientation during our life-journey. They can also give us some comfort and reassurance as we think back. It is crucial that we mark our life-journey with these as much as we can.

There is, of course, the other dimension of our journey in life. Because of the hustle and bustle of life or the pressures of work we can now and then be left feeling "off course" intermittently. This is to be expected since as we trek on in life, we do take some missteps. We often stumble and even fall. We drift now and then. We then go astray and make the wrong choices. We are tempted by shortcuts or take the wrong turn, at times deliberately. We then lose our way. Somehow moving forward becomes blurred, confusing and even wearisome. Given our waywardness it becomes a task to keep going. It could even lead to "existential angst" as described by some thinkers. Ending in such a situation we do need to be able to find our way again. Otherwise, we could end up in a worse scenario.

Fortunately for the majority of us, this is not a daily occurrence inasmuch as our attention is taken up with various things which provide some kind of direction. There are goals to be reached and tasks to be fulfilled. But there are times when we do come to the realization that "something is missing" from our lives, and we need to find it again. That can make us restless, and we begin to wonder whether there was something in the past that we had missed or overlooked. At such times, we do need seemingly to "retrace our steps" to be able to move on.

In such situations, the advice handed down to us as hikers would seem to be of some relevance: the routes we take as we journey in life, sometimes routinely, are worth examining—and re-examining from time to time. And if mistakes had been made, we need to admit those and rectify the situation as best we can. It may also involve reparations so as to set the record straight again. It could mean amending our ways.

How does one go about it? Once again, it would seem to be a call to pause and ponder. More than likely, one would think of retreats or recollection periods which devote specific times to such reflective sessions. These can indeed facilitate "re-tracing" as described here. But they do not have to be as organized or protracted as those well-known sessions. What is more important is that time is set aside to think back with a view to drawing some lessons about one's progress in life's journey.

In this respect the narrative contained in the New Testament is of particular relevance. It is instructive regarding what is entailed in "retracing our steps" as described here. As is well known, the parable of the prodigal son is about a discontented son who demanded his inheritance from his father so that he could seemingly live it up.[6] He proceeded to do just that when he got his share, enjoying his debauchery away from home. As is to be expected, however, that largess did not last long. The

---

6. Luke 15:11–32.

poem "The Prodigal"[7] by American poet Elizabeth Bishop could well be a depiction of the situation he found himself in: left in utter misery and poverty, including smells, sounds and sights. It made him pine for home and long for earlier times. He recalled the earlier happy times that marked his life then and the generosity of his father.

But it was really what made him "turn around" that would be worth our attention here. Obviously, his miserable situation was what prompted his action. Reflecting on his former plight at home and realizing that it had been a mistake on his part to forsake it in order to pursue the kind of life that he thought would bring him much satisfaction, he now realized that he had to "reorient" his life if he wanted to progress. It was not simply a matter of finding his way back home, but of re-directing and rectifying his life altogether. He had lost his way, but after some serious ruminating and resolving to do better, found his way back. He was then able to "move on" as it were. In this sense, he illustrates how important it is that in one's journey in life, one does at times step back, reflectively and resolutely, so as to be able to move forward.

Another example is worth our while considering in this instance. As is well known, sports can be a metaphor for living. Many of us are familiar with the Latin saying, *mens sana in corpore sano*. Indeed keeping our bodies healthy does enable us to have a more positive and even brighter outlook on how our life-journey itself shapes up. Various sporting activities can also encourage us to mind our bodies as well as promote teamwork. While there are also the inevitable unwelcome consequences due to failure, frustration and defeats because of its competitive nature, generally sports in various forms and types can be said to result in a certain buoyancy about life that we probably do not experience elsewhere. In such circumstances, we can find life to be uplifting.

This attitude to life and its challenges seems to have been illustrated by the Irish gymnast at the final of the men's pommel-horse gymnastic competition in the Tokyo 2020 Olympics (postponed until August 2021 due to the pandemic). Rhys McClenaghan suffered a crushing defeat in his bid to win his country's first ever Olympic medal in gymnastics. He had been a leading contender until then, having scored highly all through the qualifying rounds. Unfortunately, during the finals he lost his balance and fell off the pommel horse. It was a bitter disappointment and seemingly the end of his dreams. But having composed himself, he had a

---

7. Bishop, "The Prodigal," *New Discovery*, 19.

brief word with his coach, and then he made his way back to the pommel horse. He returned to where he had stopped, not to a victory at his sport, but to the kind of motivation that can be a model for us.

During the interview arranged almost immediately after his performance, he converted the negative to a positive.[8] Highlighting his past accomplishments but accepting his present faulty performance, he analyzed and explained what had happened. But he quickly added that he was now looking forward to a return as "a way better gymnast, a way better man" despite or because of his earlier failure. His goal has always been to break down barriers and surpass his achievements. He intended to continue doing just that. Indeed, he may have fallen, but he "retraced his steps" and then resumed his sporting journey—and his life-journey, one could add.

As we ourselves continue now with pondering on life a further question is: can the concept of creative synthesis advance our understanding of our journey in life? Can it facilitate us to re-trace our steps? Can it help us to move on and stay on track? It had been suggested earlier that it could serve as a map. Would having some kind of a life-map provide some assistance so that we can take stock?

We will recall that creative synthesis, the life-map suggested earlier, is a coming together in a fresh way of all that has existed or occurred previously. There is no mere repetition but rather a certain novelty. If this concept is to assist us as we make our way in life, we will need to find out how it can provide some re-orientation as we go along as well as how we should proceed when we encounter anything that will impede our progress.

Shall we move on then?

---

8. *Irish Post*, "No medal, but Irish gymnast Rhys McClenaghan wins plaudits."

Stage Four

Staying on Track

7

Tunnels, Crossroads, Detours

As we make our way in life, charting our routes so to speak, there are further comparisons which we can draw between our life-journey experiences and those on our ordinary trips. The nature of the travel, the construction of the road or path, or the alteration of the route can make a difference to the progress made and to the quality of our travel. Similarly, our various experiences and our responses to these as we move on in life have a way of shaping our life-journey and the quality of life, as well as the progress we make.

Sometimes the road or route that we take is a straight one, and it is really a matter of simply following it so as to reach our destination. As we would at times describe it colloquially, it is "plain sailing" after all. That kind of journey inevitably makes one long for similar ones in the near future. At other times, however, the road has certain twists and turns, and our manner of traveling involves much more attention and care. It may even mar the anticipated joy. There are occasions, for instance, when our travels involve going through a tunnel, arriving at a crossroad, or following a detour. These require changes in our manner of traveling and may even put a stop to the progress we are making.

Such "tunnels, crossroads, and detours" are in life, too. They present us with some problems, and our response to these can often make a difference to the kind of life we live. Thus, it will be worth our while in this instance to examine how tunnels, crossroads and detours—very much a part of the landscape and of surface travels—can offer valuable lessons that we can learn about how to deal with some of the challenges confronting us in life.

If one is traveling on roads which skirt around mountains, one can expect that at some stage, one would be going through a tunnel. This is particularly the case with surface travel throughout continental Europe. Doing so cuts the journey time considerably. It has therefore some practical advantage compared to the long haul on the surface roads. It can also be less expensive generally. For most of us, it is simply a development in traveling that was bound to happen insofar as it makes it more convenient. For a few, however, the experience can be also exciting and fun. For them it can be worth adding to the account of the travel, especially when one relives those moments in the narration to family and friends about one's travels.

But this construction on the route also has some drawbacks. While for the majority of us, as was already noted, it is simply a fact of traveling, there are some for whom the experience of going through a tunnel can be unnerving because the lack of daylight, despite the presence of artificial lighting, somehow cuts one off from rather familiar surroundings. It is quite understandable that they would become nervous. Even for the majority of us, going through a tunnel which stretches for a considerable length, makes one ask: How long will it be before we reach the exit? When will we see the sunlight again? Relief comes when signs appear indicating that one is almost there.

That negative experience can be a graphic way to describe the roughness of life: it is like "going through a tunnel—with no light at the end of it" is frequently heard. Unlike being in the presence of one's natural surroundings, the journey inside these tunnels with only the noise of motor or train engines breaking the silence can make one apprehensive. At times life is indeed like that. The experience of seemingly going through life's tunnels could be isolated moments. Or it could be for a much longer spell. But these occasions can and do provoke us into wondering whether there is more to life than experiencing such moments or spells, particularly if they are not isolated or brief. For some, regrettably, protracted periods of low mood or depression can be overwhelming. Going through such a tunnel in life is not to be welcomed at all.

There was a particular experience of going through a tunnel that has left an impression on me. It was during an excursion arranged by the summer language institute, this time in Austria, which I was attending in my youth. The plan for the group was to see the historical and cultural sites of a town a good distance away. As any such participant at these courses knows, these outings are always part and parcel of the program, adding to the enjoyment of attending foreign-language courses.

I was looking forward to the trip because we had been informed that it involved going through a long tunnel—a rather new experience for me at that time. I was, of course, also anticipating the satisfaction of finally seeing the historical and cultural sites about which we had heard so much in our classes, an excitement which I shared with the other students.

The weather conditions on the day of the excursion, however, proved to be less than favorable since dark clouds were already in evidence as we hit the road in our tour bus. Sure enough, torrential rain was soon dampening our spirits; and some of us would rather have stayed behind. But to our surprise our tour guide who was also our language instructor was optimistic as he commented on whatever geographical spots were still visible to us through the fogged-up windows of the bus. His enthusiasm, we soon learned, was based on his knowledge and experience of the weather conditions which lay ahead of the tunnel that we were going through. The weather on the other side of that particular mountain, he explained, was usually different from the one we were leaving. He beamed a rather beguiling smile at us.

And sure enough, once we were on the other side of the mountain, having tunnelled our way there, bright sunshine was indeed beckoning us to the warmth of the other place which we were about to visit. So different indeed from what we had just left behind.

Our language teacher during that tour gave me a lesson which he probably had not intended. It may have been merely a passing remark on his part to rescue the day; but somehow in his optimism he had also managed to communicate the role and importance of fostering hope as we go through life. It was one of those lessons which somehow stretch beyond one's expectations or even well-laid out plans. I seriously doubt whether it had even crossed his mind at that time, but I did learn something about life due to his attitude and outlook while in the tunnel. Much later on I came across in passing a similar attitude in one of Tolkien's characters who insisted that the shadow is merely a passing thing since even darkness must pass, giving way to the sun which will shine out more brightly.[1]

When I recall that isolated experience and reflect on how it can apply to our journeys in life, it leads me first of all to note that there is a marked difference between being merely optimistic and being hopeful. The former communicates a personal attitude while the latter pins one's outlook on some external basis. That distinction would not have been uppermost in our minds at that time; but as I ponder on it several years later, it did make a difference to the way our trip turned out.

Let me explain. Optimism on our part is important because it helps us to weather the storms of life despite their menacing presence while any hope we entertain needs to be rooted in something external to us. The first is somewhat subjective while the second is more objective. There has to be a firmer basis for hoping, not just a certain attitude or outlook. Our teacher-tour guide was optimistic, and he conveyed that to us in the tone of his voice and in his countenance. But more importantly, his reassurance of better weather conditions once we were out of the tunnel showed that he was hopeful, too. Somehow, his earlier experiences could be relied upon. He passed on something that made us look forward to a changing fortune on that trip.

One's attitude and outlook in life do contribute to the positivity of our life-experience. What we bring to our journey has an impact on its quality. Does this mean that we have always to be positive or optimistic? That would hardly be possible, realistically speaking. Nor would it necessarily be helpful either because it would blind us to the negative side of life. We also need to see the dark side of life's tunnels and in that way be more able to appreciate any ray of light that seeps in.

Such a double-sided experience can also be thought-provoking and may even make us appreciate more the positive side of life, no matter how scanty that may appear to be when going through a troubled patch. The contrast between these two sides of life well-pictured by diagrams and colors of yin and yang, dominant in the Chinese way of thinking of reality, is real—but our perspective can shape our response to it. Having an optimistic view is to allow the more positive side to dominate and

---

1. Tolkien, *Lord of the Rings*.

regulate our conduct—which could include dealing with, and lessening, the negative side. It is a commendable starting attitude.

Taking this point a bit further, however, we can detect a notable difference between having an optimistic outlook and being hopeful insofar as the latter entails finding real grounds for entertaining hope rather than simply adopting a certain attitude. As we turn our attention now to our life-journeys, we could ask: on what can we base our hope? Should hope be simply a matter of relying on someone's word and authority, for example a truly trusted leader or guide? At least, if that were the case, it would not be a merely subjective decision on our part, which could be prone to constantly change. But then, the question of credibility comes in. There has to be a good and plausible reason for placing our trust in that person or her/his authority. For many that is sufficient, but not so for a number of us. We want a firmer foundation.

Or can one hope because that is how it is in reality? As we have noted already, there has to be some objective basis for hoping. Insofar as we go through the *tunnels* of life, we could ask what grounds could we have for looking forward to what is ahead, especially since the darkness that we at times experience in our life-journey would appear to present a different scenario. Why should we accept that what awaits us is different from what we are experiencing—that there is a light at the end of life's tunnel?

Previously, we had reflected on the philosophical explanation of the workings of reality in terms of creative synthesis. We need to recall that reflection as we focus now on the basis for hope. It was affirmed that there is always something innovative, unexpected, and fresh in the way reality shapes itself—even if it is also the case that whatever happens comes about as a result of what had transpired in the past and is shaped by it. If indeed this is the case for everything that happens, then we have to accept that no matter what will happen it is not exactly as we have known it in the past. There is at all times an element of unpredictability, no matter how small it is. There is always a certain trace of freshness about the way things turn out.

It may not sound convincing at times, but actually history bears this out. It does not merely repeat itself, despite the view held by some regarding events. It also liberates itself, perhaps not completely, from the burden of what has transpired. There is always a certain amount of novelty even if we do not clearly notice it. Change is real, as Heraclitus had argued, and although the change may not always be for the better, in most instances it is. This is not to say that there is always progress—if by that we mean that it is always noticeably so. But the fact that it is not simply a rehash of what has transpired leaves open the possibility that there will be an improvement, no matter how minimal it is.

Despite its usage in common parlance, hoping—it should be emphasized here—is not simply waiting for things to turn out. It entails actively seeking and working for the improvement that one has in mind. Hope is about channelling change for the better—as we do with the flow of water. It is not simply waiting for it to occur. There is hope because there is the real possibility that we can always make a difference. I would like to think that the former American President Barack Obama's words, quoted many times: "Yes, we can!" are more of a challenge and not just a reassurance. Using once again the terminology that we had come across previously, we could add: reality is truly creative because it is not simply a bundle of syntheses. Our innate creativity puts us in a position to effect change. Indeed, we can.

It should be added further that hope is not the same as confidence, either. The latter rests with the individual's feelings of sureness that things will work out as intended or planned. But as was noted previously, there can be no guarantee of that happening simply because of the openness of what is to come. We can direct it somehow, but the end-result cannot be entirely what one wants. To hope is to work actively towards the improvement that one has in mind. But it is dependent on a number of factors, too, including our co-operation. We have—all of us, individually and together—the capability of shining a light even while still in the darker tunnels of life. And the actual working out of this claim is dependent on our input into the creative workings of reality.

But is that enough for us to entertain hope? Would it not be better to be more realistic and accept things as they are, rather than as we would like them to be? Are we not deluding ourselves into thinking that things can still be better? It would, admittedly, be extremely difficult to convince those who are really down on their luck or have lived their lives in utter deprivation that there is a real basis to hope. Sometimes, it seems to be even patronizing to speak of a better future when their present is utterly miserable.

That is the difficulty of speaking of hope. It should not be merely about lifting up one's spirits. That is also the problem, as we have noted, when one is simply taking someone's word for it—unless of course the speaker or the source is beyond reproach. That is an even greater challenge if one were to claim—as is being done here—that there is reason to be hopeful because change, including an improvement in one's lot, is possible. *Change is real, but progress itself needs to be made.*

If all this is to be of assistance to us as we travel on life's highways, it will be worth our while reiterating and noting more precisely a few observations. Change can be for the better, not just because change happens; but that betterment will be brought about if we exert an effort towards its improvement. If creative synthesis is how reality works, then change itself takes place outside of our control. But improvement is dependent on how we—you and I and others—exercise our creativity. While entertaining hope is partially dependent on the nature of things and happenings, it becomes truer the more we let it be actualized.

What this means is that the reality of hope is anchored to the cooperation of each of us and of all of us. Thus, as we pass through the tunnels of our life-journeys, our exit and the kind of welcome we get are dependent on what we have contributed to it ourselves as well as what others in the past and in the present are adding to it.

All this may still come across, especially since it is based on a contemporary scientific finding and a certain philosophical thinking, as rather far-fetched to be of any practical use in our daily lives. But there is something in its favor; namely, that it is not merely a consolation or a crutch, despite what some critics say, just as our teacher-guide's words were not meant merely to keep our spirits up. They were backed up by what he knew and had experienced. I recall Martin Buber maintaining that hope imagines the real. Pinning our hope to the workings of reality, and more importantly, attaching it to our sense of responsibility as individuals and as members of society at least show us that there is a realistic *reason to hope,* to look to the future rather than be merely burdened by the past as we live in the present. Going back to the phrase used in our previous recollection, it helps us to "move on" indeed.

This realism was borne out in our experience of the outlook—and expectations of the people of Tacloban and Guiuan, both of these in the Philippines. These two places were thoroughly devastated on November 8, 2013 by Typhoon Haiyan/Yolanda, the strongest typhoon in history ever to make landfall. When we visited these places a few months later, we could see the vast devastation at firsthand: almost everything had been ripped up and broken apart by the ferocious winds and heavy rains.

Several thousand people had been killed and countless others left homeless. The destruction was total and merciless. One was left speechless amidst the ruins and in the face of such a catastrophe. Any recovery, not to speak of some improvement, was unimaginable.

Yet there was a very notable attitude among the people. They showed resilience even as they observed what had happened to them, to their loved ones and to their land. There was a realistic acceptance of the enormous task ahead of them. Nevertheless, in conversation with some of them we noted that their folk-tradition likens them to the native bamboo. Pliant and bending with the oncoming wind, no matter how ferocious its strength is, the bamboo nevertheless straightens itself back up, having allowed the wind to pass by. The slogan *Tindog Tacloban, Bangon Guiuan* (Stand up, Tacloban/ Arise, Guiuan) became their rallying call to everyone. They were indeed like their bamboo, bent and shaken; but they were also determined to recover—to snap back. Like their bamboo, they explained. They were determined to recover. They did not want a handout but a hand-up. They welcomed and appreciated the external support to prop them up so as to stand erect once again. But they wanted to be agents and not merely recipients.

And they were heard by themselves—and by millions of others, locally, nationally and internationally who all came to their aid. And indeed world-wide co-operation lifted their spirits and helped them out of the truly long and dingy tunnel of life that they were going through. A few years later, when we returned to visit the place and the people, it was as if that horrific event had not happened at all. It was incredible. Even nature, especially the coconut trees, had also heard their rallying slogan. What had been downed by the terrible winds was once again erect. The optimistic attitude of the people, but more importantly their hopes grounded in their own strength plus the co-operation of innumerable others, stood by them. The marked progress in their situation was truly remarkable.

It made us recall Emily Dickinson's poem on hope[2] and how appropriate it was to the situation which we had witnessed. She compares hope to a feathered bird. It rests permanently in our soul, singing all the time and inspiring us. It seemed to us that these people had sung along with the bird. The sentiment expressed in the Irish poet Moya Cannon's poem "Flowers know nothing of our grief"[3] also resurfaced, pointing

---

2. Dickinson, "'Hope' is the thing with feathers," *New Explorations*, 49.
3. Cannon, "Flowers know nothing of our grief," *Collected Poems*, 82.

out for us that indeed as these people showed, hope is never dead "until this bewildered earth stops throwing up roses" around us. It looked as if their bamboo trees—crops, fruits, flowers and spirits—would shoot up again. And they did. Indeed, it was a confirmation that hope requires our active participation for it to prevail.

The world has been going through yet another tunnel in our life-journey—this time, dug up by the pandemic COVID-19. One is immediately reminded of Albert Camus's novel *The Plague*. This present-day threat, unlike the one in Oran in Northern Algeria, on which Camus had based his work, is so widespread and so pervasive that it is truly frightening. Somehow, a reference to Pandora's Box and its menacing contents, particularly with their release to the world, easily come to mind. To some who are especially vulnerable, whether because of age or for health reasons, this present-day threat represents a menacing incursion into their daily lives and even presages early death. There is no denying that it has, and continues to have, a detrimental impact on practically everyone's life.

While there have been reports of the devastating effects of this pandemic in the various countries affected, there have also been glimpses into, as well as protracted coverage of, how those in the frontline have been dealing with it. Side by side with the atrocity of the virus has been the unselfish work of those who have been involved in alleviating the human situation. These individuals, groups and officials are keeping up the hopes of all simply because they are confronting the threat. Rather than taking a wait-and-see attitude, those involved have been actively seeking an improvement in the situation.

Nancy Stewart, when celebrating her 107th birthday, wrote a message of hope to the Irish people. She has lived through two World Wars, the war of independence, the civil war, the Spanish flu epidemic, the Cold War, the Wall Street crash and the great depression, the financial crash of 2008 and now—the pandemic: "We will get through this!" indeed, she claims. After all, she is living proof of real survival amidst disasters. Having lived through a similar experience and a bout with COVID 19, Sister André, Europe's oldest surviving person, gave a similar message just before her 117th birthday.

The "shining of the lights" evening on Easter Saturday 2020 in Ireland met with a lot of support. The gesture was to encourage hope and solidarity among the people. Similarly, the cancelled Eurovision 2020 song-contest was substituted with a television programme "Europe Shine the Light" that featured songs and uplifting messages from the contestants of the various participating countries. Hotels in various cities in Asia turned on their "smiley" lights to brighten up the gloomy atmosphere as well as to express thanks to all those who were working hard to lighten up those feeling abandoned and lonely. Pope Francis's message *Urbi et Orbi* delivered at the Vatican was a strong assertion of the hope that Easter brings. But it was also a powerful challenge to countries in conflict to channel their energies instead into restoring peace and coming to the aid of those afflicted.[4] Other religious leaders communicated a similar message to their members and followers.

That inspiring experience in the Philippines of meeting the buffeted victims of nature's fury and the destructive side of the sea and presently of the ongoing threat of the corona virus throughout the world somehow remind, and to some extent confirm for us, that there is some light at the end of life's tunnels. Also, the tunnel may seem long—and the going is truly tedious—but it does end somewhere and somehow. However, we do have to co-operate and exert effort while going through it, as these people did and are doing. We do need to help the light enter the tunnel. We ourselves may even have to tunnel our way out, so to speak, and not simply pass through these tunnels.

The message of Camus' novel referred to earlier appears to align itself with that point. While change always happens because that is how reality comes about, it can only be for the better if we contribute to its transformation. We should be positive as much as is possible; but more crucially, we need to add our share to the task of transforming lives for the better. Then and only then will our hopes be realized. Despite the enormous challenges in life, we can be hopeful indeed. There are good reasons to look to the future with some hope even as one faces calamity.

One will recall that at the bottom of Pandora's box was hope.

We will continue this comparison of our life-journey to our road trips and the challenges that lie ahead of us by taking another but similar route.

4. Pope Francis, *Vatican News,* April 12, 2021.

Aside from going through tunnels in our travels and on our life-journey, sometimes we do end up at *forks and crossroads*. As many road-users can tell us, it is helpful when there are signs to guide us in which direction we should continue. Depending on where we want to go, the sign can point towards our destination. In this way no guessing or even imagining is necessary thus facilitating the travel.

But sometimes, when we arrive at a crossroad or a fork in the road there are no signs. We are left with no way of knowing which direction to take. Should we just continue straight on? Or do we chance taking the road on the left, or should we opt for the one on the right instead? We may have a destination in mind but which way to get there becomes somewhat problematic. Or perhaps we are just out for a ramble with no specific itinerary, yet the crossroad or fork in the road puts us somewhat in a quandary because it presents us with alternative directions. We have to choose one since we can only go one way. But what would we be missing then?

In this situation Robert Frost's poem of the quandary confronting him when he arrived at such a spot and how it affected his life is especially instructive in this scenario.[5] Faced with two roads diverging and being unable to travel on both and after looking hard down one as far as he could see, he opted for the other. Knowing that he would never be able to return despite some interest in the first one, he took "the less travelled one" instead since it seemed to him to be more attractive. He remarked that that choice made all the difference to him.

My continued curiosity about that "difference" which he does not reveal in the poem has succeeded in imparting a lesson to me about life. In my opinion, Frost captures very well the impact of decision-making in the face of alternatives, the so-called forks in life. On our life-journey we are indeed faced with decision-making, some trivial but others momentous.

As human beings we are guided by instinct as well as by reason. As we have noted previously, we are also free beings; consequently, we have the opportunity to choose even if one has to admit that sometimes the choice is restricted or even taken away altogether. There are times, too, when decision-making is onerous, and we would even prefer if things were simply laid out for us, particularly if they meet with our approval

---

5. Frost, "The Road not Taken," *Robert Frost: Selected Poems*, 77.

anyway. Making up one's mind can be agonizing. But those times when we have to choose or make a decision regarding alternatives—at various levels, including the route that we want to take in life, well symbolized by Frost's poem—then it is a much greater challenge. As it was for Frost, choosing alternatives ahead of us can make a difference to our lives, some of which can be life-altering.

We could, of course, simply follow our instincts or refrain from making any decision and just go ahead with whatever opens up for us. Deciding on one alternative calls for much thought, and we do not always have that luxury. That may, however, be fool-hardy. We may still have to decide at any rate. Sometimes we learn from past experience and draw on it even if what lies ahead is not completely the same. At least, we have something to go by. We could also seek advice and evaluate the advice before implementing it. We could weigh up the possible consequences ourselves and check how it would work out if we were to opt for one choice rather than the other.

We may have to take on board after all that even if the chance to decide may be a valuable gift to us humans, it also makes demands on us and has consequences for our lives. We may as well face that reality. The crossroads and forks in the road that lie ahead on our journey in life have a way of warning us about this important point.

But there is something more in Frost's poem which I would like to believe is even more significant; namely, his decision to take the "less traveled road" which made a *difference* to him. That difference takes various forms. But a consequential one, it seems to me, in the context of this reflection on our life-journey is the moral impact that our decisions in life makes on us, on society and on our world. In daily life whether as ordinary individuals or as professional people we are more used to measuring and weighing up what would happen if we were to choose one over the other. But there is something else that should concern us as human beings and precisely *because* we are human beings; namely, the moral import of our decision-making. It means much more than what we should do but rather what we *ought* to do in that scenario. Given the import of Frost's decision I would like to interpret the "difference" that it made to him as having such a moral significance, at least as far as this reflection on our life-journey is concerned. We could call it a "moral compass" to direct our decisions, actions and intentions.

We need to explore this point further. Decision-making in life always entails a choice between alternatives, very much like the fork or the crossroads in the road when we travel. There are so many factors that we have to take into account. In addition, we have to weigh up the significance of the decision itself. We regularly do this in daily life. For instance, we look at what is involved and what the consequences are. We balance the pros and cons. Ordinary living as well as work scenarios require that task of us. Rash decisions are rarely recommendable although admittedly there are times when we must make them because of the restricted time-factor available to us.

But what is at times missing in decision-making, regrettably, is the moral factor. It is more than just the question of what we need to do, or which action is better or more urgent. And it is certainly more than just what we want. Instead, it is the important consideration of what is the right thing to do. There is reason to believe that it is, seemingly, the less-traveled road in life's journey. And yet that is what distinguishes us as humans from all other creatures because only humans are in a position to consider what *ought* to be done. This is distinct from, although related to, the question of what one should do. The latter implies a task or an assignment that needs to be carried out while the former also charges us with a certain amount of responsibility or accountability. It is a significant difference.

Why?—we may ask. Being confronted with the task of choosing what we ought to do is much more than just facing the dilemma of which road to take. The moral impact weighs heavily on the shoulders of human beings. We are tasked with this responsibility which can indeed be burdensome because we have, as free beings, the ability to choose as well as to think. Which path to take, from a moral perspective, means that we have to consider the nature of the action we have in mind, our motivation, the consequences of our decision and so many other factors. It seems as if Frost does indeed remind us, even if he had not intended it in this way with his poem, that such a decision makes a difference to us as human beings. As we travel on life's highways and by-ways, the moral factor should loom large. As has already been pointed out, this is what distinguishes humans from mere brutes.

The "difference" that Frost's decision made for him and its vagueness can be likened to, one would be inclined to think, how incalculable and how indiscernible at times this so-called moral import is in our life-journey. It is not simply an either-or situation as it is at the fork in the road. There are, of course, helpful signs that point in certain directions since both history and education, particularly ethical teachings, can provide us with some guidance as to what the right or moral decision is. They are significant resources that we can invoke. We do have to admit, however, that unlike being guided by the signs at crossroads or the fork, merely following directions in this case is not sufficient if we want the moral factor to make that human difference. In the end, as human beings all of us have to undertake that task ourselves of taking into account the moral factor if we are to stay on track and make a "difference" to our life-journeys. It is an important challenge to each of us, and we ought not to shrug it off.

The moral difference has been the subject of much deliberation by thinkers down through the ages and in all walks of life. Despite its closeness to religious belief we should not mistakenly believe that the moral demand is one that is imposed on us only if we believe that there is a God. What we ought to do—that is to say, the right deed that should be done—is a fundamental challenge to us because we are endowed not just with the ability to think rationally but also to act freely.

There are variations of this so-called moral factor depending on whether one follows the ethical theories of Immanuel Kant, John Stuart Mill, Thomas Aquinas, John Dewey or several others in history or today. But irrespective of what is emphasized: the act itself, one's intention, the consequences, one's attitudes and so on, the crucial factor is that it makes an important "difference" and is not simply the result of a choice.

Moreover—and this is where creative synthesis can once again come to our aid—that so-called difference can be actualized if we choose to exercise our creativity in such a way that it brings about the positive development of those concerned. Human creativity is what puts us in a strong position to contribute to the welfare of everyone as well as of the world we live in. It can make *a truly significant and noble difference* to us all and to our journey in life.

We will close in more on this observation a little later. At the moment, however, this may be an opportunity for us to take yet another direction as we continue with our reflections on our life-journey. Since we want to stay on track as we move on it is important that, if possible, we clear the way ahead of us of other distractions.

In our travels we are sometimes forced to take detours as well. They can be annoying, particularly if we are pressed for time, despite the fact that often there may be good reasons for re-directing us. But even a road that is regarded as a safer alternative does not always prove to be helpful as far as we are concerned. This may be because we end up in unfamiliar territory, and that realization can be frightening. Often one has then to rely on one's instincts, rather than on experience. Being taken away from the planned itinerary can also be disappointing, particularly if one had intended to see specific sights and sites or do certain things along the way. There can also be extra expenses because the detour can be much longer than had been taken into account in the costing of the original journey.

Similarly, *detours* in our life-journey can take various forms and have different effects on us. But whatever they are, they can thwart the best laid-out plans, leading to disappointment, frustration or even anger on our part, especially if these are imposed on us. It is as if doors are being closed, sometimes in our face. We are being robbed of any satisfaction, success or benefit as we travel on life's roads.

Are there reasons then for welcoming "detours" confronting us or doors closed in our face? As we travel in life, we often like to think that it should be as we want it to be. There is something rewarding in being able to say that we did it our way or that was our strategy. We have ambitions, dreams, goals, and so on. We may have put much thought into planning our life-journey; therefore, any deviation caused by outside forces can create much turmoil and upset. Circumstances, however, may dictate a change in the route we are taking. Somehow, that is beyond our control. But at times the actions of others, the consequences of their decisions and, unfortunately, the thoughtless and wicked deeds of some, have a way of upsetting our plans in life. Often, it is a matter of merely making some changes to our plans; but at other times, these have a way of derailing them altogether. More significantly, it is taking away our liberty and freedom, our ability to plan our course ourselves. We might even end up once again in a situation reminiscent of Heidegger's complaint about being "thrust into this world" without being consulted. Are there good reasons for the detours that we have to take because our intended route in our life-journey has been interfered with?

Perhaps the straightforward answer is simply to acknowledge that that is life. There is a lot of unpredictability and forces outside our control.

Going back to our earlier reflection on the creative nature of reality, we will recall that there is an aspect of life that is simply unforeseen and unforeseeable. "*C'est la vie!*" is a commonly heard explanation. Sometimes it is—hard as it may appear—simply due to "outrageous fortune" or simply, tough luck. An integral aspect of living is, like reality itself, the role that luck plays, as the American philosopher Charles Hartshorne, would put it. There is bad as well as good luck. It is not consoling, and it is a hard pill to swallow on life's journey. But that is simply the state of affairs with reality itself.

But this does not mean, and should not mislead us into thinking, that it is a matter of simply accepting everything that life throws in our direction. That would be sheer fatalism; or worse still, it would be ignoring that, as was also noted earlier, we do have some control over what happens in life. Complete passivity or total detachment is not the same as a certain amount of resignation in the face of forces beyond our control. Creative synthesis, as we have seen, involves also taking some control in the redirection of events as they occur.

Facing detours, as it were, is an integral part of living. No matter who we are or where we come from, such a situation seems to be the lot of human beings after all. Perhaps, if we cannot note the difference between what is delightful and what is saddening, between what is satisfying and what is disappointing or what is helpful and what is useless, then it would not matter. But we can because as human beings we have been endowed with the ability not just to think but also to distinguish. It may be a gift but for some it is more like a curse, as Sartre describes this mark of human beings. It can even make us resentful. Our life-journey can become unpleasant or even burdensome due to this ability of ours. One may wish that it were not true and that it would happen to no one in life; but unfortunately, that is not the case.

There is also such a thing as a bad lot, described by the ancient Greeks as misfortunes allotted to them by the gods. Or it is regarded as the bad karma that we have inherited from the past. We do not have to subscribe to those descriptions to realize how misfortune seems to be the plight of individuals or of peoples. We do not have to go back in time or to travel elsewhere to know that there is much to be regretted and even much more to be resentful about as we face an uphill journey because our life-itinerary has been forcibly re-directed. If that is not our choice, why are we left in this situation? What becomes of our so-called choice in life?

But there is a side to these detours that can be unseen initially but turns out to be even more than welcome. It is as if being re-directed, without our consent or prior information, is meant to open up another route in life for us to take. Detours in the long run may even be welcome. In fact, they can bring some relief. After all, road works, accidents, flooding and so on can be dangerous to one's travel, and being directed to an alternative route should not only be expected but also much appreciated. The longer route may even prove to be less costly after all. When all things are taken into account, the detour forced on the traveler may even be the better alternative. Sometimes, it may open up worthwhile sights that one would have missed if there had been no detour.

Strange as it may seem, facing closed doors or being forced to try another way can also result in a more positive experience. They cause us, even against our will, to deviate into strange territories which nevertheless provide alternative opportunities. It is as if closed doors lead to other doors, opened because the first ones had been closed. It is as if—recalling once more the concept of creative synthesis that we had come across earlier—there is always something unexpected and that something turns out to be even better than what was originally planned. That point was well illustrated for me during that summer hitchhiking trip in Germany: unable to get a lift to my planned destination, I met and befriended the couple heading in the opposite direction instead—much to my delight and gratitude.

Oddly enough, Robert Frost's personal life illustrates quite well that "having to take a detour" or facing closed doors may in the long run be a very welcome one after all. Having tried his hand at farming and unable to interest publishers in the USA to publish his poems, he had to divert, so to speak, to England. It was a detour in his life-journey that was not just a welcome break but also a most rewarding one. He met and befriended other poets and literary people in that new country. It made it possible for him to fulfill his ambition which had been frustrated while in America. His poetry soon met with the success that eluded him in his previous life.

On his return to America he was already an acclaimed poet who was sought after by publishers and readers. His literary reputation blossomed. One wonders whether that would have happened had he not been "diverted" in his life-journey to another country and other surroundings. Such detours in our life-journey can at times be the unexpected break that can lead to more fulfilling lives.

This is not always the case, one would have to admit. But given that such re-routings of our life journey are a reality and that at times they end up to be fine or even rewarding, there is room for stating that we should be patient or resigned. However, as we have already noted, that is only one aspect of life, as expressed in the notion of creative synthesis. It would be closer to the reality if we also head towards the creative side of reality, and therefore also of life. What this means is that while recognizing that there is a dimension to our life-journey that is outside our control or is forced on us, it is not the totality of what life offers. Detours, just as they do in our travels, can allow us to do other things, take a welcome break or even re-invigorate ourselves. The change of direction may lead to other routes which would have otherwise been unknown to us.

There is, however, still another challenge thrown at us by the detours in life, irrespective of how they come about. It is the chance to capitalize on them, so to speak. As creative beings, we can re-arrange our lives, refresh ourselves, take control of the situation, and so on. There is an ancient saying worth recalling here: "*Carpe diem!*" It is a well-known slogan, not always used as intended. But I should like to think in the present context that seizing the day is a challenge to incorporate into our lives in a positive way whatever has happened. It is putting the onus on us, creative beings, to make use of the detours to locate other possibilities on life's highways to fulfill ourselves. It is to look forward rather than merely backward. In the good sense of the word, it is to "capitalize" on these situations.

This observation was well illustrated in the way a detour was forced on, but accepted imaginatively by, certain countries, groups and individuals affected by the COVID-19 pandemic. The health authorities in these countries strongly advocated what was termed "social distancing" in order to stave off the spread of the virus. This resulted in the banning of large gatherings in private and in public life and even in the locking down of communities and of nations. The pandemic definitely made inroads into practically all countries. It made terrifying incursions into the daily schedules of people and blocked them from carrying on with their lives as usual.

That situation resulted in several closures. This forced the populace in a number of countries whose doors had to remain closed to pry open alternative ways into the outside world. The residents of apartments in some towns in Italy and in Spain used their windows and balconies to sing out to their neighbors and to the streets below in an attempt to cheer one another up and to express their gratitude to the health workers. In France, a resident in a group of apartments utilized their courtyard to project a film onto one of the walls for the entertainment of the residents who watched it from their balconies. Orchestras, operas and various musical events whose scheduled performances had to be cancelled opted to stream their offerings instead, lifting up the spirits of many viewers and listeners. A few restaurants, rather than remaining shut, ventured into the delivery service instead—to the relief of many.

The cancellation of all sports events made team-players and supporters rally together to channel their energies towards helping out with the distribution of meals and other such jobs. Cabin staff in Sweden, who were furloughed because of the cancellation of flights, were re-directed towards nursing homes where, after a few days' training, they could put their professional training and skills hitherto serving passengers, into much needed assistance in these places. Creativity was certainly evident in the way all of them tried to overcome the obstructions to their routines.

The closed doors of schools, colleges, and universities as well as the locked portals of churches, mosques and temples, meant looking for another avenue to deliver instruction and to conduct worship. It certainly opened up the possibilities offered by technology and mass media. Education and worship took another route and continued to deliver—in another form. The detour taken was yet another illustration of overcoming an obstacle thrown on life's highway. The new route turned out to be effective in maintaining some services in a different way.

Interestingly, but just as effectively, sports clothing companies and garment manufacturers, technological companies, distillers and breweries in different parts of the world took another route to bring their product to the public. The lack of demand for sporting and other kinds of garments was countered by the need for personal protective equipment (PPEs) for medical staff, making it possible for those companies to divert to filling that need, much to the relief of the employers, employees and of course, the overworked health staff and volunteers. Since there was a lack of medical equipment, including ventilators and protective masks, those engaged in 3-D printing turned their attention instead to working out the possibilities of meeting that demand and supplying the required products. A Belgian company diverted its workforce to making transparent face masks to accommodate lip-reading. A rather interesting case was the costume-company which had designed the garments worn for the film *Chernobyl*. They made imaginative use of the clothing worn by the actors. These were now particularly useful for the health workers, in the real-life situations, to whom they had donated their product.

The demand for sterilizers and alcohol-based hand-sanitizers was such that shelves were emptied of stocks a few minutes after deliveries. There was a world-wide urgent demand which could not be met. At the same time, the government-imposed closures of restaurants, bars, pubs and other eateries as well as large gatherings meant that there would be no orders for alcoholic drinks, either. This was when the creativeness of a distiller in Ireland and elsewhere came to the rescue. The switch-over to using their facilities to produce, at cost-price, the much-needed sanitizers meant that they were able to utilize their alcohol to respond to the demand—and their detour into that territory led to making a crucial difference to the impact of the virus both on the company and the general community. A Protestant minister compared the welcome turn-around to converting swords into ploughshares in the Old Testament and to the fishermen becoming fishers of men in the New Testament. Also, the unsold beer during Australia's lockdown, instead of going to waste, was converted into renewable energy to power an essential water-supply plant.

All these "detours" became alternative routes to take as people coped with the pandemic—in a rather creative way.

In this reflection, we have given our attention to tunnels, crossroads/forks and detours which we encounter on our land trips. Traveling in life we meet these, too. As we move on, they present certain difficulties, causing us to pause or even halt. In pondering on these challenges, we noted how they are like some of those problems thrown in our direction as we go about our lives. They are a part of living, the given as it were. Often they are outside our control. But how we respond to them can make a difference to our lives and the lives of others.

Turning to the notion of creative synthesis, we learned that there can be a (creative) way of dealing with these in our life-journey and that the so-called given (synthesis) can even be utilized to take us in another direction that may in the long run prove to be a better alternative after all.

8

Obstacles, Hurdles or Barriers?

"We were stopped in our tracks!" That is an utterance, adopted from some of the misadventures during travel, which we also hear so often regarding certain experiences in life. It expresses our surprise, our resentment, and even our horror that what confronts us prevents us from moving along in our travel. There are many reasons for such a situation, of course. But the result is the same: what is ahead is in our way, preventing any further movement on our part. Whatever form it takes, it is not even redirecting us. It is actually blocking our path. That can be frustrating indeed.

Again, we will note that there are similarities here between our trips on the road and our life-journey. There are times, too, when what confronts us in life is immovable, and thus we are prevented from moving on. When traveling on life's roads, highways and byways, we do encounter sooner or later several blockages in various forms which impede our progress. At times, the situation is simply annoying and we can put them aside. Or we can shrug them off and then carry on with something else. But at times they stop us altogether, and they demand much more attention and effort on our part. Such situations can even be menacing. There are occasions when it would seem that we would have to retreat or accept defeat since there is no way we can deal with them. That dire situation in life can have a psychological impact on some of us inasmuch as we could feel defeated.

The challenge, it would seem, is to identify the cause of these obstructions in life and then decide on what would be the appropriate strategy in the particular situation. It may appear rather imaginative, but it may just serve our purposes in this instance to think in this way: just like what lies ahead of us on the road as we travel we could identify the blockage in our life-journey as an obstacle, a hurdle or a barrier. Our way of dealing with it would then depend on which it is.

There are indeed some similarities between life and our travel situation in this respect. Progress on life-journeys is halted because of certain external causes not of our own making, one may even add. Often it seems that despite our best efforts there is no forward-movement and no breakthroughs either. It can be frustrating. At times it is like running into a wall or against the force of the ferocious winds of an oncoming storm. What do we do in these situations? Do we turn back or stand still? Should we fight? As we continue with these reflections on our life journeys, we would do well to take note of these *obstacles, hurdles* and *barriers* that we meet and need to overcome in life.

The German family who were staying in the same boarding house where my fellow students and I had lodgings while working in the car factory for the summer were particularly friendly. They were on a walking holiday in picturesque Bavaria. Given the father's rather stressful job in Düsseldorf, having the time to explore the countryside and to engage in conversation with us seems to have been the right kind of break for him and his family. They were delighted to meet with us from time to time, especially since we were all trying to improve our conversational Deutsch, which we soon learned is rather different from Swäbish, the local dialect in that part of Germany.

One particular incident, which at that time seemed innocuous enough, nevertheless somehow got lodged among my memories of those summer months. The mother mentioned that on their walk the previous day there was what she described as *Hindernis*. Not knowing what it meant, I asked her for the English translation. But it was the young daughter who came to my rescue. Rather than translating the word for me, she simply made a fist of her left hand; and then using one finger of her right hand, she drew a path with it around her left cupped hand, pointing to it. "*Das ist ein Hindernis!*" It was a very effective explanation, and there was no need for any translation or elaboration.

What she did not intend with her rather simple maneuver was that she had actually conveyed to me a particular route that we can and probably should take when we are confronted in life with something that impedes our progress. I mulled over that lesson for some time. Blocked by an obstacle in one form or another we do not always have to confront it headlong. Rather it would be more advantageous to simply go around it, and in that way we can continue with our journey. Going around whatever it is that is obstructing our way can at times be an effective move.

Here are some examples that aptly illustrate this observation. In a world that is very male-dominated and replete with stereo-typing, women writers in the past have had to resort to using male names to get the same work recognized. They exemplify very well how obstacles placed in one's way do not have to block one's progress after all. One goes around it and follows a different path—even to great success. Mary Ann Evans, for instance, used the name of George Eliot, having been encouraged by George Henry Lewes, an English philosopher with whom she was romantically linked, when she published her best known works which include *Middlemarch,* widely regarded as one of the greatest novels ever written.

Today, J.K. Rowling used the same technique. Her work has definitely been extremely successful, but it seems only because faced with the problem of the non-acceptance of a woman writer among some of the reading public she had skirted around that obstacle. In this way she succeeded more than if she had spent her energy on forcing the issue. Some would even claim that she beat would-be foes at their own game.

That strategy of "indirect action" can be likened to a judo maneuver which one uses to overcome the opponent. Instead of forcing oneself headlong towards the opponent, one capitalizes on the strength of the opponent to overcome him/her. The trick seems to be to use it in such a way so that it adds to one's own capabilities. It is the indirectness of the strategy that provides an advantage. As we had noted earlier, Taoist philosophy likens its approach to hard obstacles to the way water, drip by drip, erodes even the hardest stone. It takes much time and patience, of course; but it can be more effective than directly pounding the stone.

In an extended sense, such technique and thinking would somehow support the action of going around an obstacle rather than confronting it head on. It should be stressed that yielding, rather than attacking, is not the same as surrendering yet it can be more productive. Swerving from a path being blocked by an obstacle may be a more intelligent and productive option, as any driver of a means of transport would confirm.

There is also another indirect way of winning over one's opponents to one's side by taking the trouble of first examining the problem from their point of view and then pointing out how it can be complemented, rather than rivaled, by the opposite one. This should not be equated either with surrendering one's original position altogether simply because this recourse to indirectness does not compromise one's standing or uprightness. No, indirectness is definitely not in the same league as forgetting or ignoring or setting aside one's principles or standards. The latter would be regrettable. In fact, it may even be unsuccessful. In comparison with direct action, the indirectness of this more diplomatic approach shows respect for the opposite view as well as indicates a genuine effort to understand it first.

All these options may not convince some people, admittedly; but at times it is worth recognizing that indirectness, "going around" or "taking a side road" can also be a way of dealing with some obstacles in life's paths. Being direct in one's action or tackling the obstacle headlong and head-on may turn out to be even problematic for us. In such cases, going around it may be the better course after all if we want to continue with living our lives satisfactorily or achieving the desired results.

In fact, the option of going around an obstacle, *ein Hindernis*, may be the more successful alternative because removing it may not be a truly viable option. Realistically speaking, at times it would take a Samson or a Hercules to get rid of such an obstacle. It does not, however, mean that one should not deal with the problematic blockage on the road, but rather that resolving it may call for a more indirect action. There is a common saying that can be of use here: "We may have to work our way around this."

To return to our use of the concept of creative synthesis as a life-map, it would appear that dealing with some obstructions (the synthesis) lying on our path calls for a rather "creative way" of doing so. Looking for other options instead of the direct one can be an effective way of sorting out a problem. It is not giving in to the might or force of the obstacle—hence, it is not a surrender, it should be emphasized once again. But it is seeing another way out of the situation by finding a more efficacious alternative.

Admittedly, that strategy may not suit some people—individual temperament, background and capability differ among us. Indirect action, such as the option of going around the obstacle, may even appear to some to be cowardly. However, it should therefore be added that such indirect action is merely one option among others, but one which is nevertheless worth considering, depending on the situation. Deciding on that course of action is strategic rather than conclusive. The "tangential approach" favored by much of Asian culture could bring about the results desired or needed; but, of course, it is not for every situation.

Let us switch over now to looking at other blockages on our life-journey. After all, just as in our road travels we meet them, too, in life. There are times when progress in our respective life-journeys is stopped by what turns out to be more of a hurdle, rather than an immovable obstacle, in front of us.

As is well known, hurdles are used in some races. The athletes line up at the starting point at some distance from these hurdles which are placed at regular intervals on the allocated lane. Before they reach the finish line, they must jump over the hurdles which are intended to slow down their progress. Unfortunately, these can also stop them from reaching the finishing line although the intention, of course, is to jump over them. Whoever succeeds in clearing these hurdles and reaching the finish line first is the winner. Watching such a race can be exciting, particularly if one is cheering on someone who is a friend or who represents one's country or organization.

There is something about jumping over hurdles that can provide another lesson to us on how to deal with blockages along the route that we take in life. As in a hurdle-race, rather than fighting whatever confronts us or whatever is obstructing our path, an alternative is to jump over or to rise above it. While the obstacle remains, it no longer stands in our way because we have gone beyond its reach as we continue with our life-journey. Are there occasions then when, once again instead of directly engaging with whatever prevents us from moving ahead, we take an indirect action, but this time surmounting it, so to speak? What are the hurdles that stand in life's lanes? If these are the "syntheses" facing us and obstructing our progress, what "creative" action can we take in dealing with them?

Before we proceed with our inquiries some reminiscences of mine may help us catch our breath, so to speak, for a few moments. I have always been fascinated by Mt. Fuji in Japan whether in pictures or in reality. Seeing it from the bullet train for the first time was a truly breath-taking and memorable experience for me since I had heard so much about it. Rising so majestically above the clouds, it seems to be unhindered by anything on the ground or in the atmosphere. It is as if it is sending the message that by towering over whatever is down there, it succeeds in retaining its beauty. It always makes me think of Mt. Mayon in the Philippines, seemingly holding forth above the landscape dotted with coconut trees, banana plantations and rice farms. Its beauty is untouched by its surroundings because it has risen above them. With both of these natural beauties their peaks appear to be unmarred yet rooted in the same spot from where they arise.

Similarly, an incident from one of my explorations in times gone by had such an effect on me. It dates back to my boyhood days in the Philippines. It was a time of adventure: hiking, camping, outdoor activities—and even getting lost! On one of those trips we made our way through a lot of overgrown grass, swaying coconut trees and thick plants. We did not have the benefit of a map since it was outside the borders of the town. Besides, part of our training was to learn how to cope under these circumstances. We had taken the trouble of placing signs along the way, like breaking some branches and then using them as arrows pointing the way back. We had even placed some rocks on top of these to ensure that they would not be blown away or disturbed. We were, so we had been instructed to keep in mind, *exploring* rather than *trailing*. It was intended to be an adventure. The difference in the nature of that particular trek made it even more exciting to us, young ones.

The going was great until it hit us after a considerable amount of hiking that we were lost—with the realization that soon there would be no daylight to illuminate our way back home. Somehow, the terrain had started to look very unfamiliar, and the noises we were hearing were ominous.

And we were getting tired. Of course, we were supposedly prepared for such a predicament; but we could not hide our growing fears, especially since we had different views on where to turn and which direction to take.

That was when the decisiveness of our leader came to our assistance. Instead of insisting that we go one way rather than another, he decided to climb a tall coconut tree. He seemed to do it with ease, too. When he reached the top, he assured us that he could see the far-off road from there so he called out to us to form a line in that direction. We immediately jumped into action to implement his instructions. The way back turned out to be a more direct route to camp.

He rescued us that day, much to our relief, and, needless to say, that of our families. To us, youngsters, he had provided an exciting tale to share, sometimes with additional imagined details on our part, of course. But more importantly, it taught me that there are occasions when, as he did when he climbed up the coconut tree to scan the "terrain" from that vantage point, one should "rise above" the situation, very much like Mt. Fuji and Mt. Mayon.

As athletes do when faced with the hurdles on the tracks and they jump over them to continue running, sometimes a better strategy in the face of a challenging situation is for us to transcend it. In this way, it has not taken control of us but rather we have overcome it.

In this respect, I often wonder how Nelson Mandela was able to deal with the traumatic experience of being incarcerated for several years. One would expect some bitterness, resentment or even anger. After his release, he opted to use his time to serve his country instead rather than seek vengeance. He rose above his personal tragic experience to forge his way ahead, with some success, so as to remove the much-hated regime of apartheid in South Africa. His line of action in dealing with a personal obstruction was to treat it like a hurdle so that he could serve his country better. He refused to stumble because of it, but chose to rise above it instead. For him, principles of truth and reconciliation were what mattered more in resolving the situation. The act of "rising above it" made it possible for him, seemingly, to view the landscape from another angle—a lesson that I had learned from our hiking leader who climbed up the coconut tree to scan our surroundings when we were lost.

Similarly, the Armenian tragedy, about which we heard while on tour in that country, and the attitude adopted by some in Armenia, left a deep impression on us. Whatever the facts and the interpretations of these—there has been a prolonged effort to have the slaughter of millions in Armenia by Turkey classified as a genocide which the United States under Pres. Biden has recently done—it was rather the way in which the country has seemingly risen above the tragedy that has left an impression on me. The words of our tour guide still ring in my ears: in building the memorial which stands erect in Yerevan, the capital, they wanted to "rise above that lamentable part of their history." In doing so, they also hope to "liberate" (rather than exonerate) the perpetrators. Not surprisingly, there is much controversy throughout the world about its history and its commemoration. But what is worth thinking about, when confronted by such a blockage in one's own life's journey, is the possibility, without denying the horror and suffering, of "rising above it" and therefore to let it be more of a hurdle rather than an insurmountable obstruction.

In these cases it is not a matter of who wins but rather of not letting the perpetrators gain the upper-hand after all. It is not so much a question of triumph as it is one of moving on by moving up. It is transcending the fray rather than being sucked into it.

Recently in Ireland news spread about the tragic deaths of three young children at the hands of their mother. It was overwhelming—yet, rather unexpectedly, also inspiring because of how the father, Andrew McGinley, seemingly rose above the tragedy because he wanted to keep the happy memories of the fun-loving children and of their devoted mother, who had been diagnosed with a mental disorder.

In the interview on Raidió Teilifís Éireann, Ireland's National Public Service Media, and in the Irish national papers, he recalled those memories created and left behind by the kids.[1] As their father, he wanted to preserve them. He explained that his children would not want him to be angry—besides, he believes that anger is a negative reaction—but to move on instead by following through with their childhood projects and fulfilling his promises to them. Puzzled and deeply hurt, he paid tribute to their mother who had been a loving mother, a hard-working professional nurse and devoted wife until then. He said that he needed and

---

1. *Irish News*, "RTE Interview with Andrew McGinley."

pressed for answers beyond the mere psychiatric diagnosis and treatment that she had been receiving then as to how she could have changed with the passage of time.

His case is definitely worth listening to. It is certainly thought-provoking. Many have admired his stance and his courage, and they have expressed their sentiments on social media. He had rightly won a lot of support. More to the point in the present context, however, his attitude of rising above such heart-breaking circumstances, which he refuses to let stall him, is truly inspiring.

As we resume our reflections now, we could liken some of the blockages in our life-journey to hurdles to be dealt with. It is not so much for people to jump over them as runners do, but to rise above them, as the above examples did, so as to have "the upper-hand" as it were. We will not necessarily overcome or subdue these; rather, it is a matter of not allowing them to block our way completely. History is replete with facts and stories of individuals, communities and nations doing just that in the face of much tragedy and horror. It is as if there is a refusal to be intimidated by such obstruction. More than that, it is denying any victory to whatever is standing in the way of our development as truly human beings.

But in what way should we think of this manner of dealing with such blockages? With tragedies, is it a matter of simply casting them aside? That would hardly be realistic since they are truly real after all and present a threat to our progress. In the case of other human beings placing such impediments in our way, is it a form of forgetting and carrying on? That, too, would not appear to be a real option since the obstruction of our progress in our life-journeys should simply not be tolerated. And there is also the important factor of ensuring that justice is served. Once again, the difficulty here is deciding whether "rising above" the obstruction is the right course of action.

We need to delve into that point more forcefully. But first, we should examine how human beings can "rise above" such impediments. There is a word derived from Latin that can assist us with this task; namely, "transcendence" implying "going across, beyond, and even above" the obstacle. It is related to another word; that is, "ascend" or climb. This is more than a play on words since human beings have it in their nature to be transcendent, to be able to go beyond, to reach across and to rise up.

We are used to thinking of our nature as rational; in fact, human beings are defined by their so-called rationality. We have been stressing that point here. It implies being able to reflect and to choose. But it is also within our nature, unlike other creatures, to be able to go beyond ourselves, to reach out, and to long for more. This gives us the ability to rise above what is and seek out not just what we want but also—more significantly—what ought to be.

The common interpretation of human rationality, to define who we are as human beings, does not do justice to this innate ability of ours since it is too much concentrated on our ability to know that we know. This "reaching out" or transcendence should of course be guided by our ability to think and to decide. In other words, it is rooted in and should be guided by our rational nature. But it is much more than that. "Transcendence" in much of philosophical usage, as in Kant's or Husserl's use of that term, is associated with knowing in the first instance, but it involves being able to know *beyond* what is.

But here I propose linking it with Hartshorne's notion of creativity (as was discussed previously in an earlier reflection). Our creative nature enables us to transcend, that is to say, to go beyond what has happened or what is presently the situation. There is a certain novelty, a freshness that comes about because of what each of us adds to it. As Hartshorne puts, it is "reality plus one" since we add to it by our exercise of creativity. Admittedly, it is only partial since it is based on and makes use of what is already there. But we contribute to it with our own exercise of creativity. We make our respective contribution rather than merely inherit what has been passed down to us. This is why we ourselves can "go beyond" whatever has been placed in our way and is now stopping us from proceeding.

How does this aid us with our present reflection on some of the hindrances in life? That we can, so to speak, take control of them rather than let them get a grip on us is vitally important. We can rise above them, we can jump over them as we do with hurdles, and we can transcend them. Or we can even use them as stepping stones towards something more acceptable. Of course, it is easier stated than done. And it requires more than courage to do so. But it is, needless to say, up to us. It can undoubtedly be difficult to let that be the case. And yet, there is something very human to be able to say when confronted by such impediments: "I will not let this be my undoing, I will not let this take hold of me, I will rise above it," or some such bold statements.

Several have done it before us—Nelson Mandela stands out as an example—and their decisions have propelled them to get on with their journey and to make tremendous progress while enhancing the lives of others. And then there is the example set by those who rose above any hurdles standing in their way due to accidents or to circumstances of birth, physical or mental, which appeared to limit them. It is simply awesome to watch them succeed in whatever they have set their minds on. The Special Olympics are always inspiring. The same can be said when one meets these individuals in daily life. Even if they were not aware of it, they had truly transcended the situation. And we have to some extent benefitted now, and continue to do so, because they had done so. Our individual impact on humankind—when we exercise our creativity—is not to be underestimated.

Let us ponder further about our trek in life in the context of the blockages impeding our progress or even stopping us altogether. We note once again that the existence of these impediments can indeed be problematic: what should we do with them or how can we eliminate them? Some are intractable obstacles, others are more like hurdles.

In tackling the situation, a more successful move at times is to be patient, to see how it will develop, and to think further about it. We also have to find out whether there are resources available to us, whether we have the capability ourselves to deal with it or perhaps enlist help. Or it may just go away with no action on our part. What stops us in our tracks in our life-journey may, in fact, despite appearing menacing initially, melt away given time, very much like a giant snowman right in the middle of a narrow road. Indeed, we can be grateful that not all situations, even grave ones, truly prevent us from making inroads in our journey in life.

But there is another kind of obstructions, one which simply needs more direct action on our part. Unfortunately, this other kind of situation is definitely nothing else but a *stopping-block*. There is no way of removing it, of pushing it aside, or of overcoming it. It is not an obstacle so there is no point in merely going around it. And unlike dealing with a mere hurdle, we cannot simply rise above it. One's options are limited in this instance. Worse, if one does not actively seek to remove it, it will prove detrimental for all.

Slavery, abuse of human rights, oppression, poverty, various forms of discrimination and countless others are such obstructions. These are genuine barriers, and they prevent our development and can even dehumanize us if we do not seek actively to work against them. Direct immediate action seems to be the only option unlike with the other situations, when it is more prudent to consider a more indirect one. One has to deal at once with these as well as plan long-term strategies with the intention of eliminating them altogether.

Here are some more examples. Our times have been marred by several terrorist acts which have resulted in the deaths of innocent people in London, Berlin, Paris, Christchurch, Vienna and in so many other places in the world. Whatever the motivations of those perpetuating them, their acts certainly put an end to the lives of those who are not party to their grievances. Allegiance to a cause, without considering the negative effects on others, is doing them, their loved ones and society in general a grave injustice. Furthermore, one would have serious doubts as to whether the cause is truly being served in the best way.

Something similar, even if not on the same scale, can be said about those who victimize others because of their race, gender, sexual orientation, religion and other factors. Today there are increasing incidents of cyber-bullying, facilitated by the wide-spread use of social media. No matter which form it takes, blocking the improvements in life or putting up barriers such that targeted people are restricted from making any progress in their life-journey, whether in the context of jobs, careers, professions, or reputation is to hinder or even halt altogether their full development as human beings. It may not necessarily cut short their lives, as terrorist acts often do; but it puts something that is integral to their lives to an end. This cannot be allowed to continue. All these, and similar evils, have to be eradicated, rather than merely tolerated.

The difficulty, however, is how to go about addressing the problem, eliminating the cause or stopping it from continuing any further. What we can be sure of is that any such attempt to block our journey in life demands urgent action on our part if we truly care about enabling all of us to develop as human beings in our journey in life. Solutions will vary not just because situations are different but also because we have diverse views on the matter.

Despite these disagreements there may be some common basis nonetheless for insisting that the removal of the effect starts with knowing and dealing with the cause. Unusual as it may seem, there is some justification for maintaining that these situations are brought about because of human ignorance or prejudice as well as malice—or to use a more contemporary term, a certain "mindset" that pervades one's actions. While acknowledging the difficulty of specifying the action that should be taken to address each of these situations, we can at least examine these kinds of barriers to our journey in life.

Recalling our earlier reflection on the moral import of our choices in life, we can now follow it up with some thought given to the role that ignorance (or warped thinking) plays in leading one to the wrong choices and deeds. The examples cited above show this to be true. A particular comment, carried by the international press, by a relative of one of the victims of the racial terrorist in Hanau, Germany recently is illustrative when he wondered "what is going on in that person's mind" to lead the perpetrator to such a barbaric act. *Warped thinking is a real foe.* It can lead to malice. Consequently, it demands correction if we are to tackle the effects, both immediate and long term.

It is necessary to unpack this suggestion if we wish to proceed any further. As we have already been noting, we are used to believing that human beings stand out in creation because of their rational nature. Whatever interpretation we give as to what constitutes rationality, a common understanding is simply that we can think, we know—and we know that we know. But that gift of being able to know needs to be nurtured. We do not come into this world, laden with all kinds of knowledge, despite what some thinkers claim. The description of *tabula rasa*, a blank sheet, is apt, it seems to me. This is why most of us feel strongly about the role of education, starting in the home, continued in schooling, and lasting throughout our lifetime. In fact, some would even maintain that education, that is to say, gaining and expanding one's knowledge, should never stop. That is simply our make-up as human beings. There is a given seed in our lives, but it has to be nurtured and nourished. There is an inherited synthesis, but it requires a creative development. For this reason, *educating ourselves is a constant process, not a finished product.*

The problem, of course, is that not every one of us has the opportunity or the inclination to pursue education in its various forms. Acknowledging this lacuna, Michael D. Higgins, President of Ireland, has made literacy and education one of the key themes of his Presidency. He has spoken publicly and frequently about the need to cultivate independent thought and ensure access to life-long learning opportunities. In his view schools are not places to educate future workers but to empower future-engaged, informed and active citizens. This in turn will result in the democratic functioning of communities and societies.

In the context of our reflection here we need not consider the nature of education itself. Crucial as it is, that is too broad a topic for now; hence, we would want to narrow it down for present purposes. Since what we are concerned with here are the barriers being strewn in our path which block or even terminate our development, in what way can education be of any relevance in this context?

The claim made earlier was that the ignorance and malice of those who engage in those heinous actions play a large role in motivating them. Any direct action aimed at stopping those who inhibit or cut short the development of others as noted earlier should also address, even more so, what leads them to engage in this kind of activity. It is thus not only what they are doing—which requires our immediate attention to stop it—but *why* they are doing this. And to know that is to get at the source of their action. Dealing with what prompts their course of action entails addressing it at the roots rather than merely the branches, so to speak.

How does education, that is to say, in relation to what we are considering here, play a part in this? There are many views of its role and tasks, of course. We do not have to detail them here. But there is one that seems to me to be quite relevant to us in the present context. Martin Buber, the Jewish philosopher and mystic, associates education with moral development.[2] It is the association of learning with *taking responsibility* that—it seems to me—strikes the right note for this reflection.

Education is far from being merely the acquisition of "knowledge" as important as this may be. It is more about widening one's vision so that one can go beyond mere instincts and self-interests. It is coming to the realization that one's presence in this world can make a difference to the

---

2. Buber, "The Education of Character," *Between Man and Man,"* 132–147.

world—good and bad. It is enabling one to choose, as well as know, that which can contribute positively to our development as human beings. It is scrutinizing one's mindset because one cares about how one should act. It is widening one's horizons to include all those who inhabit the same world.

In stark contrast to indoctrination, education respects human beings who are endowed with both reason and free will. Education, properly understood and practised, is not patronizing or brain-washing. Instead, it is about *enabling* our minds "to look beyond" oneself and "to look out" for one another. Will this ensure that the barriers we noted earlier will be removed? That would be too much to expect. After all, as individuals, we have different views on practically everything. What has been asserted will simply be brushed aside by those who are already intent on their plans.

But an important step that we can take to remove barriers which block us in our journey in life is "to open our eyes" or better still, "to look out" for everyone. To do that, we have to critically check out the viewpoint that is prompting or even urging the destructive action. It is to leave behind prejudiced and narrow views so that we can act in a more responsible manner. It is not just to nip the problem in the bud but also to untangle its roots as well. In that way, we will not merely survive, but more crucially, will even thrive.

This means, expanding on what Ellen Johnson Sirleaf, former President of Liberia, Africa's first female elected president and Nobel Peace Laureate, had pointed out in the Webinar on gender equality in leadership, we have to create structures so that the change can take place. And we need to provide resources, as Mary Robinson, first female President of Ireland and United Nations High Commissioner for Human Rights, had added.[3] That course of action is true for all of us no matter what scene it is—if we value our development as responsible human beings. It is about letting our so-called "moral coat collar" get a grip of our activities.

On this point, there is a lesson that we can learn from the experience of some Latin American strategists influenced by liberation theology. The oppressive situation of countless numbers of poor people which hinders their human development and the imbalance between the poor and the

---

3. "Global Leadership and International Co-operation in the Context of COVID 19 and Beyond," Webinar chaired by Dr. Robin Niblett CHG, Director and Chief Executive Chatham House, July 10, 2020.

wealthy were mainly due to the reckless work of those who wanted to enrich themselves. Supported by the authorities who wrongly and selfishly believed that their nation would prosper and would have an economic standing in the world, this blot on their landscape blinded these perpetrators to the sad plight of the majority of their own people.

In response to this unjust situation, some believed that the only way to tackle the problem was to rise up in arms. They were convinced that freedom from poverty and oppression could only be won through armed revolution, which to them was the only available route to directly tackle and transform the situation.

But some thinkers in their group thought otherwise. For them, the first step that needed to be taken was at the grassroots level. It had to start with those who were being victimized. In the view of these thinkers, the victims should become aware of their oppressed lot created and perpetuated by those who sought to keep them in that state. "Conscientization" was necessary. Enabling them to arrive at this point through seminars and meetings was important since "being aware" is an initial stage in one's assessment of the situation. A focused method of educating them about the situation was important if they themselves were to be the agents of change. Liberation from their miserable lot entailed active participation on their part. That is essential, these thinkers firmly believed.

Changing this landscape, however, was not just left to those already oppressed. The oppressors also needed to be made aware of the consequences of their selfish desire to enrich themselves. Educating them, as it were, was also important to effect the change. What was required was the rectification and transformation of the situation itself: the lot of the oppressed and the oppressor, rather than a reversal of roles. That is a crucial difference from the thinking of those who chose the other option of revolution instead of education.

Similarly, Helder Camara of Brazil rejected the use of violence to effect change. Opting to side with the poor, he warned those seeking change in the political situation of his country of what he referred to as "the spiral of violence." Instead, he called for transformation, which included a revolution of the mind, a change of heart and a cultural upheaval, all of which were to be peaceful. Violence leads to violence, he maintained, rather than to the desired transformation.[4]

---

4. Camara, *The Spiral of Violence*.

A similar direction seemed to have been taken in Indonesia by a couple of families who had become victims of violent and tragic bombings in their country. A recent BBC World News report[5] followed these families who had been trying to come to terms over a number of years with the horrendous deaths of their loved ones and with their own painful experiences. In particular, the young children had undergone personal difficulties and needed some answers to their predicament. Arrangements were made for these families to meet with the convicted perpetrators of the bombings to help them to understand each other's perspectives. It was a question of coming to grips with the mindsets and what lay at the back of these.

In almost all of the cases, prompted by the searching questions of the family-members the conversations provided a re-thinking of the perspectives which had led the bombers into taking their action. The realization of the effects on these families was some genuine awakening for the bombers. Erasmus's observation, in an adapted version, that "*Malo accepto stultus sapit*" shows that one can learn or become wiser from knowing and acknowledging one's mistake or evil deed. In turn, as it happened in this case, it can lead to a change of heart and forgiveness. Just like retracing our steps, it is a form of "moving on" that we had already talked about.

Direct action to break down barriers but also in a peaceful manner was the strategy chosen by Mahatma Gandhi with *satyagraha*. The Sanskrit word means "holding onto truth," or grasping it. The force of the truth, as he explained and employed it, leads to a particular form of non-violent resistance. In his case it was directed at the oppression felt by his people under British rule. Unlike passive resistance, it actually advocates resisting that which kept his people in what he regarded as their slavery.

This form of opposing human rights violation, directly but non-violently, was also employed by Martin Luther King and John Lewis in the USA and by others. That tactic has been referred to as a "stern love" of non-violent resistance and was combined with a "walking protest" of the civil rights movement. It is peaceful but not passive. As John Lewis put it, walking can be a peaceful act of defiance and can lead to "good trouble" in the hope of a reversal of the situation. In Nelson Mandela's case it was "a long walk to freedom"—as his autobiography describes it.[6]

5. BBC, "What Would You Say to the Men who Killed your Mum?" aired February 17, 2020.

6. Mandela's 1995 book was made into a film with the same title in 2013. It is a

The People Power movement of the Filipino people resorted to a similar tactic to topple down the then president, Ferdinand Marcos, who had been accused of obstructing the people who wanted to remove his martial law rule which was perpetuating their oppression. Taking the name of the scene of the protest march, it has been known as the EDSA Revolution. Similarly, the Velvet Revolution in Armenia was a direct, but peaceful, way of bringing about a welcome change in government and also a more acceptable manner of dealing with the country's problems.

These strategies involved some form of "educating"; that is, "liberating from ignorance and malice" those who were responsible for the abominable effects of their actions. In these examples, it was a matter of bringing forward the moral argument, rather than using force. What we can learn from those situations is that resolving conflicts is more a matter of drawing together of what is setting us apart. Educating both sides of the divide is, strange as it seems, directly dealing with the barriers which block any advancement. It is tackling the effect by targeting the cause itself. By confronting the mindset which underpins the misdirected behavior it is exercising our "creativity" in a productive manner. It is re-igniting what should continue to light our way as we travel together in life.

At the same time, however, we should not neglect to exert effort to obstruct the results of questionable ways of thinking. It calls for direct action aimed at eradicating the effects. We cannot simply ignore the unfortunate and unwelcome "syntheses" blocking us; that is to say, the effects of warped thinking, prejudice, discrimination and false ideas. How specifically that would work out depends on what is achievable in particular cases. But it is crucial that we do not merely tolerate what harms others in any way, but instead actively seek out the causes with a view to eradicating them.

In this reflection we examined different blockages which lie in our path as we seek to freely develop ourselves as human beings. These thwart our attempts to progress in our respective life-journeys. We explored different procedures to deal with them depending on whether they are obstacles, hurdles or barriers, While the paths we need to take may differ due to the nature of these blockages, what they have in common is that

---

British-South African film directed by Justin Chadwick from a script written by William Nicholson and starring Idris Elba and Naomie Harris.

these should not obstruct the wish and the right of any of us to move on in our life-journeys. Creative synthesis as a map on our life-journey can provide different routes to where we want to go and assist us to stay on the right track.

Stage Five

Taking Stock

9

Co-Travelers

Companions or Competitors?

GOING ON A JOURNEY is usually a pleasurable experience. There is so much to see no matter where one goes. In fact, it is quite common to talk of a trip of a lifetime, the expectation being that it would be most enjoyable and truly memorable and that it would be to some longed-for destinations. That enjoyment is enhanced when there are others also traveling with us, particularly if they share our interests and plans. We can then relish the travel experience and celebrate our togetherness as well.

In contrast, traveling on one's own can be a lonely experience. Unlike business trips which are planned to achieve something and hence, often more convenient on one's own, vacations, pleasure trips, tours and so on are quite group-oriented. Of course, it may suit certain individuals, particularly the more adventurous type to go solo. But somehow those traveling alone miss out on a valuable aspect of the travel. While sometimes decision-making is made easier if one does not have to be bothered consulting anyone else, it also means that there is no one with whom to share the excitement of the trip, the grandeur of the sights, the pleasure of the experience and the camaraderie of one's companions.

This is one reason why a journey differs from a race despite the presence of others; that is to say, fellow-runners. There is obviously company, too. But the main rationale of racing is to be competitive and to defeat the others. Reaching the finishing line first involves beating the other competitors. In such a situation one is very much focused on the task ahead. One wants to outdo the others. In this sense, the more one knows the weaknesses of the competitors, the more one can capitalize on these so as to surpass them. Rivalry is rife, and the other runners are there to be beaten. The thrill of the race becomes more intense the more one nears the finishing line—which necessarily involves outdoing the other competitors.

There is something in this comparison that can be a lesson for life and how we live it. As we continue with our reflections on our life-journey, we now turn our attention to those traveling with us, no matter who they are. If we regard life as a race, then these others are competing with us. They are our rivals, and the more we outrun them the better we will feel. On the other hand, if life is a journey, then they are our companions. We share the world with them, and we help one another out.

So to what extent are our co-travelers in life *companions* or *competitors*? In what sense is traveling alongside one another in life a matter of sharing with, rather than outdoing, one another? Is it a matter of being "near rather than merely next" to one another? What does it entail? Does it mean we need always to walk at the same pace to move on?

Suppose we pause for a few moments before proceeding to explore those points. Some youthful experiences and lessons I had will, hopefully, refresh us during this momentary stop.

An enjoyable experience for me during the summer months was attending foreign language schools in continental Europe, particularly Germany, Austria and Spain. Not only was it a break from the pressures of academic work required by the university, it was also a change in routine. Of course, the main thing at these language courses was still academic work. After all, there were the classes to attend, assignments to fulfill, and language labs to visit. Some of these courses are intensive, and so more learning has to be squeezed into such a short period of time. And being in the country where the language that one is learning is spoken is also the chance to imbibe its culture firsthand—and that requires some time, too.

But such language courses had another attraction as far as I was concerned: the opportunity to meet students from various parts of the world. The international nature of these courses meant that sometimes one would be meeting a participant from a country unfamiliar to me, and it would be a novel experience. Others would, of course, have hailed from better known nations.

What turned out to be an even more enjoyable and equally fruitful experience were the sessions outside the classroom: whether it was the cafés, the walks, the evening get-togethers that some of us would organize by ourselves and for ourselves. We wanted the time to be enjoyable as well! What was singularly interesting was that at such language courses sometimes the only way to chat, exchange views, share jokes and pursue other activities together had to be conducted in the language that we were studying. That meant that we were learning one another's grammatical mistakes! But it was fun, and we managed to form friendships that way. It was always a diverse group, and the nature of the grouping enhanced our enjoyment.

As I reflect on those summer months, when I traveled to a foreign country to study the language spoken there, I came to realize that the objective of learning the foreign language was at the same time the opportunity to experience diversity. The participants were all individuals from different backgrounds, and yet we were enjoying one another's company because of our common goal. We studied, we did our assignments, we attended classes; but we also found time to enjoy our togetherness.

The first group of activities at the language institute necessitated individual work, but the second kind called for some bonding and relishing one another's company. In fact, that enjoyment was due to, when I think about it now, our diversity: culture, language, interests and other factors. It was the common goal of studying the language that brought us together in the first place but it was our diverse composition that united us during the time we spent there. Since then I have had numerous exposures to and experiences of dealing with a diverse body of students, people and professionals; but that youthful experience still stands out in my memory and probably formed a certain outlook on my part.

One would hardly credit that kind of experience as significant as one journeys through life. Yet it was, because it was a chance to realize that we were not competing with one another as in a race but rather that we were accompanying one another to reach our common goal. Instead of hindering our progress—and enjoyment—our different backgrounds provided the setting for commonality.

In contrast, at times in life in our rush to get ahead or to the top, we brush against each other, we shove and push, we step on one another, and some even trample rivals down figuratively if not literally. That period of study during the summer months showed that differences, in whatever form they are, do not have to set us apart. They do not have to have to be discarded, either. In fact, they also contribute to making the experience even richer as I learned in no small way in the company of a diverse foreign-language student body.

The summer months as a student also provided me with the opportunity to travel farther afield. A new experience for me then was the train journeys on the continent of Europe. One particularly enjoyable route, as far as I was concerned, was the train journey from Düsseldorf to Stuttgart, both in Germany. At that time, it was the scenic route along the River Rhine that captured my imagination, particularly the old castles visible across the body of water. It was one of those journeys where one could spend the hours of traveling just looking out of the window.

I had the same experience when, instead of flying, I took the 7-hour train journey from New York to Vermont in the USA. The chance of seeing the autumn foliage en route was too irresistible for me. I was certainly rewarded as the changing and colorful landscape along the route was truly spectacular. Instead of turning to my reading material, I simply gazed at the passing scenery in awe throughout the journey.

Several years later, on various train journeys in different countries I still have the habit of looking out of the train window to catch a glimpse of the passing scenery. This time, however, the added years in my age made me more reflective. On one occasion on a train journey in Poland I noted that the seat arrangement on the train gave two passengers the choice of sitting next to each other or facing one another. That may not be a particularly eye-catching observation. But as I watched my fellow passengers, I noticed that those seated together were catching the view of the outside world from the same perspective whereas in the case of those facing each other, one would see the view as it was about to pass by whereas the other would catch a glimpse of the same view after the train had passed it. Two different but compatible views of the same reality. Differing perspectives yet a certain commonality.

It seems as if because of where we are, we differ on how we see the world. But it is the same world; and it is the same object of attention, even if it is observed from diverse angles. Yes, sometimes even a mundane train journey can teach us that we can converse, see the views, and share experiences despite looking out from our respective positions. In fact, sometimes the differences in what one sees or had failed to see can liven up the conversation. Similarly, in our journey in life, there are different angles from which to view the surrounding world, and they do not have to mar the journey itself. They do not have to detract from the specificity of the perspective either.

Another wonderful chance afforded to me on train journeys in continental Europe was the experience of crossing borders. At that time, there were passport checks—this was pre-Schengen—and that can be a nuisance as it causes delays and not a little anxiety. The thrill, however, was crossing into another country with a different language, currency (before the euro, that is), culture, and people. It was like setting foot in a new world.

On one occasion, my companions and I hopped off the train in Hendaye, France, having secured our hostel accommodation there because we wanted to explore the surrounding area. But we soon discovered that the cost of meals there was a bit beyond our reach. On the other hand, across the border to Irún, Spain, shopping for food and other groceries suited our meager budget.

So we hatched a plan to beat the system and to take advantage of the disparity in prices between the two countries: we stayed in France, crossed over to Spain, shopped for groceries in that country, and returned to France. Of course, we had to show our passports there and back, but that was no problem. The border police soon got used to seeing us with such regularity that eventually they would just wave these starving students on.

Diversity, even if only in the cost of groceries, does not have to be a barrier after all—a small point perhaps, but good enough for us at that time. And another lesson that diversity could be turned to our advantage.

Keeping the issue of diversity and the topic of companionship in life in mind, let us now ponder on what deserves our greater attention as we travel together on life's highways and by-ways. There is a philosophical dictum that what is distinguishable is separable. The point is that if we can distinguish one from another, this means that we can separate them. This has led to dualism: a popular philosophical viewpoint, both in Western and Eastern thought, that splits matter from mind, body from spirit, and so on.

We do not have to be bogged down by this dictum or its advocates, as far as this reflection is concerned. Unfortunately, however, since it seems to be at the back of the minds of those who insist that being different amounts to being a separate entity, it cannot be completely ignored either. This has implications for how we view ourselves and our lives inasmuch as it can lead us to conclude that our differences from one another imply our separateness, that being different from you indicates that I am not you and therefore that I am separate from you. That may seem obvious, but it requires further critical attention because it has a way of spilling over to how we treat one another.

Like many influential ways of thinking that have become rather entrenched or like many other statements or beliefs, if these are taken for granted, they can cause some problems for the way we live. In the present case, they can result in racism, discrimination based on religion, gender or sexual orientation and so forth.

The relevant point here is that just because someone is different from us or looks different from us or hails from somewhere else should not lead us to discriminate against her/him/them. What makes them different is simply what is *distinct* about them. But they are still like all of us, human beings. That which stands out as different is the distinctiveness of the other party. It does not and should not separate that person from any of us. In other words, features shown in various ways may be distinctive, hence recognizable; but the reality is common to all.

The noted Armenian-American novelist, playwright, and short-story writer William Saroyan refers to every man and woman as simply a variation of ourselves.[1] Maya Angelou, celebrated American poet and civil rights activist, remarked too that we are more alike than unalike, even describing us all as "family"[2]—there is much truth in that point of view.

Going back to what we had inquired about at the start of this reflection, this means that irrespective of our distinctiveness (which should be valued), we are companions in the journey through life. We are not rivals

---

1. William Saroyan (1908–1981) was an Armenian American author. His writings dealing with daily life, with its ups and downs, are famous.

2. Angelou, "Human Family." Maya Angelou, who died in 2014, was an acclaimed American poet, storyteller, activist, and autobiographer. Her most famous work is *I Know Why the Caged Bird Sings* (1969).

or competitors. We are traveling together rather than racing against one another.

Does this amount to saying that we are devaluing what is distinctive about us? That is hardly the case. The two perspectives of the train passengers facing each other viewed the passing landscape differently. It does not lessen their enjoyment of what they saw. In fact, it added to their being able see something that the other did not. My co-participants at the language institutes which I attended let their respective backgrounds enliven and inform our get-togethers. In the other example, the distinctive features of the adjoining European countries added to the "smart" way that we dealt with our impoverished lot.

Granted that these are not the most valid arguments in support of the points being made here, they are nonetheless lessons worth pondering on. Sometimes it is the small things in life that can cast some light on the important lessons we should learn about life. *Lessons in life are lessons, too, about life.*

There is a notion that has been gathering a certain amount of attention in contemporary philosophy and which is particularly relevant to us here; namely, "the other" as an issue. Rather than spending time elaborating on that topic, for our purposes here we could concentrate instead on the related issue of "the otherness of the other" inasmuch as this is what seems to put the other at a distance from me. To rephrase what we have already come up with earlier, it would mean that it is the otherness of the other that makes the other distinctive, rather than separate while sharing an underlying commonality between us.

Moreover, turning to the other, we noted, does not after all constitute a threat to oneself but rather allows one to have company as one travels on life's highways. As was already noted, that which makes the other different or its "otherness" merely distinguishes rather than separates him/her/them. Despite the diversity, there is a common bond among us.

But how should we understand this? After all, since we are all individuals, are we not like islands, separated from one another? The numerous islands which dot the Archipelago Sea in Finland would certainly give that impression. That is certainly what one notices about them, especially from the air. If we as individuals are like these, how should we relate to one another? As I recall our visits to the various islands scattered in the Philippines and those in Greece, their uniqueness is rather striking. In fact, one of the attractions is precisely that they are different from one another. Are we not like these, each of us endowed with individual traits and gifts?

However, if we look much more closely at the sea that surrounds the islands, including those mentioned earlier, we will notice how the seawater has a way of preserving the individuality of the islands while maintaining their closeness at the same time. John Donne's famous assertion that no man is an island, entire of itself, points out that each of us is a piece of the continent; that is to say, a part of the main and thus we all affected by what happens to a part of it.[3] While likening us to islands in the sea, William James, the American philosopher, adds that we may be separate on the surface but really connected in the deep. Deep down there is a shared bottom, a link.[4] Comparatively, we are only islands on the surface. In this sense the sea has a way of showing us that while each island is *distinctive* it is *not separate or cut-off* from one another after all. There is something down there that unites them all. Perhaps it can teach us about our own situation: each of us is *unique but also connected*.

Can we say the same thing about our co-travelers in life? Is there a common bond that unites us all? How do all these observations aid us to regard one another as co-travelers, rather than competitors, in our journey in life? Taking up the notion of the otherness of the other, we could rephrase that last question by asking: *how* are we to acknowledge the otherness of the other? Doing so will affect the kind of response that we give or should give to the so-called other, thus taking into consideration our other concerns regarding this matter. Without necessarily specifying strategies here, we should nonetheless address the more general issue of what is involved in *acknowledging,* rather than merely, accepting or tolerating the otherness of the other.

Acknowledging in this instance, compared to simply accepting, implies a further factor as one is confronted by the otherness of the other. It indicates that one is much more aware of, and receptive to, the

---

3. Donne, "For Whom the Bell Tolls."

4. This observation is attributed by Rev. Candace McKibben to the American philosopher, William James, who established the philosophical school of pragmatism and is considered one of the leading thinkers of the late nineteeth century, in her article, "Like islands in the sea, our connections run deep."

presence of the other precisely because of her, his or their otherness. It is certainly more than merely tolerating the other. What then is involved in acknowledging the otherness of the other? To help us understand this point better, the word "recognizing"—or better still, the Latin word *recognoscere*—can be useful insofar as it alerts us to another important consideration; namely, that turning to the other, in fact, allows one to know oneself again. There is a sense in which acknowledging the other is also recognizing oneself.

That may seem odd at first. But somehow, despite the obvious differences we note between us and the other, we do notice a certain familiarity simply because we realize that in some respects the other is like ourselves. We are all human beings. It is in this sense that we begin to see ourselves *in the other*. It is not a diminishing of oneself and of one's own values. Instead, in the process of recognizing the otherness of the other, one gets to see oneself from another angle. It is a significantly different view of oneself. Hence, it is not merely seeing oneself in the other, as in a mirror. The act of "recognizing" the other, and what it involves, is an act that brings to the fore what is implicit in oneself, which one would not be able to do otherwise. To Socrates's advice that one ought to "know thyself" we could add that in recognizing the otherness of the other, one does get to know oneself better or at least in a different light.

Recognizing the otherness of the other, as the term "recognition" also implies, is attaching a value to it. Acknowledging it involves respecting it just as acts of recognition in other contexts, e.g. of someone's achievements, indicate the high regard that one places on whatever it is to which one has given recognition. This is why it is more than just accepting it in the sense that one has had no choice. It is not drawing it to oneself only to have it be put aside. Acknowledging is actively accepting and valuing the other *in its otherness*. It is to see the distinctiveness of the other, allowing it to be itself. It is first of all a "letting it be" rather than "making it become" oneself. It is to make an effort to learn from the other precisely because it is an *other*. It is a realization that the other does have its own worth, rather than requiring an imposition of one.

Acknowledging the otherness of the other, however, is more than just recognizing and affording it respect. Also implied and required is a response. It is therefore more than noticing it as one does when one catches a glimpse of something on the horizon or from the train window. The response is, of course, the most intricate part of acknowledging the otherness of the other since one is meeting and is now engaging with it. What makes it so is that the manner of response would vary from one individual to the next and from one situation to another. It is not uncommon that there are heated debates and continual controversies regarding diversity. Many, on the other hand, would insist and argue that respecting the other should not be taken to mean that one does nothing towards or for the other.

But how should such a response take shape? Let us "invoke" again the help of one of the foremost Jewish thinkers of our day: Martin Buber. He refers to such an encounter with the other as a "dialogue" in a more fundamental sense.[5] According to him, the basic presupposition for dialogue to exist is the very openness of one's being. It is actually "communion" insofar as it entails the encounter of beings in their openness.

What is important is that each becomes aware of the other as other, a partner, rather than as an object. In dialogue the I encounters the other in his or her very openness, and the I addresses them as such. The I does not ask what impression one's speech and being will make on the others for it is to their very being that the I turns. This I does not forfeit the other's person: he and she remain the same. Neither does the I leave its ground in order to meet the other, says Buber. The I does not, so to speak, trade in its uniqueness when it turns to him or her. The I and the other, therefore, remain distinct from each other; yet, between them is a definite relationship. One can also add that there is attentive listening to the other and in this way, a genuine conversation can start.

Because genuine dialogue is communion, it takes place in spite of conflicting opinions for it is independent of them. Neither of the participants needs to give up his or her point of view, insists Buber. In fact, essential views demand that whoever holds them maintains his or her stand. Accepting one's partiality as well as the limitation imposed by the other participant, he or she may still cling to his or her own viewpoint.

This difference of opinion should not, however, shut down the openness of each to the other. This point must be understood well, Buber warns, for otherwise dialogue may be interpreted as hemming in those who engage in it so that they find themselves not bound to say everything which in all righteousness they should say. One's basically different

---

5. Buber, *I and Thou* and *Between Man and Man*.

view about the subject of the conversation may even urge one to aim at convincing the other of the righteousness of one's way of looking at the matter. This desire to influence the other, however, does not mean the effort to change the other, to inject one's own "righteousness" (as Buber would say) into him or her.

As we have seen, genuine dialogue cannot come about unless one affirms and accepts the very otherness of the other. For Buber, this strictness and depth of human individuation or what he calls "the elemental otherness of the other" is not merely a starting-point to be discarded at a later stage, but is recognized and confirmed at all times. When one desires to influence the other, it means making an effort to allow what is right to grow amidst the diversity.

We can even go further and claim that the otherness of the other can illuminate and even enrich one's self. To throw some light on this claim, we can enlist once more the help of Mencius, who teaches that the self is actually developed as it turns to the other, rather than when merely engrossed with itself.[6] In this respect, there is much in his way of thinking that can be likened to that of Buber. We will see immediately that his view not only differs from narcissism, but it also challenges the isolationism that appears to result from the axiom "distinguishable, hence separable" that was already shown to be questionable.

Like Aristotle, Mencius starts with what humans have in common with non-humans; but unlike him, Mencius singles out the heart, rather than rationality, as the distinguishing feature of humans. Although this forms a small part of human nature, he maintains, it is nevertheless unique to humans. But by "heart" is not simply meant the biological organ that living creatures possess. For Mencius it is the source of morality. Moreover, he holds that the function of the heart is to think, not conceptually but morally. At the same time, this way of viewing the heart and its function shows that Mencius, like his contemporaries and unlike dualistic thinkers, does not separate the physical body from non-physical activities. He holds that human beings who merely look after their physical needs are no more than mere brutes. In fact, he maintains that humans who care more about their "higher desires and needs"—foremost of which is morality—do develop their human nature more fully, as the sages do.

6. Mencius, *Mencius*.

Mencius maintains that the essentially moral nature of the human heart, is bedded in four incipient tendencies: "compassion," "shame," "courtesy and modesty," and "right and wrong." Compassion is the germ of benevolence; shame, of dutifulness; courtesy and modesty, of observance of the rites; and right and wrong, of wisdom.

Each of these tendencies is significant in its own way. Compassion, which makes humans empathize with one another, is the strongest motive to moral action while the feeling of shame makes them aspire to be better human beings and to advance morally. The observance of rites, which is also highlighted by Mencius, is more than the dutiful fulfillment of rituals—a practice attacked by Confucius's critics. In Mencius's development of this teaching, the tendency of courtesy and modesty is a restriction on self-aggrandizement. It prompts one to be more other-centered. The tendency of right and wrong is what helps humans to distinguish right from wrong and to approve what is right and disapprove what is wrong. Mencius stresses that this tendency, while it does not necessarily mean doing what is right and avoiding what is wrong, does account, in conjunction with the sense of shame, for the realization that what one has done is right or wrong.

Mencius is careful to point out that these tendencies, while containing the germs of moral activity, do need to be nurtured and developed—and this is where his insights are especially relevant for our purposes here since this can only be done by "turning to the other." Otherwise, contrary habits will take over. All he is claiming is that they are pre-conceptual and pre-action. He understands them to be natural in human beings. No one is, in his view, devoid of these, no matter how transitory or momentary they may be.

Mencius thus provides us with an account of human nature as having an inborn moral capacity. This capacity is shown in the four tendencies that he has identified as present in every human being. They do need to be developed actively, or at least unhindered from burgeoning into fulfillment. Ultimately, however, they are all one and the same inasmuch as they are what help the human individual to become moral. In short, Mencius maintains that human nature is at heart good. Since humans have the built-in capacity, it is within their reach to exercise benevolence and to train themselves to make the correct responses.

Mencius's insight into what is imbedded in human nature which needs to be cultivated somehow makes me link it up to a certain extent with a remark made by the commentator on *Michelangelo's Pietas*, a documentary shown on Sky Arts. He maintained that the famous sculptor somehow already saw in the marble block in front of him the marvellous statue hidden, as it were, in the piece of marble but which needed to be brought out by his artistic chipping. He worked on it carefully and gradually so as to make it visible for everyone to admire. Somehow like the innate goodness of humans affirmed by Mencius, the beauty in the marble block needed to be, as it were, "led out" by Michelangelo. His efforts brought the Pieta to life. The result is definitely stunning and awe-inspiring as any visitor to St. Peter's Basilica in the Vatican, where it is on display, can attest. Seeing it in actuality is certainly an awe-inspiring experience and well worth having to stand in line outside in the Square in front of the basilica—both of which we did!

Returning to Mencius's insights, we could ask further how one develops these tendencies which mark a "gentleman" off from the "small man" as described by him. According to this Chinese sage, the former pursues morality above everything else while the latter concentrates on self-interest to the detriment of morality. The two goals are not necessarily incompatible; it is what dictates one's ultimate action or what is given priority that differentiates the two kinds of individuals. The gentleman follows his "heart" earnestly while the small man gives in too readily and constantly to his desires or the lesser parts of his nature.

Mencius does not see a necessary opposition, therefore, between looking after one's own interest, e.g. profit or one's welfare, and pursuing the demands of moral living. Again, continuing the Master's practical view, he accepts that adequate physical nourishment and the satisfaction of all basic material needs are part and parcel of human nature. Only when they stand in the way of the moral quest must these be relegated to a secondary place or even sacrificed.

He stresses that morality is our proper end as human beings, unlike other beings for whom those base needs and desires are dominant. Consequently, the *junzi* as Confucius described a moral person, on the way to becoming a sage, seeks morality out and pursues it wholeheartedly. In a tone reminiscent of Kant's standpoint, Mencius regards the pursuit of morality itself, rather than its achievement, as the most important human endeavor. In fact, seeking morality is already being moral.

Mencius pursues the question of what makes humans, who are inherently good, nevertheless go astray. On this point we will recall our previous reflection on what drives some to inflict harm on others. This can happen because of the individual's habits formed by the choices made as well as through interactions in the socio-political environment which serves as the context in which those choices are made and activities carried out. On the other hand, Mencius also argues that it is within the individual's innate capacity to turn to inner resources or to "invoke" them so as to withstand those obstacles and even overcome them through assiduous moral strivings. Mencius advocates that one can master one's emotions and desires or channel them so that one makes moral existential decisions that will promote one's moral growth. Again, it is within one's inner resources that one can interact with and respond to the various challenges in one's society in a moral way.

In short, Mencius's message is one of hope, based on a certain faith in human nature. It is echoed by what we have already heard about our creativity and how we exercise it.

There is something more in what Mencius has to say about human nature that is worth pondering about here; namely, that we can go out of ourselves seemingly or that we have the capacity to "reach out" to others. Furthermore, if we recall, such a move develops our humanity in the view of this Chinese thinker.

But before making that point more explicit, I would like to show how his observation about our ability to reach out always makes me imagine the way bridges connect two territories and provide passage between them. In this way traffic in both ways is facilitated and enhanced. Both sides also benefit from the interconnection. Bridges, no matter what kind of construction they are, seem to concretize for me the act of "reaching out" that we humans should be encouraged to do.

For generations, San Juanico Strait sliced the two adjacent islands of Samar and Leyte in the Philippines. It is quite narrow, but the only way inhabitants of one island could cross over to the other was by sea—in rather old-fashioned ferries. It was a dangerous crossing, particularly when there were typhoons or even simply strong winds. Besides, they were slow and the crossing would take a long time. These ferries were usually packed not only with passengers but also with cargo since that was the only way to transport it.

Today there is a stunning bridge, which is presently the longest in the Philippines, connecting the two islands. Even the sight of it from either end makes one marvel at its beauty, especially now with its light shows. No wonder, it has become the pride of the people. More importantly, however, it has connected the two islands, and has made it possible for them to cross the San Juanico Strait and avail of the resources on both islands. San Juanico Bridge "reaches out" and offers opportunities to the inhabitants.

Bridges, like the one between Samar and Leyte, are not unlike what Mencius was referring to about human nature. That is to say, the potentialities in human nature, once they have been actualized, bring about much good for both oneself and the other. We also need to "reach out" and by doing so develop ourselves. Human beings can and should be like bridges, rather than walls. The interconnection, rather than the division, between and among individuals lets them grow in their humanity. While each of us should understandably address our respective concerns, we ought also to reach out to the other. As human bridges the interaction between us has a way of transporting "the goods" to both sides.

This observation was well exemplified in the "Black Lives Matter" protest organized following the incident between an African-American man and a white policeman in Minneapolis, USA, which led to the former's death. On that occasion in London a black man, attending his first protest march, crossed the line to the opposite group in order to carry an injured white man through an angry crowd to avoid catastrophe. The photograph of his action was carried by various media throughout the world to much praise. He symbolically and literally showed how human beings can indeed "reach out" to others by "crossing the road" to the other side.

The act of "reaching out" by some unknown individual took a different form for us on our brief tour of Lviv, Ukraine's largest western city and culture center. We had crossed over the border from Poland on the train as we intended to spend a few days there. We decided to book our hotel accommodation as near as possible to Freedom Avenue, the tree-lined centerpiece of Lviv's historic Old City, a UNESCO World Heritage Site.

On the second day of our visit, having spent the evening of our arrival strolling up and down the avenue so as to enjoy the new and different experience and get the feel of it, so to speak, we opted to go on the hop-on-hop-off bus. In that way we would get an overview of the city first before deciding where to spend more time exploring. That was when we spotted the Lviv Opera Theater. We got off at the stop to check out what we could book for that evening. It was a Ukrainian folk theater festival performance that was scheduled. We looked at each other, and then after some initial hesitation decided to book tickets for two of the cheapest seats nearest the back exit. We thought that if the experience became too much for us because of our lack of knowledge of the language and the customs, we could make our exit without much bother or trouble to anyone.

Booking the tickets, however, became somewhat of a problem since the lady ticket-seller had no English. We wanted some details about the performance beforehand. Understandably, she could not provide them. There were no leaflets in English either. Fortunately, the lady behind us who was also waiting to get tickets came to the rescue—she did not speak English but had some Deutsch. As it turned out—we later on amused ourselves about the experience—we were communicating in a foreign land in a foreign language! It was enough for us to be able to decide "to chance it" and to hand over the price of the tickets.

But it was really what happened when we arrived at the magnificent opera house that made an impression on us. Having admired the achitecture, we decided to head for our seats—with a view to making a quick exit if the evening did not turn out to be what we had hoped for. The lady-ticket seller was waiting for us. She had no problem recognizing us as we stood out in the crowd. We smiled at her. To our great surprise, she gestured that she wanted to exchange our cheap tickets for two of the best seats in the opera house! Through an interpreter she explained that since we had gone out of our way to experience their culture, she wanted us to also enjoy it. She had "reached out" to us—and did it in a very pleasant and surprising manner.

As it turned out, the performance was thoroughly enjoyable. Even more appreciated, however, was her hospitable gesture. It was, for us, a lesson on how diversity can be bridged, despite language barriers.

The menace of COVID-19 has re-shaped, almost literally, the "face" of the world. Entire populations have been urged and even required to stay indoors. Streets, roads and lanes are deserted. No matter which country is being shown on the screen of televisions or the social media sites, one will be struck by how even financial and business centers are like ghost-towns. There is an eerie silence permeating the entire atmosphere. It is devoid of any activity.

Unfortunately, this situation has led to much isolation, particularly of the elderly. The threat of the virus has certainly re-enforced our separateness although this time as a preventive measure. Fortunately, a rather inspiring call has been made to combat it—a reminder that our togetherness is what truly matters, even in such circumstances. People are being asked to "stay in" and are also being urged to "look out" for one another. Neighborhood is not just a description of a locale, it is much more an illustration of what human living should be, reminiscent of what we had learned from Mencius.

"Reaching out" took another form under these circumstances. Instead of sticking with the popular ways of shaking hands, kissing or hugging, individuals have been urged to show their friendliness and solidarity in different ways so as to maintain "physical distancing" (the alternative phrase for "social distancing"). Nodding to each other or even extending verbal hellos are common ways. But some have resorted to the Asian way of placing one's right hand, probably taking the cue from Mencius, across one's heart, and nodding to the other party while also smiling. It is "reaching out" in another form. It is indicating that one extends one's empathy to the other. Or the other greeting, associated with Hinduism and practised in India and elsewhere, of placing one's open hands in front of one's body, with fingers together and pointed upwards, and wishing *Namaste* thus acknowledging the presence of the spirit in the other person or persons is yet a sign of togetherness while being distanced.

But "reaching out" was particularly palpable when in Ireland, Britain and elsewhere people, at a distance from one another, extended their gratitude to all those involved in taking care of, even at the risk of their own safety, those affected by the corona virus and to all those who continued to provide essential social and medical services. Clapping hands in unison was a most inspiring extended moment of delivering a strong message of appreciation. It bridged the physical gap and the barriers.

There were other inspiring moments in the midst of the calamity of the corona virus. One of these was the way in which individuals and groups responded to the needy and the isolated. These volunteers came to their aid by bringing to them whatever essential supplies they required. Somehow Simon and Garfunkel's popular and well-known song about being a bridge over troubled waters was being literally and physically replayed. They certainly helped the recipients of their good will and action be reconnected with the rest of society. The deed was a powerful way of healing the fragility of human nature.

Their action transports me back to the aqueducts built by the Romans. The one which we visited in Segovia, Spain, was particularly impressive, especially since it was the first one which I saw. It made Roman history come alive for me. But what impressed me even more was that, overcoming the obstacles of the terrain, it facilitated the transport of sorely needed water to the population, much like what these present-day volunteers were doing despite the risks involved. An extra bonus provided by such aqueducts is that their architecture enhanced the beauty of the surrounding area. In the same way, the much-appreciated "extended hands" lifted the spirits, not just of the recipients but also of the population as a whole.

Bridges and extended hands can "reach out" to cross the divide, thus illustrating our oneness. They can buttress our fragile human nature even if we are on different territories. We have to make the effort to cross them—creatively. We can and should be "bridge-builders" as fittingly described of Mary McAleese, who was President of Ireland for two terms and who succeeded in bringing together diverse communities during her presidency. A bridge over the Boyne Valley has been named after her.

Going back to our earlier reflection on our diversity as travel companions and keeping in mind what has been noted as its positive side, we do have to acknowledge nevertheless that it can result also in disagreements and conflicts. It is a fact of life, as Buber pointed out. We cannot ignore that at times there is much harm inflicted and injustice committed. Resolving these disagreements and conflicts would naturally be the priority, but sometimes one arrives at an impasse. How should one respond to it? This is, of course, a complex issue.

But we ought to face up to it nonetheless. Just as it would be farfetched to claim, when traveling with a motley group in a tour, that everything runs smoothly, it would be short-sighted to expect that companionship in a diverse society and a divided world does not sometimes take its toll. While diversity can and does contribute to the variety and richness of our experiences as we travel together in life, we must also be realistic and accept that our differences can also mar or even ruin our life-journey. We should face up to our differences and resolve any difficulties together, as Buber stated.

We should not be misled into thinking that the task of harmonizing conflicting interests will be a pleasant or easy one. On the contrary, as experience has taught us, we can expect that those "differences" sometimes do lead to disagreements and disputes—and lamentably, even wars. We cannot, therefore, merely gloss over these problems and issues.

But to paraphrase Joe Biden, the President of the United States, whose inaugural address, which was broadcast internationally in various television channels and covered by the international press, rings true for us all, we can be opponents but we do not have to be enemies. He added that we will have conflicts, but they should not mean waging wars, advising us to open our souls rather than harden our hearts.[7] Or as Amanda Gorman, the youth poet laureate of the USA, who recited her poem during Pres. Biden's swearing-in worded it: we need to lay down our arms so that we can reach out our arms to one another.[8] Former President Barrack Obama in a message during President Biden's celebratory concert, also televised on international channels, likewise advised listening to those we disagree with as well as to those we agree with, adding that while there can be strong disagreements between us we should recognize our common humanity.[9] In short, reminiscent of what we have learned from Buber and Mencius on this occasion: we need to give one another a chance.

In the face of conflicts a significant option worth examining is the possibility of extending forgiveness. It is a major theme, among others, in Leo Tolstoy's novel *War and Peace* and illustrated in varied circumstances by the different characters.[10] One of the characters in Fyodor Dostoyevsky's work titled *The Brothers Karamazov,* shows a reason for adopting a forgiving attitude. Zosima tells the others that forgiveness is an acknowledgement that each of us is somehow responsible for the sins of everyone else since all our actions are intertwined with one another. For that reason, no one is entirely blameless.[11] Indeed, we are all part of the resultant syn-

---

7. Biden, "Inaugural Address," Presidential Inauguration. Live broadcast, CNN, Jan. 20, 2021.

8. Gorman, "The Hill we Climb," Presidential Inauguration. Live broadcast, CNN, Jan. 20, 2021

9. Obama, "The Inauguration of Joe Biden," Presidential Inauguration. Live broadcast, CNN, Jan. 20, 2021.

10. Tolstoy, *War and Peace.*

11. Dostoyevsky, *The Brothers Karamazov,* 285.

thesis and the challenge is to creatively deal with it rather than apportion blame. Mencius has given us a lead in this respect.

A little earlier in our reflections, when we mulled over ways of dealing with whatever is blocking our progress in life, we turned our attention to the possibility of rising above the impediments which were likened to the hurdles blocking our path. In the face of diversity and differences, we must also recognize that there would be conflicts and various other disagreements, some of which could threaten the companionship described here.

As was noted, disharmony is a fact of life, and often disagreements and disputes cannot easily be resolved. We will recall nonetheless that Buber pointed out that dialogue can take place despite differences of opinion. Dialogue as well as intensive negotiations and good-will featured in reaching a peace settlement between parties which led to the Good Friday Agreement in Ireland with John Hume and David Trimble as chief architects.[12] Recognizing the otherness of the other entails the challenge of opening ourselves up to the power of forgiveness. This does not mean that we simply, as we say frequently, "forgive and forget" or in similar phrases. Instead, it is to disallow the fury to triumph, just as Bloody Sunday gave way to Good Friday.

In a different but relevant context, once again the words of President Joe Biden of the USA are particularly worth keeping in mind. During the lighting ceremony at the Lincoln Memorial Reflecting Pools arranged between sundown and dusk before his inauguration, he faced the lights which represented the then more than 400,000 victims of the pandemic in the USA. He pointed out, as cited by various international media and channels, that to heal we should remember despite the difficulty in doing so.[13]

Indeed, if creative synthesis has taught us anything, it is that whatever has happened, good or bad, remains. We cannot wipe out the past, simply because it is unrealistic to do so or even to think so. Good or bad, like footprints on wet cement, they have made their mark on the trodden paths of life. But we can and should move on.

Where does this leave us then? We can, as had been suggested previously, rise above these disagreements as we journey on with our travel-companions. We can soldier on insofar as we have not allowed the

---

12. The Good Friday Agreement, so-called because it was reached on Good Friday, April 10, 1998 in Belfast, was an agreement between the British and the Irish governments and most of the political parties in Northern Ireland on how Northern Ireland should be governed.

13. Biden, "Lighting Ceremony," Live broadcast, CNN, Jan. 19, 2021.

situation to get the better of us. We can continue in spite of the adverse effects of living in a diverse society. The pursuit of true peace and the effective resource of peaceful means are worth seeking.

But, in addition and perhaps even more of a challenge, we can—taking up what has just been suggested—forgive. We often hear that "to err is human, to forgive is divine." It may well be since it sometimes demands so-called superhuman efforts to forgive someone who has wronged us. But to forgive—even with the knowledge that the past cannot be wiped out or that the wrong done cannot be undone—is human, even if we are not inclined to believe so. It does take much effort at times. Besides, we do not always succeed in doing so since the past, especially if it hurts, has a way of re-surfacing. And yet, being able to do so is a mark of genuine humanity.

Here Mencius can once again help us to appreciate this point. He teaches us that as human beings we have the resources to be able to respond positively to this challenge. Assiduous moral strivings, which includes the act of forgiving, is—as he reminded us—the mark of genuine humanity. In our ordinary travels, we have come to realize that at times we need to unburden ourselves of too much baggage to be able to continue with comfort and success. Forgiveness is also a way of off-loading some of that burden, both material and immaterial, in life. In that way, we are able to move on.

Mencius can assist further if we do regard our fellow-travelers in life as companions rather than competitors. Even if we are not always so inclined, this demands showing compassion to others. The challenge facing us is even greater when we take into account that there are some among us who do need companionship. Its lack leads to much loneliness, isolation and even the feeling of having been abandoned. It is always a mark of the kind of society that one belongs to—something that Mencius, and before him Confucius had pointed out—when there are members who are left on the sidelines as we continue on with our own life-journeys.

It is, understandably, difficult to specify the exact measures that we must take because circumstances differ. Besides, resources are not always as readily available as one would want them to be. Nevertheless, it should not be a handy excuse for shirking our responsibilities as companions. Companionship, in whatever form it takes, is going out of our way to seriously consider "the other" as fellow-traveler. The otherness of the other is, as Buber puts it, a summons to us.

The more important and fundamental task is to turn to and—appreciate—the otherness of the other, irrespective of who the other is. The otherness of the other is a valuable lesson that all of us can learn during and for our daily lives. On this point it is particularly instructive to hear a lesson on harmony produced by the symphony orchestra: distinct musical instruments playing alongside others, do not lose their own sound while attuned to the others, but rather are enhanced by the contribution of the other sounds to the overall music. After all, to adopt and adapt a well-known saying; namely, that we may be singing a different song or dancing to a different tune, but we do share a common hymn book.

Indeed, it is important to achieve harmony just as much as unity. Pope Francis's observation made in his Christmas message of 2020 is particularly relevant here.[14] According to him, we are truly co-travelers in life, even if we come from different parts of the world. After all, we share a common nature, such that what one does always affects everyone else even if not in so explicit a way all the time. Recalling what we had learned in the previous reflection about the sea and its surroundings, we may be, due to our individual natures, like "islands" but at the bottom there is a common sea-floor uniting us all. We should strive to support the unity that grounds us all, irrespective of our differences, and not just work towards achieving some union when these seem to dominate instead. In this way, we could arrive at some harmony.

This commonality that binds us together as human beings, despite any division that may exist, was well brought out—rather imaginatively—in what some people did with the wall recently erected to separate a section of Mexico and the USA. The wall consisted of steel bars erected vertically next to one another but with some slits between them. The opening provided a good view of the adjoining country from the other side. It was these narrow openings which inspired some individuals, instead of merely peering through them, to insert strong narrow wooden bars to the other side and to attach seats at both ends—they became the see-saws for the children on both sides!

But it was what inspired the placing of this contraption that can provide some lesson in our journey in life; namely, that what one does always affects the other party just as the action of one of the players on the

---

14. Pope Francis, *Vatican News,* December 25, 2020.

see-saw lowers or raises the other. Likewise, we are, to take up the point in this context, "playmates" in life even if we are on different soils. There may be two sides to a dispute, but we are all affected by what one side does. And it is up to all of us therefore to resolve it to everyone's benefit. It is ironic that a wall intended to divide communities and not just lands can be inspiring in this way.

It alerts me once again to what the poet Robert Frost wrote about the task of mending walls.[15] In his poem about it he maintained that, despite the general observation made by the poet that there is something about a fence that we generally dislike, he was doing it at the insistence of the neighbor, who maintained that good fences can make good neighbors. The poem is very nuanced and multi-layered in meanings, well worth pondering over.

Frost may have had something else in mind. But for our purposes here there is one specifically relevant observation that I would like to make; namely, that somehow the varying, and even conflicting, interests of the two parties can meet—and be dealt with—over what in fact separates them: in this instance, the wall that requires mending annually. It is reminiscent of a scene which I witnessed on one of my road trips in Ireland. Two elderly farmers on either side of the wall which divided their lands were having a so-called neighborly chat, apparently conversing but also grumbling, even shouting and pointing fingers. It was an animated and even heated conversation by all accounts. At the end, however, to my pleasant surprise they waved goodbye to each other—one of them seemingly toddling off to his lunch while agreeing to resume their "conversation" the next day!

Somehow such a twist regarding the purpose of the wall—what was intended to divide actually unites—makes me recall once again our visit to what has been known as the Great Wall of China. In Ming times they were called "border barriers" by the Chinese. They had been built to keep the invaders away at some distance and to isolate the residents. Division and separation of the warring parties as well as the protection of the residents within the walls were the aims. As we stepped onto such a historical and monumental construction, centuries later, we could not help being awed by such a construction, especially when we considered how it was done—at such enormous cost, including human lives.

---

15. Frost, "Mending Wall," *Robert Frost: Selected Poems*, 43–44.

Our group consisted of individuals from various countries. One could not help but notice that the visitors—and there were hundreds and hundreds of them—came from different parts of the world, with one purpose: to admire and experience a wall which stretched for several kilometers. It made us wonder how such a construction, intended to divide, was actually bringing together all these people from various nations. Somehow, despite the disparity in origins there was something that united them: a common purpose and, of course, a natural curiosity.

It is paradoxical, to an extent, but also thought-provoking: even walls intended to separate us can actually be "converted" into "bridges" for us. Much depends on how we exercise our creativity in this respect. The same can be affirmed about our disagreements and conflicts. In this sense, "mending walls" is a particular challenge to our relationships with one another, as individuals but also as societies.

We should gather our thoughts together on what we have highlighted in this reflection. As we travel through life, we will notice the differences among us. We asked whether our co-travelers are companions or competitors. This is because of our diversity.

But taking our cue from Buber and Mencius, rather than allow this fact to ruin our trip through life, it has been suggested that we should take advantage of it. We should also pay attention to—and even celebrate—our diversity. We could heed the advice given by Kazuo Ishiguro, the Japanese-born British writer, in his Nobel Lecture at the prize-giving that, given the time we live in with its dangerously increasing division, we must learn to listen because we may even learn from one another a great humane vision that will enable us to rally.[16]

Once again the concept of creative synthesis, which has been serving as our travel map thus far, can be handy here—even if it comes across as rather too abstract. But it is helpful to connect our distinctiveness—what makes each of us different from everyone else—with the "synthesis" aspect of that concept and reality. What this means is that we are all products of past events coming together but at different times and occasions. I differ from you because I am the embodiment of a different synthesis. That is what makes me, me while another synthesis makes you, you. It is

---

16. Ishiguro, "Nobel Lecture."

my "whatness" or who I am. Our respective distinctiveness is what constitutes our uniqueness as individuals.

But "creativeness" on my part is how I respond to your synthesis or to your "whatness" while "creativeness" on your part can be stated similarly. It is our own specific way of dealing with each other's distinctiveness. To phrase it slightly differently along the lines of the present reflection, recognizing the otherness of the other is *creatively acknowledging the synthesis that is the other*.

10

The Footprints We Leave, The Tracks We Carve

GOING FOR A STROLL on Bray's up-graded promenade is a delight, particularly if the Irish weather co-operates as well! It makes us think back to our leisurely walks in similar surroundings in Nice, France and in Alicante, Spain as well as in other cities where we had spent a few days. Just a few meters away is Bray Head, inviting all strollers to continue on to walk towards it and uphill to see the sights of Dublin and farther afield from such an advantageous height. Even from the more level promenade the view is indeed magnificent. The sea is inviting, the peace and quiet is soothing, and the sight of flying seagulls is relaxing. No wonder, it is a popular spot for residents and visitors alike. Crowds throng the place when there are scheduled events.

When first I visited the place a good few years ago there was a sizeable number of holiday-makers from outside towns and cities mingling with the locals. I remember very well my chance meeting with a family from Northern Ireland. They told me that no matter where in the Republic of Ireland they visit for their holiday, they always end up in Bray, such was its attraction for them. For a few years, however, it had become a bit outdated and worn-looking. But today it is once again vibrant, popular and entertaining. The promenade has been reconstructed, and stretches out even more.

The Footprints We Leave, The Tracks We Carve

There is a sign, well-located to ensure maximum attention, to remind all strollers to leave nothing behind, except their footprints. The message is quite obvious, and hopefully every visitor and beach-goer abides by it. If so, then the authorities can be assured of a clean and pleasant environment for everyone who visits the place.

There is another popular spot in Morocco that has its own attraction—the long, sandy beach in Agadir. It is definitely worth a visit, at least at that time many years ago when we spent a couple of weeks there. One could go for a long walk for miles, with just the waves lapping the shore with some soothing sounds—a pleasant feeling that always makes us recall the time when we heard the Russian waltz "Amur Waves" for the first time when on a tour of Russia, Belarus and the Baltic States. During our regular strolls, we came to appreciate its relaxing atmosphere. It was also fun to see the footprints that we had made being washed away by the rolling sea, almost as if it did not want any traces left after us.

Comparing ours and other footprints on the sand before that happened, however, became a fascination for us because they gave us a clue—so we thought, Hercule Poirot-like—of who or what or how they came about. We would then concoct a murder mystery with the beach as the imaginary crime-scene. Once as we went for our early morning stroll, we recalled the story set somewhere else of two sets of light footprints on the beach, which then became only one but deeper a bit further on. It was supposedly the story of a young boy who carried his much younger brother who had become tired as they walked on. More importantly, it was an example of brotherly love.

Yes, footprints on the sand provide us with some information on what has transpired—or had been imagined to have happened until, of course, the sea-water takes over, or as picturesquely described by the American poet, Henry Wadsworth Longfellow, the white hands of the waves erase the footprints left in the sand.[1] Footprints, unfortunately, also do a lot of damage. There is understandably a growing concern that the grassy trails on Machu Picchu in Peru are left bare due to the increasing number of tourists. There are organized Inca trail treks, very popular with adventurers, tourists and visitors of all ages, as well as individual outings to see the sights of the Sacred Valley. The journey is unbelievably stunning, passing through the region's ruins, mountains, and cloud forests. The first glimpse of Machu Picchu in the early morning light is a

---

1. Longfellow, "The Tide Rises, the Tide Falls."

real eye-opener. The downside, regrettably, is that such visits, due to the huge number of footfalls, can create their own ruins.

Not as dramatic as this case, but also ruinous, are the footprints left by people and animals on freshly-laid cement pavements. They mar the smoothness of the carefully laid-out pedestrian walk-ways, but they can also make it more difficult for those who have to travel on them on wheel-chairs or with carts. They are not like those footprints on snowy paths which melt away once the temperatures rise. They are there to stay, regrettably.

Today, however, the idea of footprints takes on a different meaning—we even talk of digital footprints, for instance. Thanks to the efforts of many, we have become more aware of the carbon footprints that we are leaving for ourselves and for the next generations. It would be good if that call for more care is heeded not just by individuals and groups but also, and more importantly so, by those who have charge of cleaning up the environment of carbon emission. Climate-change affects all of us in this world. It would seem to be the case that we should not leave any such footprints after all. It is a call that needs urgent heeding and requires immediate change in our lifestyle—a challenge to the world-leaders meeting for COP26 in Glasgow, Scotland.

There is something quite thought-provoking about footprints, particularly about what the sign in the Bray promenade advises. The message of that sign should make us think further about the footprints that we do leave behind to stay, whether on Bray's promenade itself, or the grassy footpaths of Machu Picchu or newly-cemented footpaths lining the streets. Unlike the footprints on the beach in Agadir, which are washed away by the sea, the indelible carbon emissions that we are discharging into the atmosphere causing climate-change have such a lasting effect. That, too, should make us reflect seriously about what we are doing and how we are contributing to it.

Similarly, whether we like it or not, as we go through life there is always something that remains about us and from us. The world is different because we have embarked on our life-journey. There is a trail that has been marked by what we have done. There are footprints that we, and only we, have left behind. They are forever etched on life's paths.

Indeed, leaving our footprints is indicative of how we human creatures like to leave our traces after us. We like to make marks somewhere, somewhat, somehow. And we have various ways of doing so. At times, we fancy ourselves as being immortalized in this way. There is a sidewall in one of the student bars in the university town of Heidelberg, Germany well known for the etchings made by the young drinkers, in pairs, to perpetuate their time together. It gives them a reason to return years later—that is, if they are still together!

Despite the common expression that the past is past and that it is easy to forget it in most cases, there is such a thing as the immortality of the past. Whatever has occurred, no matter how far back it is in time, continues to be in existence. We do not and cannot cancel it out, even if no one remembers it. The past still impacts on the present; it cannot be undone.

We will recall from our previous recollection how this point was made by Charles Hartshorne. The philosophical phrase which he coined is "creative synthesis" which in the present context has been serving as road-map for us. The past, according to him, consists of all that has happened coming together and staying together; hence, it is a synthesis. It remains stuck in and thus partially determines any future outcomes. Another way of understanding this view is, as was suggested earlier, that the past is immortal insofar as it becomes part of the present and has some influence, no matter how small it is, on the future.

That may be worrying, but it should not necessarily be. It simply means that what we contribute to the whole of reality does matter after all since it determines it to some extent. There would be a real difference in the whole of reality if it had not been done or had not happened. It could even be encouraging because it amounts to realizing that what you and I do is never duplicated, and therefore there is something original and personal in whatever we do in life.

This has some implications, of course, for how we value our life-journey. We may have been "thrown" into existence, to repeat what Heidegger has remarked; but once we have indeed appeared on the world stage, our individual performance adds something, unduplicated, to it. Shakespeare described our presence in this world as players standing on a stage. It would mean then that every actor and performer, that is to say you and I, makes a difference to the entire drama unfolding on the world stage.

If indeed we are all travelers in life then the quality of the tour itself is marred or enhanced by our contribution to it. Due to human activities there is a contrast between the litter strewn on neglected sites and the scenic beauty surrounding us. As we continue on life's highways and byways we will note that, like the litter thrown, the waste scattered around, and the destruction caused, our acts can damage the atmosphere for us and for everyone else. Yet when someone actively cleans it up the difference is striking. Small acts can and do make a big difference. At the same time, the good that results because of our deeds will brighten and aid all of us to live better and to have more productive lives.

If that is the case, it would indeed be much more gratifying if we were to leave the place more pleasant and beautiful than when we had arrived. We will not just have good and happy memories, but we will also have left behind a better world for everyone. It would be of some consolation to realize that all that was possible because we came this way. It is different, and for the better, only because we have turned in this direction.

Tracing the footprints in various sites and locations, which we have been engaged in, directs us now to the broader but related topic of what further lesson we can draw from them. Let us pursue it then by examining certain slogans or sayings along the way.

There is a popular saying that we are all familiar with; namely, "following in someone's footsteps." We use it in various contexts; for example, children emulating their parents, a protégé carrying on the master's work or a fan duplicating an idol's achievements, and so on. There is also some truth in holding that, given what was said earlier, we all follow in someone's footsteps, for good or bad.

The corollary to this is to say that we somehow create, or at least help shape, the pathways to be followed by those who come after us. If it is true that what we do adds to the construct that is reality, if indeed every deed of ours attaches itself to what later generations inherit, then we need to consider the kind of inheritance we are leaving behind. One of the important tasks then as we go on our life-journey is to consider, and consider well, what we are leaving behind.

That question is more than merely asking how we will be remembered—in itself an important consideration—but, more significantly, how we are living our lives now in such a way that others after us can be grateful not only that we have cleared the way, but that we have also paved the route so that their own life-journey has become more pleasurable and fulfilling. Naturally, the specific answer will differ from one person to another; but the relevant observation remains: whatever it is that we are doing will influence and impact on the lot of those following in our footsteps—that is to say, the "syntheses" that we are leaving behind. In this respect what Greta Thunberg, the teenage Swedish environmental activist internationally known for challenging world leaders to take immediate action against climate change, has left a lasting mark on our minds.

This, of course, raises the question: what kind of inheritance should we build up? That, once again, will depend on individual tastes, capabilities, resources and capital. But no matter what it is, it is crucial that we work for the improvement of all peoples' lives. It should also mean that not only should we not damage the world, but that we should also enliven it, so to speak. It is important that whatever we are engaged in continues to improve the life-span of all those who inhabit the world. It also entails that the accumulation of our achievements is not left in the hands of only a favored few but serves all.

Talking of footprints also brings to our attention here another well-known saying which is also quite relevant: "walking in someone's shoes." Doing so somehow sensitizes us to the situation. There are variations of this phrase; for example, the American Indian version of not judging anyone until you have walked in that person's moccasins, or the Chinese teaching, drawn from Confucius, that one develops sympathy by walking in that person's footwear. Although that advice is of course meant to be symbolic, it can also be an eye-opener. Somehow, one's perspective on different matters can be changed because it is not merely about looking at the situation but also about feeling it. The change in footwear, especially if it is not one's own, has a way of not just enlightening us but also making us feel even more empathetic about someone else's plight. We will recall that Mencius describes compassion as "the germ of benevolence" which needs to be nurtured. Compassion, he tells us, is what makes humans sympathize with one another and is the strongest motive to moral action.

There is a particularly comical one-man show, written and performed by Mikel Murfi and was showing at various stages in Ireland. Called "The Man in the Woman's Shoes," it follows the character named Pat Farnon, in his five-mile walk to do some business in town and back to his cottage. What is of particular relevance to us here is that it helps one to appreciate, which of course owes much to the actor's skills in taking on different characters, how the change in footwear makes a difference to how one views life and its demands.

What is the point in all of this? Suppose we retrace our steps to find out. We had observed that the footprints we leave behind are at times shaped by the footwear we are wearing. But if we care about the kind of footprints we are making, then we could perhaps say that walking in someone else's shoes can help us leave a different set of footprints. Depending on the comfort and discomfort felt in someone else's shoes, one could be more appreciative of what the original wearer feels. As the character in Murfi's show reveals, doing so could help the other wearer feel and relate to others differently. It helps us to go beyond ourselves to connect with others. It could make us more sympathetic and understanding—and that can make a noticeable change in the kind of footsteps that we ourselves leave behind us.

There is yet another consideration that we ought to make as we continue mulling over the kind of footprints we are making if we care about those sets which we are leaving behind. We should extend it to realizing that we do owe a lot to those who have preceded us. In some cases we may have stepped into their tracks; in others we simply followed the route they had laid out for us. Following footprints should refresh for us therefore the sense of indebtedness to those who had preceded us. Sometimes these footsteps are giant ones, important ones or of the heavy kind such that they do get noticed. In this case, our gratitude to them—for the syntheses which they have created and we have inherited—is very much in place.

But there are also footprints which are simply there—unnoticed and yet influential. George Eliot refers to them as "unhistoric acts."[2] In an oft-repeated observation this author remarks that the reason why our lot is not as bad for us as it could have been is half-indebted to those whom Eliot describes as having lived faithfully a hidden life and are resting in unvisited tombs. Their footprints stay with us and have improved our lot, nevertheless. Even if they remain anonymous they, too, deserve our thanks. We have truly been the beneficiaries of achievements which sometimes escape our attention. Moreover, one could add, these unsung heroes certainly encourage us to do the same and leave something worthwhile for those who come after us.

Gratitude is definitely one of the lessons which the ancient educator in China, Confucius, wanted to instill in his students. When he was asked by them as to why he exhorted them to mourn their dead parents for three years, he remarked that this is because children owe the first three years of their lives to them. It is a specific way of honoring them, he added. Fortunately, for the majority of us, because of the care and concern shown

---

2. G. Eliot, *Middlemarch*, 873.

to us by our parents, they definitely have earned our gratitude. Sadly, this is not always the case given the plight of so many uncared for and mistreated children all over the world. But the reminder to show gratitude to all those who have helped us with our first steps in life—as well as in the remainder of our life-journeys—ought to be foremost in our minds. It is a way of carrying on with what had set us up in the first place. It is also a powerful incentive to spread that good deed even further. It is the best way to give thanks to those who have *enabled us to enable others*.

In this regard, the story that my older sister narrated to me as a young child is quite pertinent. She was treating me to a *halo-halo*, a favorite Filipino drink/snack, as a bribe to accompany her on a window-shopping spree. Between sips of our refreshing drink and before I had time to scoop out the various pieces of fruit at the bottom of the tall glass, she asked me what I wanted to become when I grew up. I shook my head. So she said that we could go on an imaginative trip to the gates of heaven. She offered no other explanations.

St. Peter *daw* [so the story goes] was welcoming the new arrivals that day. According to her, St. Peter was very impressed with the first one, a lawyer, who had devoted himself to championing the oppressed and the disadvantaged and had succeeded in rescuing them from their plight. The second also drew a lot of praise from him since as a medical doctor she had worked tirelessly in a voluntary capacity to attend to those who were unable for financial reasons to go to a hospital. The third arrival was a businessman, who had turned his successful ventures into a financial haven to the advantage of those requiring much-needed assistance to keep them going in life.

St. Peter welcomed them all, thanking them for their labors, and opened the gates of heaven. He was about to close these when a fresh arrival, an elderly lady, caught his eye. He paused and, after greeting her politely, asked her what she had done in life. She smiled, and remarked that as a long-time educator while on earth she had taught and had encouraged the three, and others besides, who had just preceded her to pursue the paths of service in life. That drew a big smile on the face of the gate-keeper of heaven who promptly opened the gates even wider. He invited her to step inside where her former students and a just reward awaited her.

It was much later in my journey in life that I got to grasp and appreciate what the story was about: the elderly lady had provided her young charges the impetus to be other-oriented in their choice of a career. She had "enabled" them to accomplish what they had done, i.e. become sources of assistance to and strength for others! Although apocryphal, its lesson is definitely worth taking on board, and hers is a trail worth following during our earthly pilgrimage. Indeed, the story-teller herself became a lawyer, then a judge and a law professor.

This next episode is from real life, this time a journey to outer space. It has been jogged from my memory by the recent passing away of Michael Collins, the NASA astronaut who was the command module pilot of Apollo 11 when it was on a mission to the moon in 1969. It, too, illustrates for me what "to enable others" means.

Left on his own, circling the earth, while his colleagues Neil Armstrong and Buzz Aldrin explored the moon and left footprints there—an achievement described as "one small step for man, one giant leap for mankind"—he was truly an important part of the adventure. He may not have shared the spotlight then and later and did not step on the moon himself, but he had certainly "enabled" the feat to take place and his fellow space-travelers to achieve what they had done. Without his co-operation, this adventure would not have happened. Dubbed as "the forgotten astronaut" but justly honored, Collins had left a different kind of "impression" on and of the moon landing.

His contribution to that most memorable event somehow reminds me of John Milton's well-known words—despite having been written in another context: "They also serve who only stand [or sit] and wait."[3] It was just as crucial to its success. One does not have to be in the limelight to achieve that.

As we continue to mull over lessons to be learned from the footprints left behind, we should also turn our sights to include those who are not leaving any footprints anymore, as it were. This is particularly true of the *los desaparecidos* of Latin America and elsewhere. They have been taken away by political forces and, despite much effort on the part of their families and of their supporters, there has been no trace of them. Everything on them, including their footwear presumably, seems to have

---

3. Milton, "On His Blindness," *The Penguin Book of English Verse*. 147–148.

simply disappeared. That scenario has been repeated several times in different parts of the world, including with the kidnapping of the young students in Sudan and in Ethiopia.

The apparent disappearance of the footprints of those who had been incarcerated by the Nazis, having transported them to concentration camps, has nevertheless left an imprint on the minds of people. The footprints may have vanished literally, but their sad legacy has been perpetuated by the piles of shoes which confront visitors to the camps. Seeing them at Majdanek and at Auschwitz, both in Poland—as we did on a couple of occasions—was illustrative of the cruelty of a segment of the human population. It tested the validity of the philosophical axiom: *Homo homini lupus est.* Regrettably, we humans do act like wolves at times. At the same time, it was also a summons that such deeds should not be tolerated or repeated at all. The shoes of the victims piled up high for all to witness have a way of leaving a lasting impression for the whole of humankind.

Then there are those who, seemingly, have only footprints on their paths to nowhere because they have been left homeless for various reasons. The sight of individuals, some of whom are shoeless, walking aimlessly on the streets and then desperately looking for shelter for the night on pavements is not just pitiful but is also regrettable—regrettable because it seems that we have not cared enough to share the goods of the earth. There was that old lady in Los Angeles who kept pushing a supermarket cart containing her belongs and who had only plastic bags to keep her feet from the heat of the roads and pavements. It is a sad scene that regrettably is replicated several times around the streets in a number of countries in our times.

The flight of the migrants escaping from the fear of persecution in their own country and braving the elements in order to find refuge in other countries leaves behind a different set of footprints. Often these are lost at sea or washed away in the floods. At times, there is a trail in the paths left behind as these migrants walk barefoot or hang their footwear around their necks.

But irrespective of how they have traveled, this is yet another rebuke to us that if the migrants are companions in life's journey, rather than competitors out to run us down, then we do need to think seriously about how that unfortunate situation can be resolved. Just because migration is a fact of life and has been an integral part of human history should not make us callous to this type of movement of individuals and groups. It should not lead them to such a destiny either. Instead, their trail should guide their footsteps to a decent destination.

Footprints, and the kinds left behind, are graphic reminders that there are times and occasions when we need to exercise our "creativity" continuously. Our moral sensitivity should prompt us to "step in" at times. As human beings, we ought to care enough and respond to that situation. We should "step up" to our moral responsibility. We ought to make that moral difference, which we have earlier associated with one of Frost's poems. We could even, so to speak, walk the extra mile.

This last consideration leads us to push on with our examination—this time of the tracks that we ourselves carve out in our life-journeys and which subsequently become the trails for others to follow. In turning at this juncture towards the future we should also face up to the challenge of facilitating the life-journeys of those following our trail. It is matter of caring about what we ourselves leave behind us.

Again Robert Frost, the American poet, can provide us with a particularly appropriate setting and insightful lines. He tells us in one of his poems that as he travels back home, he is sorely tempted to stop and admire the woods which are lovely, dark and deep. But he pulls himself back because of the promises which he needs to keep. He remembers the miles he has to go before he sleeps.[4]

Like a wake-up call, the sentiment expressed in those lines rouses us into realizing our obligations to others. Those who come after us are indebted, good or bad, to how we have lived up to our responsibilities in life and are often impacted by what we have done or left undone. Like the footprints we leave behind, the tracks we mark out for them will determine to some extent how their life stories will unfold, or what trails they can pursue.

Unlike the footprints in our own travel, however, the tracks we carve for those who come after us are still ours to make *now*. It is the present time but with a view towards the future. This point should make us more careful and more caring. Our gratitude to those whose work, study, accomplishments, and feats in the past have opened up more trails for us to follow should provide us with the incentive to do the same for

---

4. Frost, "Stopping by Woods on a Snowy Evening," *Robert Frost: Selected Poems*, 130.

our successors. The promises we need to keep may not be explicit and publicly made, but our responsibility as fellow-travelers should nudge us in the same direction. What kind of pathways are we marking out for those who come after us? What type of route are we opening up for others to follow? What quality of a journey lies in front of them because we have gone ahead?

Along these lines of thought, I recall a game that we used to play in my elementary school days. It was an exploration of unknown paths, terrains and destinations. That can be both exciting and terrifying. For youngsters that can be a real challenge. What these were depended very much on what the leader would have in mind for us to discover. The game-plan was for him to trek ahead. Then the rest of us would follow the trail that he had laid out for us: full of surprises, twists and turns, and even bodies of water to cross or brambles to cut down. It was even more fun if the whole affair took place on uncharted territories since it would also provide a few scary moments worth re-telling. The leader would leave signs and signals as he moved on which we had to decipher and interpret so that we could catch up with him.

One thing that I had come to appreciate even then, in addition to the fun and excitement of the game, was that he was opening up our view of unfamiliar spots since trailing behind him also entailed stopping now and then—not just for rest—but also to admire the landscape as well as to reap the benefits of the track that he had made out for us and to make our own discoveries. Following the leader's footsteps had its rewards. I sometimes wondered whether he had planned it that way.

Another experience comes to mind in this context, but this time when I was a young student in Ireland. Once I was driving to the west of the country to visit an ancient site. I had been looking forward to this trip. Everything was fine until I hit the country roads: unfamiliar territory and narrow roads, with no one in sight to help me out. But at least, I consoled myself, there were the road signs for me to follow—until I realized that having done so, I ended up in the same spot a couple of times! Little did I know that a popular youthful prank then was to turn road signs around—and as I learned afterwards—so as to introduce travelers like me, it seems, to the entire countryside, or at least most of it.

Finally, in frustration, I drove on for another mile or two until I spotted a farmer. Fortunately, he was taking a break from his toils and was leaning on a wooden gate next to the road. I asked him for directions. He sighed as if to indicate to himself that I was yet another lost soul, a familiar sight to him it seems. But it was his version of giving directions that has stuck with me ever since. Pointing to the road ahead, he told me not to take the lane to the left, and then further up not to take the next right, and finally not to take the small turn toward the left as I neared another old farmhouse.

I thanked him politely but was left wondering how that would bring me to where I wanted to go. I did arrive at my destination, as luck would have it. It was much later on, however, when it dawned on me that by telling me where *not* to go, the farmer was actually pointing me in the right direction towards my destination. He had directed me, indirectly it seems, to where I really wanted to end up. I chuckle now as I took that lesson about life as indicating how even a negative can lead one to something positive: *not taking a wrong turn is already placing one in the right direction.*

How do these experiences aid us with our present reflections, or do they? Hopefully, they do. As we consider the tracks we are carving ahead and as we continue with our journey in life, we ought to be aware that, like our leader's advance trails and the farmer's road warnings, the signs we are drawing, the trails we are blazing, the sights we are highlighting, and other deeds we are committing can and do make a difference to those following us. If these are all for their benefit, if they assist them to make progress, if they contribute to their appreciation of life and their surroundings, then we have truly provided a satisfying lead. Similarly, if we take the trouble of warning them about the pitfalls along the way, the mix-up in the routes, or the wrong direction to avoid, then, strange as it may seem at first, we have also made it possible for them not to get lost and even to advance further.

As a whole, there is something about making tracks, literally and symbolically, for others to pursue that can be nerve-racking, particularly if one takes into account how they will affect others. But it can also be satisfying and gratifying. There is something about it that deserves our careful attention since whatever we do does add to the quality of the life-journeys of others as well as ours. In that sense our "creativity" is indeed something to be treasured and put into valuable use.

There is still another layout on the road that should make us think about the tracks which we ourselves make during our journey in life. Sometimes on our ordinary treks we come across well-worn paths. Somehow, on seeing them, we experience a certain familiarity with them because we realize that so many others before us had trodden on them.

There is one such path that skirts around the local cemetery in a nearby town providing a short-cut to the graves in one of its sections. Many prefer to take it rather than walk along the boundary wall to the gated entrance since it takes a considerable amount of time to do so. Such well-worn paths are therefore understandably popular. But more importantly, these provide an added advantage: a right-of-way simply because the frequent use of it had given the walkers the right to take that route, even if it passes through someone else's territories.

In such a situation certain concessions and compromises have to be made, of course, to protect one another's rights and avoid conflicts. But to what extent does this, in the present context, provide us with yet another area to be explored here as we ponder on the paths we are making on our life-journey?

There is something about a repeated action—in this case, frequent footfalls—which becomes habitual: not only is it taken for granted but somehow it also becomes acceptable often by default. In most cases, this situation brings about a lot of benefits; for example, one does not have any more to exert so much effort thus freeing one to engage in other activities. It becomes taken for granted. The trouble with this is that the same situation, unfortunately, also applies to misdeeds. Done repeatedly and generally, they somehow become acceptable conduct. Such entrenched practices may even give one a so-called "right of way" whereas they should be eradicated, and not merely tolerated. The excuse, often heard as justification that "we have always done it this way" does not make what is suspect acceptable. We have noted this point earlier, but it is worth bringing it up here.

Examples of this repeated practice which is often overlooked and sometimes even accepted would be: discriminating for suspect reasons, cheating as a way of life, impoverishing others for one's gain, "waylaying" the innocent or the vulnerable, and so on. Because they have become so ingrained in some societies, the opposite practice, that is to say, opposing these acts or practices, may even become suspect. Helder Camara, late archbishop of Brazil, was known for saying that when he was giving bread to the poor, he was hailed a Christian. But when he was asking why these people were kept poor, he was branded a communist. Poverty for some, it seemed, had become so much part and parcel of his society—and yet its cause needed to be overcome. But not much attention or care was being given to it.[5]

Seemingly, such situations over time had provided, wrongly, a so-called "right of way" and had become simply one to be taken for granted and impacting present victims. However, perpetuating these situations is misdirecting society now, with repercussions for the future. The track being carved out by the oppressors leads eventually to society's demise.

We should now halt momentarily to ponder more on what has been illustrated above; namely, what is entailed by our need to face up to our responsibilities to future generations. We have already taken into account how we are contributing to climate change because of our way of life. We have also seen that our footprints, in various forms and sizes, remain forever in the paths of those who are traveling in life, too. But we still need to explore more what the onus of responsibility really entails as we carve the trails ahead of us. The salient point here is that it is not just about our activities; but, more crucially, it revolves around our sense of responsibility to future generations.

Let us take a closer look then at what is involved as we turn our attention more explicitly this time to "the promises that we have to keep"—taking up once again the cue provided by Frost's poem. It is, of course, very difficult to spell out what those specific "promises" are. After all, we have varying views not only on what we regard as responsibilities, but we also have even conflicting interpretations of what is involved in "keeping our promises" as we walk on life's paths.

But there is a philosophical description which we can use in the present context; namely, "moral sensitivity" (or what Mencius refers to as "heart") as it can throw some light on what has just been discussed. What this means is that we can live up to our responsibilities or keep our

---

5. Camara, *The Spiral of Violence*.

so-called "promises" by developing what is being described here as our moral sensitivity.

Moral sensitivity, which can help us stay on the right track, is much more than moral sentiment or feeling since it is not merely about how one feels about the matter. Neither is it exclusively an intellectual ability that helps us to distinguish between what is right from what is wrong. Nor is it simply a decision we make freely as when we choose between alternatives.

And yet all of these come into play here since moral sensitivity is ultimately based on our very humanity. That is to say, as human beings, we possess feelings, imagination, intellect and free will; and when we ask what is ethical or moral and what is not and then draw a conclusion, we make use of all these human gifts. Moral sensitivity is nurtured, rather than merely learned. It is about wanting to do what is right instead of merely abiding by what is acceptable.

First of all, the word "sensitivity" is based on the way we reference the word "sense" inasmuch as it is a term with different meanings, each of which we can avail of to understand moral sensitivity as used here. Let us examine these meanings more closely.

"Sense" in the first instance refers to our five senses that put us in contact with the outside world. Secondly, that word is also used to refer to someone having "sense," by which is meant that that individual does not just know but also has the right knowledge. Thirdly, it can also mean simply "in a particular instance" as when we qualify a statement or claim that we make when we say "it is true in this sense." But "sense" finally can also have a stronger meaning: namely, as a more or less coherent overall view as when we talk of "life making (or not making) sense."

Now the phrase "moral sensitivity" draws on all these meanings. It is, first of all, through our senses that we accumulate experience, including moral experience, of the world around us thereby situating us to respond accordingly. However, "moral sensitivity" in the ethical context, as it is being used here, is more than mere sense experience because additionally we require the right knowledge, and not just any knowledge, so that we will act ethically. We also need, secondly, to be aware of the particularity of a situation so as to be able to judge the appropriateness of our judgment or decision. For instance, situation A may have to be judged differently from situation B even if there are similarities between them. But, thirdly, we should be informed by an overall perspective that helps us not just to situate the particular moral situation or context but also to judge it more coherently and consistently. We cannot simply regard every situation as completely different from other situations. There is a certain commonality.

Now the various uses of "sense" and their applicability to the phrase "moral sensitivity" come into play when we are considering whether an action or behavior is right or wrong. What this means is that ethical thinking—the "moral" aspect of the phrase—is not solely a cerebral activity. It is not just in the mind, in other words. Rather, it is a rational activity that involves all the abilities that we human beings possess, including of course the use of our intellect as well as our senses.

The sensitivity that has been described here and used accordingly is of the moral kind. It is an integral one which makes it identifiable with our humanity. Moreover, when we engage in ethical thinking in various situations because we want to live up to our responsibilities, we draw on various sources, including our gender, culture and religion, for instance. Ethical thinking helps us to appreciate our own status as agents and recipients: beings with "moral sensitivity" that needs to be developed so that we can indeed give a responsible response to the challenges of personal and societal life.

This is why education or nurturing throughout our lifetime plays a crucial role in cultivating moral sensitivity and ethical thinking. This is not exactly the same as schooling although that, too, has an important role to play. What this means instead is that as we travel on life's highways and byways, we should realize that, like Frost, we have promises to keep and that therefore we should also cultivate our abilities to live up to them. Crucial to it is developing our moral sensitivities. We "owe it to ourselves" as a matter of speaking. If we care about the tracks that we are charting as we journey in life, we cannot ignore this important task.

In this reflection we have examined the kind of footprints that we are leaving behind. They remain after we have left life's trails just as those before us had left their imprints. That fact of life carries a certain amount of responsibility, the "promises" which we need to keep. The footprints that we ourselves are following in our life-journey should make us think about what we ourselves are stepping into now and about the tracks that we are carving for those after us. After all, we have the creative power to do so. That should be imprinted in our minds.

Borrowing but adapting to our context the advice given by the chief superintendent to one of his officers in the Canadian TV series *Murdoch Mysteries*,[6] we should try to provide incentives for others to follow in our footsteps, rather than to shelter in the shadows that we had cast. Doing so can change our world for the better and make it brighter for everyone hopefully.

---

6. *Murdoch Mysteries* is a Canadian murder-mystery television drama series shown on various networks throughout the world.

Journey's End

Homeward-Bound!

We would not be too far off the mark, it seems, were we to presume that as we travel, irrespective of the mode of transport, our minds would inevitably turn towards our final destination. There would be much anticipation on our part. This is particularly the case if the place of arrival is new, or if the plan is to enjoy ourselves, or if we will be joined by friends or family, and some other similar considerations. For some, the excitement builds up when the announcement is made that the plane would be landing in a few minutes or when one catches sight of the port of call. What would it be like when we get there? Would it live up to our expectations?

It is different, of course, if the reason for our travel is business or professional. In that case, we would want to have organized ourselves properly to ensure that the trip would be a successful one and that its purpose would be achieved. Probably the place of destination would not have the same significance as the event itself. Preparation is therefore much more crucial in this case to ensure a hoped-for outcome.

There are some similarities once again between our mundane travels and our life-journey. In a sense, the latter combines what we have noted above both regarding pleasure and business trips. Additionally, as we reflect on our life-journey, we do have some apprehension, too, about the end-of-the-line, so to speak. In fact, it is probably felt even more. This is why our final end and destination in life are the concern of many and the subject of much speculation as well as of religious belief.

Answers vary, of course. At the same time while this topic occupies the thoughts of such-minded people, so do one's mode of living and one's arrangements for it. Accordingly, there is also much attention given to how we can prepare for that final moment. It would be rather presumptuous to believe that all of us regularly think about where our life-journey will finally take us. Nevertheless, it is true that now and then that thought does surface and may even occasionally preoccupy us.

Indeed, at times we wonder what is down the road for us when we have completed our life-journey. Where are we finally heading? What awaits us? How do we prepare for it?

As we review our reflections on our life-journey at this juncture, those questions are to be expected. Earlier, we had paused and we had pondered as we traced the way ahead of us. It would be worth our while to heed the advice, given in another scenario, of one of Shakespeare's characters: "Go wisely and slowly. Those who rush stumble and fall."[1] I like to think that this advice would be a wise way of implementing a slogan we learned at school: "*Festina lente!*" (Make haste slowly). After all, as was affirmed throughout in this book, life is indeed a journey, not a race. There is much to preoccupy us along the way and they would seem to require our more immediate attention.

In this set of reflections, we had asked questions, we had examined some of the challenges which arise along the way and we had sought advice from those who had preceded us. Our life-journey has been described here as an E.P.I.C. trek *(evoke, provoke, invoke, convoke)*. At the start we had looked into the possibility of a life-map, similar to the maps we use when we are on our trips. Our hope was that such a map would facilitate the task of charting our route through life's highways and byways and assist us to confront the challenges ahead of us, and somehow even broaden our horizons. Our route took us all over the landscape as well as along bodies of water inasmuch as we wanted to draw inspiration from various sources as we "move on" and pluck "thoughts" to nourish us along the way.

We turned to the philosophical concept of creative synthesis, articulated by Charles Hartshorne and developed for our purposes here as

---

1. Shakespeare, *Romeo and Juliet*, Act II, Scene III, *The Complete Works of William Shakespeare: Comprising His Plays and Poems*, 903.

a life-map. Descriptively, creative synthesis shows how the various events come together (synthesis), shape the present, but still leave room for the future (creative) to develop. It explains how there is an "already" which we have to accept but also, and more importantly, that there is a "not-yet" awaiting our own contributions. While we cannot undo the past, we can correct it, build on it, or improve it or make amends—for a better present and a brighter future. In this sense it provides some basis for a realistic hope but at the same time offers a significant challenge.

It was suggested that this philosophical concept can also help us acquire an understanding of our life as a journey and, to a certain extent, enable us to cope as well as deal with what lies on its paths—both challenging and satisfying. It should prod us on to make it fulfilling for everyone. In addition, moral sensitivity, rooted in our nature as humans and not merely creatures, could provide the *compass t*o direct us on our travels in life.

With creative synthesis as "guide" lighting our way in a sense, we probed into some of the challenges in life described as "tunnels, crossroads and detours." We also tested its applicability to our encounters with the "obstacles, hurdles and barriers" which block our paths. We turned to it for guidance on how we can regard our co-travelers as companions rather than competitors. Putting this suggestion into practice can help us, it was claimed, to develop as truly human beings as we turn to one another and share with others our very humanity.

Creative synthesis, applied to how we live, alerted us also to the kind of footprints we leave behind and the tracks we lay out for those following us. Global warming, for instance, is no longer just a reminder—it is the stark reality which demands our immediate action. Throughout our exploration it was also asserted that finding meaning in life entails creating purposeful goals for all of us. And in so doing, our life-journey itself may be made meaningful or at least somewhat purposeful.

Inevitably, however, at this stage in our itinerary our thoughts will turn to our final destination, despite any hesitation or reluctance on our part. Immanuel Kant's third question: "What may we hope for?" resonates with the thoughts and feelings of many nevertheless.[2] Similarly, William

---

2. The first and second questions which Kant famously maintained as the most fundamental are: (1) What can I know? (2) What ought I to do?

Shakespeare's more poetical observation expresses the sentiments of a number of us: "... what dreams may come when we have shuffled off this mortal coil, must give us pause."[3] How should one envision it? Given the limitations of human knowledge, that would be an extremely difficult task. Nevertheless, there will be varied answers depending on the belief-systems to which we subscribe in life, of course.

Let us look into some of those. When Confucius was asked by his disciples what he knew about the after-life, he replied that it was practically nothing. He urged them instead to concentrate on this life and how we should live it.[4] Many would align themselves with his view. It is good advice. Nevertheless, we cannot help but wonder still about "the beyond" somewhere. Albert Camus described our time on earth as being in "exile" from which we are liberated at our final moment but with nowhere to go[5]—a description that would likewise find acceptance with a number of people.

In contrast, Socrates firmly believed in the afterlife and the immortality of the soul, a belief that leads to a particular way that life is to be conducted in the here and now. Even if not exactly described that way, various cultures, primitive, traditional or developed would agree with that view. C.S. Lewis for his part also expresses what several are inclined to believe when he remarked that if we are not thoroughly satisfied with the pleasures of this world the chances are that we have been made for another.[6]

For his part, Gabriel Fauré, the renowned French composer, captures in his entire *Requiem* a sentiment, shared by many, of a very human feeling of faith in eternal rest. In another context Charles Dickens puts the same thought in one of his characters who looks forward to going to a far, far better rest than he had ever known, a much quoted description of the afterlife.[7] The same sentiment is expressed by W.B. Yeats in his "Sailing to Byzantium": feeling the weight of old age, he longs for his soul to be released into "the artifice of eternity."[8] What it is, of course, remains to be seen. And that makes us even more curious.

3. Shakespeare, *Hamlet*, Act III, Scene I, *The Complete Works of William Shakespeare: Comprising His Plays and Poems*, 960.

4. Confucius, *The Analects*.

5. Camus, *Exile and the Kingdom*. Although fictional, this book describes for him the human situation.

6. C.S. Lewis, *Mere Christianity*.

7. Dickens, *A Tale of Two Cities*.

8. Yeats, "Sailing to Byzantium," *The Works of W.B. Yeats*, 163–164.

But, irrespective of these ambiguities, somehow the suggestion that the end of our life-journey, is in fact more like a home-coming or a return is one that can be sustaining and welcoming for all of us—and yet challenging at the same time. This turn-around in our reflections here may be unexpected but may be more reasonable after all. In addition, this suggestion is not as strange as it may initially strike one. In fact, one will find it affirmed by various teachers, be they religious or secular, but expressed in different ways.

One will recall that Plato's term for our sojourn in this world was *anamnesis,* a recalling of home. Christianity has taken that on board with its belief in death being an eventful journey back to the Creator. Similarly, although interpreted differently, Hinduism affirms that life is to be practiced in such a way that one's *atman* becomes re-united with *Atman*. For the faithful believers in Islam, paradise awaits them. Rumi, a 13th-century Persian poet, mystic and scholar who transcended boundaries with his teachings and writings, described the grave as after all "only a curtain for the paradise behind." He wonders why we think separately of this life and the next since "one is born from the last."[9]

What is involved then in entertaining the suggestion of a homecoming at the end of our life-journey? Even in our ordinary travels to distant lands or shores, despite the thrill and the novelty of it all during the trip, there is some excitement in the realization, at least for some of us, that "it is good to be going home." The lyrics and the music of "Going Home" sung by the British boys choir Libera, express that feeling and relief shared by many that the end of one's journey in life means "no more fear/no more pain/and no more stumbling by the way . . . real life has begun."[10] It is in this sense that many, whether religiously-oriented or otherwise, do regard our life-journey as a return journey to where we have come from. Thus, our arrival terminal, in fact, can be compared to our departure point The chorus of the Hebrew slaves in Verdi's *Nabucco* certainly captures the sentiments and longings of many who are pining after and yearning for their return home.

9. Rumi, "When I Die."
10. Libera, "Going Home."

There is significance, it would appear, in realizing that we are "homeward-bound" as we travel through life.

But there is a marked difference, and an important one at that. It is of particular relevance in this final reflection. After all, no return to one's home from any trip is ever the same. A trip has a way of providing us with new experiences definitely, fresh perspectives perhaps, and important lessons at times. This is especially true if one has been away for a long period of time. The travels of Ulysses, even if fictional, illustrate how prolonged travel can be character-changing as well. As every *balikbayan* or returning émigré can vouch, while the departure from, and the return to, home may be from the same place, one is not, or expected to be, the same individual as before. Accordingly, such a homecoming has its own significance, depending on the kind of traveler one has been.

This is even truer with our life-journey. Inasmuch as it has been compared to the trips we make in life, the suggestion being made here is that it can indeed be regarded as a return trip. Irrespective of backgrounds or life-styles, our life-journey also has a way of transforming us, hopefully for the better. Our arrival, following our journey in life, is itself therefore a *kairos-moment*.

Let us probe further into this, keeping in mind that the so-called homecoming depends on *how* we have traveled on life's paths before that moment. For this reason, it has been suggested here that as we go along, we reflect on our life-journey with a view to making that arrival more meaningful and purposeful. Gabriel Marcel's *homo viator*—a singularly apt depiction of our human nature in this context—finds fulfilment in living a life that responds positively to the gift and challenge of existence.[11] Once again, hopefully creative synthesis as a life-map helps us to understand and appreciate that point.

And yet the critics of those whose sights are firmly focused on the beyond are partly right in insisting that we should turn our attention to this world instead of the next—to *existing rather than exiting*. They do have a valid point, it must be admitted. Indeed, as we learned with the concept of creative synthesis, we ought to because this is where we are situated. Whatever we do now remains and adds to the whole of reality itself. We should not forget that this world is after all our stage, and we as

---

11. Marcel, *Homo Viator*.

actors have to play our part well while waiting for the final curtain. Even the spiritual writer and monk, Thomas Merton, is known to admonish that we should embrace the present even if we do not know where we are heading. That advice can be helpful in enabling us to treasure whatever lies in front of us right now.

Irrespective of which of the two points of view just outlined we align ourselves with, our life-journey is in fact a *waiting-time,* as it were. Let me explain further. It must be stressed that in this context we ought not to equate "waiting in the meantime" with merely "hanging around" or "putting in the time" or simply doing nothing. Aristotle warned that no individual who does nothing ever attains happiness—or finds true fulfilment. Neither is it to be equated with a life-style of indulging ourselves: "eat, drink and be merry for tomorrow we die," or "chasing after the rainbow" despite the many "evocative" attractions littering our way. Nor is such waiting a matter of re-enacting the scenes and playing the parts as described by Samuel Beckett in his play, *Waiting for Godot,* uncertain as to how the drama would ultimately unfold.

Instead, that waiting-time, that is to say, our life journey, is an *opportune period*. The constant challenge to those anticipating that moment of "home-coming" mentioned above is to prepare for it. For those who insist that the here-and-now is our actual destination and that is what "homeward-bound" journey means for them, it is a matter of achieving whatever its goal is. In the time of our life, William Saroyan, the Armenian-American writer, advises living in such a way that there would be no ugliness or death for ourselves or for anyone who comes our way.[12] Instead, we should seek goodness everywhere, bringing it out of its hiding place and freeing it—as we noted Mencius urging his disciples to do. Zen Buddhism, for its part, advises its practitioners to spend their time concentrating on achieving the final goal of "awakening" through a life of meditation, tranquillity as well as compassion. The important thing to keep in mind for either perspective—and to live accordingly—is that it is a valuable opportunity.

Earlier in this book it was suggested that now and then we should make the effort to be *free from* everything else so as to be *free for* such a task. We could undertake it during this waiting-time by actively seeking

---

12. Saroyan, *In the Time of Your Life.*

comma-moments to punctuate our lives thus enabling us to think and act as conscientious and responsible life-travelers. We noted that such *silences* dotting our way and lighting up our footpaths can provide not only *sense* but also *strength*. Such comma-moments can also be the break we need to re-orient our lives and look for different or alternative directions no matter how we interpret our "homeward-bound" trip.

Now and then in our travels we consult our maps to check whether we are still on the right road and heading towards our planned destination. In like manner, the opportunities to look back at and evaluate the past can help re-direct our way forward. We ought indeed to "seize" those moments. Along the way we can continuously, so to speak, "charge" ourselves so that we can then be in a position to "discharge" our calling in life. We should not just, as the oft-quoted saying goes, "talk the talk but walk the walk."

Moreover, and more crucially, we have been reminded all along in our reflections here that as "creative" beings each of us has it in our power, despite variations, to make a positive contribution and to make a difference during our life-journey as well as to the kind of life-journey it turns out to be for ourselves as well as for those around us or who follow us. How we take advantage of whatever is at our disposal during our travel in life would understandably vary since a lot, of course, depends also on what is available to us. But creativity empowers us all—in our specific way—to *form* ourselves, *reform* society and *transform* the world.

As we face the continuing challenge to enhance the quality of our life-journey it will be worth our while to draw again from our travel experiences before we wrap up. In this respect, there is something that we can learn from the stopovers which often are part and parcel of long-haul flights or from the time spent at ports-of-call by cruise-liners. On those trips, while waiting for the onward travel to one's final destination, one could simply hang around airport terminals or decide to stay on deck. But one could also regard these as a chance to see more or do more while traveling to one's destination. How we utilize those in-between periods can make a difference to our life-journey.

I recall the time when we availed of the opportunity afforded to us to tour Belgrade necessitated by a three-day stopover in that city because of the flight arrangements of the then Yugoslav Airlines and to do the same in Karachi due to a similar set-up by Pakistan Airlines, both times on our way to another country. In addition to visiting some spots, even if only briefly, as well as broadening one's horizons, such intervals during one's travels to somewhere else can be uplifting and rewarding. In fact, there have also been occasions when these were especially welcome since somehow the stopover turned out to be the chance not merely for some sight-seeing but even to renew friendships or help out in various ways, as has happened on several occasions during our travels.

Our life-journey, too, offers similar intervals which are varied opportunities to exercise our creative powers over our own lives as well as those of others. They are stopovers, not a complete stoppage, which means that we do continue with our other activities. As in those travel breaks it is truly a matter of *stepping out* rather than of doing nothing or staying back. Moreover, such activity is *intended* rather than merely accepted. In the matter of our lives, in comparison to our trips, a lot more is of course required of us.

In this regard, existentialists have stressed the choice that faces us in making our earthly existence more meaningful and that it is ours to make with as much resolve as we can muster. Indeed, "to exist" (as the Latin word *existere* suggests) is not merely "being in sitio or standing still" but more importantly "coming out or going forth" (the variant *exsistere*=to come out, brings out this meaning more clearly). As we travel on in life, we need to face up to its challenges by taking initiatives and not just expecting developments to happen. It is a matter of acting rather than merely re-acting. Our creativity empowers us to do so, but we must put it into effect. We will thereby be stepping up to our moral responsibility as *human* beings.

Another consideration worth making in this context is that waiting before reaching one's destination can also be an opportunity for sharing. During our travels, exchanging stories or experiences—at least, for most of the time—is not just a way of passing the time but it can also be openings towards new horizons. Admittedly, not everyone likes to be hearing seemingly endless travel anecdotes but on occasion, listening to co-travelers encourages one to seek out new travel episodes, too. Often it is also a matter of sharing one's resources with the others whether because of need or simply out of generosity. Travel difficulties can be overcome or at least eased somewhat in addition to the pleasure shared with them.

This last point takes me back to those hitchhiking days as a university student—"ride-sharing" would probably be a more appropriate term today—referred to at the beginning of this book. Those drivers on their way to their respective destinations stopped briefly and opened their car doors to provide me with the chance to arrive at my own destination. Although at that time, it proved to be simply a convenient and cheap way for me to get to where I wanted to be, the experience—when I look back on it now—was a lesson on *sharing* one's resources and company with others. It may have seemed like a relatively small bit of hospitality on their part, but it *enabled* me to reach my goal. That meant a lot to me. It made waiting patiently at the roadside worthwhile as their gesture provided me with more chances to enjoy my journey and arrival at my destination.

It seems, as I reflect further now, that our respective life-journeys could also be—if we take the trouble of sharing what resources we have—a way for others to advance on their own journeys. After all, we are co-travelers; in fact, as we have noted previously, companions rather than competitors even if at times and in certain circumstances we appear to be that. *Progress is not to be measured on individual scales only, but also on the quality of life for everyone.* It is so important to look out for, rather than race against, each other. Life is not a solo run either. Whatever we do affects us all. And what we leave behind maps out the journey in life of those who follow us.

A rallying cry during the COVID 19 pandemic, exhorting everyone to care for one another and to follow the guidelines to suppress the spread of the virus was: "we are in this together." We are indeed companions in our journey in life, and we need to care for one another and for the world we live in. It is to *recognize*, and not just tolerate, everyone.

At the same time, it is essential to realize that every one of us has something valuable, no matter how small, to share. It also implies a certain entitlement on everyone's part to the goods of the earth because we are all its inhabitants. As we have learned from Buber, Mencius and others, we enrich ourselves, too, while enabling others. This was well illustrated and concretized by the Nobel Peace Prize committee when it awarded the 2020 prize to the U.N. Global Food Programme. It showed an awareness of the urgency to heed world problems. The head of that organization used that opportunity to urge billionaires—and others—to step up to that responsibility of relieving the hunger experienced by those who had become victims of wars, conflicts and other tragedies throughout the world.

What is of particular relevance to us here is its lesson: the waiting-time of life, that is to say, as we move along in our life-journey, is also meant to be "sharing-moments" among travel companions in life, including—and even more so—with those who for various reasons have "fallen by the wayside" no matter in what context or who caused the situation. The phrase associated with the well-known American entrepreneur, Bill Gates, can serve as a useful rallying cry: "Giving while living."

Still another observation could be added here as we continue to compare the time we spend on our ordinary trips and on the homeward-bound life-journey. On the trips we make to various destinations, most of us are likely to pick up souvenirs to remind us of the various sites we had visited. Others enjoy keeping diaries or travel journals to jot down their travel experiences. Still others preoccupy themselves with buying gifts or presents for those left behind, for family members and friends when they meet them upon their return. Somehow the idea is to treasure or share the memories we have of those trips and to anticipate the joy of giving.

In like manner, our life-journey is full of these activities, even if not as targeted as these. What this means is that whatever we do *during* our journey in life is putting together the legacy we will be leaving behind. The care and attention we give to assembling souvenirs or gifts, the compilation of diaries and the noting of journals can be likened to how we shape our legacy to those after us. Both the tangible and the intangible "products" that have arisen from our differing ways of exercising our creativity will be part of the syntheses that will result.

As a travel-map of life, the notion of creative synthesis can teach us that ultimately it is not what we acquire or possess but what we do that shapes our life-journey. In this respect it would be helpful to constantly and regularly remind ourselves that *while* on our life-journey—during the so-called "waiting-time"—we have been given the chance to make a positive difference to the world because we have passed this way and have trodden on life's paths. The footprints we ourselves leave behind will remain and will alter the course that others will follow in life.

Kamala Harris, the first female, black, south Asian-American to hold the position of USA Vice-President, rightly urges us in her message during the Inaugural Concert, broadcast in various international stations, not just to look at what has been but at what can be.[13] The young poet laureate Amanda Gorman in her poem for that same event, also carried

---

13. Harris, "Inaugural Concert," Live Broadcast, CNN News, 20 January 2019.

by numerous international presses and stations, echoes that cry to move to what shall be rather than to march back to what was.[14]

One should add that as we forge ahead through life's paths, we may even be spurred on to walk that extra mile with our co-travelers or to become vehicles for peace in the world. That is our gift and privilege. It is a more fundamental challenge—and arguably, more rewarding—than simply caring about how we will be remembered by later generations or what kind of artefacts we are putting in place. Expanding on Amanda Gorman's advice, we should aim to leave behind a world better than the one we have inherited. Our "todays" are the scene for us to work towards a better "tomorrow"—for all.[15]

At the start of our explorations there was an invitation to you, the reader, to pause and ponder and thus to create an opportunity to reflect on life while we carry on with the daily business of living. The hope in doing so was that our reflections would provide some "thoughts for food" to nourish us on our journey, and even more significantly, that the period spent doing this would spur us on to creative, responsible action.

However, the book is not meant as, and cannot be, a recipe for any specific action as such because that varies from one person or group to another and from situation to situation. Additionally, the direction we individually take or the route we choose in life depends on many factors. It is not possible, nor should it be expected in a work like this one, to deal with all the challenges we encounter or find strewn in our path as we journey in life. Hence, the approach taken here was more descriptive and reflective rather than prescriptive.

These reflections merely "point the way"(as Martin Buber characterizes his philosophy)[16] or provide "restful stops" rather than prove or argue a particular view-point. After all, regarding life with its unexpected twists and turns, it is ultimately more a matter of *thinking through* many issues ourselves—a challenge to us all as thinking beings—rather than of convincing everyone to think in the same way. Life itself is full of complications and challenges as well as satisfactions and rewards. Where it is

---

14. Gorman, Live Broadcast, CNN News, 20 January 2019.
15. Gorman, Live Broadcast, CNN News, 20 January 2019.
16. Buber, *Pointing the Way: Collected Essays*.

possible, however, we can on the whole benefit from more reflective stops and sharing our insights.

After all—to remind ourselves once again—life is a journey, not a race. It is not a solo run either. Surprisingly, at times one needs to slow down so as to make real progress. *It is during moments of stillness and silence that we become attuned to the sounds, those which truly matter in life.* We may even thereby be able to plot our journey more clearly and more meaningfully. When we pause and ponder we can then mark out what is indeed important.

Afterword

Glancing Back, Looking Ahead

THERE ARE INNUMERABLE INDIVIDUALS throughout history and in our present times whose deeds and decisions have a way of making inroads into our journeys in life. They have made an impact on us all. Sometimes they even contribute to the quality of our lives and the routes we take. But because they remain unnamed or unknown, they cannot be explicitly thanked. I want to rectify that anomaly since that good fortune has definitely been mine, too: *kayô kaya ako* (you are, therefore I am).[1] *Madamo nga salamat!* (Many thanks!).[2]

There are, of course, others who have always been on our side and are known to us. Over the years the support of my family and friends and of various academic institutions, grant bodies, scholarly societies, professional associations, scholars, colleagues, editors, publishers and students throughout the world facilitated my journey in life and my travels and made them truly rewarding. I have expressed my appreciation of their support and have put on record my sincere gratitude to them all on a number of occasions. The publication of this book provides me with yet another opportunity to acknowledge my indebtedness to all of them.

I am grateful to Cambridge Scholars Publishing for allowing me to draw on certain material contained in my earlier books with them. This has been published here with their permission. Furthermore, their kind

---

1. See footnote 11.

2. This is in Waray-waray, the language commonly spoken in Eastern Visayas, Philippines.

gesture has facilitated the expansion and further development of some of the themes in a new context. At the same time, I want to express my gratitude to Wipf and Stock Publishers and their staff for providing the opportunity to share with readers this set of reflections—a "resource" hopefully—on our journey in life. I also wish to acknowledge the much appreciated encouragement received from Mary McAleese, Former President of Ireland; from Paulus Budi Kleden, Superior-General of the Divine Word Missionaries who serve world-wide; and from John Cobb, prominent American theologian of Claremont, California. Their endorsement of this work is truly encouraging.

This work, as has been the case with all my other publications, has benefitted from the wisdom of so many others in the past and in the present. I am truly thankful to be able to draw from that wellspring and to walk in their footsteps. I do wish especially to reiterate my expression of gratitude to my wife, Marian. Not only has she been my companion and co-traveler in life but she has also been an active collaborator in my thinking and published work, including this book. She has played an important part in shaping and transforming my thoughts as well as in enriching and enlivening my written words. *Go raibh maith agat.*[3]

The invitation to join me on this reflective journey was extended to readers of various backgrounds, irrespective of any religious affiliation or none. After all, even if we hail from diverse backgrounds, we stand on common ground that is truly vast. As we journey on in life, we encounter others coming from somewhere else, but sooner or later we find ourselves taking the same highways and byways. It is illuminating to hear one another's tales and to take note of them as we travel together. There is much that we can learn about life in this way.

This book was written in the hope that it would be of interest to all readers, irrespective of background. Despite our differences in that respect, we are all on a journey in life; and there is much that we have in common. Having paused and pondered here, however, those readers who are philosophically-oriented may wish to pursue further a more systematic and extensive treatment of the themes touched on here, as well as others, in my scholarly books, particularly in *Society in its Challenges* and *Ethical Contexts and Theories*.

3. This is a Gaelic expression of thanks to an individual person.

But there may be some who would appreciate giving more attention to the religious dimension and to listening to the religious narrative along the way. In fact, for them the journey in life is a religious pilgrimage or a journey in faith. To those readers, I would like to extend another invitation by pointing them in the direction of my other books, particularly *From Suffering to God* and *From Question to Quest*, both of which were co-authored with Marian. Others may be more interested in my *Religion, Reason and God* and *The Christian Message as Vision and Mission*.

Other readers who may prefer a more literary trip as they reflect on their life journey—living has been likened indeed to writing the chapters that make up our book of life—may find our trilogy of novels more to their taste: *Those Distant Shores*, *That Elusive Fountain of Wisdom* and *This Deep Pierian Spring*. These provide instead a narrative version of the journey of life at different stages through the dialogues and life stories of the fictional characters.

The writing of this book was completed during the imposed lockdown of the country resulting from the pandemic COVID 19. This dire situation has paralyzed nations and has caused considerable and untold personal, social, economic and financial misery throughout the world. It has resulted in the tragic deaths of millions throughout the world and untold misery to those directly and indirectly affected. It continues to do so, and one sincerely looks forward to an end to it and wishes that a recovery for all will be in sight.

However, it did bring about, too, a growing realization of a global commonality and companionship—the saying that "we are all in this together" has been a constant reminder—and an explicit caring attitude which concretized a gesture of generosity on the part of individuals, groups, corporations and nations. In this respect somehow the importance of following a "moral compass" and taking personal responsibility for the common welfare, became more than just a talking point.

The pandemic has shown itself to be bigger than a health problem; it has also resulted in an economic crisis. After all, we are truly a worldwide community; and financial narcissism has a way of hurting us all. Even in this context, we are co-travelers. Co-operation, rather than competition, does have its advantages—even in monetary terms. Referring to the availability of the vaccine to poorer countries, the IMF has argued that a global recovery from the economic downturn caused by the pandemic can only be achieved when there is world-wide attention to the health of all countries. It has therefore urged wealthier nations, for their own good, to contribute to the expenses of sponsoring vaccines for deprived nations. It is encouraging to learn that recently the G7 nations have heeded that call and have decided to donate vaccines to them. One would sincerely wish that more attention would be given to this urgent mission and that the desired results would be achieved.

With the situation caused by the pandemic there has additionally been a realization of the importance of having what has been termed a "road map" provided by the health and public authorities. It is expected to guide people's conduct as they maneuver their way in the changed and changing terrain, described as "the new normal," trespassed by the virus. It also challenged the creativity of many who, impeded in their usual routine, channeled their expertise into rather innovative ways of dealing with specific issues or situations arising from the pandemic. In this scenario one cannot help but be reminded of some of the observations made in this book about our journey in life itself and its challenges.

It also seems that for some the enforced curtailment of personal and social lives as a way of halting the spread of the virus created a rather unplanned opportunity and the environment to re-examine their priorities and re-evaluate the paths which they had been taking in their journeys in life. Somehow, it made them appreciate the need to "pause and ponder" while dealing with the situation. Many discovered—or re-discovered—not only the health benefits but also the psychological rewards arising from their walks, on their own or with a companion, which they undertook because of the restrictions. While one would value that welcome opportunity and would wish that important practice to continue, as has been suggested by this book, one would, nevertheless, wish that the context had been different. One can only hope that the longed-for change of scenario will take place in the very near future but that the practice of "pausing to ponder" would continue.

As hope takes over and brings its solace, there is a sense that somehow, despite the toll exacted by the pandemic on the lives of people, it is still true that despite the changes in their lifestyle, they will continue to affirm life itself. To borrow a saying used in another setting, *Vita mutatur sed non tollitur*. The pandemic may have altered the course of living, but it has not blocked it altogether. Furthermore, there is indeed an urgent need to consider a change of direction in the way we conduct our lives

Afterword

and the goals we set up for ourselves. Perhaps, another route in life may be in place.

Along these lines, one recalls what the poet Percy Bysshe Shelley wrote, that if winter comes, spring cannot be too far behind.[4] Coincidentally and happily, the long-awaited vaccines are now making their way in some countries to the population, very much like the sun's rays as they reach out to the various nooks and corners of the world.

Indeed, looking ahead in our journey of life—and pausing to ponder during our "comma-moments"—we should continue to bear in mind time and again that *creative synthesis* which pervades reality can reassure us that while the past is inherited and accounts for the present, we can help shape the future. And even if we may have to admit that at times life seems to be more a *Gift* (German), it is to a considerable extent truly a gift. It should be treasured; but more significantly, our creativity should be put into efficacious use. That is our choice as well as our responsibility. As a life-map this way of thinking can deepen our understanding and motivate our actions. It could stir up hope and may even bring about more positive results.

As we now resume our life-journey on our respective routes towards our own individual destinations it may be appropriate to draw a couple of lines from an oft-quoted traditional Irish blessing as a parting wish: "May the road rise to meet you./May the wind be always at your back."

Let me add my own *farewell*: I hope that we will all *fare well* in our life-journeys

---

4. Shelley, "Ode to the West Wind," *The Penguin Book of English Verse*, 284–286.

Selected Bibliography

Angelou, Maya. "Human Family." In *I Shall not be Moved*. 2. N.Y.: Penguin Random House, 1990.
Aristotle, *Nicomachean Ethics*. N.Y.: Macmillan, 1989.
Arnold, Matthew. "Dover Beach." In *The Penguin Book of English Verse*, edited by John Hayward, 344–45. Harmondsworth, U.K.: Penguin Books, 1970.
"What Would You Say to the Men who Killed your Mum?" BBC Programme, February 17, 2020.
Beckett, Samuel. *Waiting for Godot*. London: Faber and Faber, 1972.
Biden, Joe. "Inaugural Address." Presidential Inauguration. Live broadcast, CNN, Jan. 20, 2021.
———."Lighting Ceremony." Live broadcast, CNN, Jan. 19, 2021.
Bishop, Elizabeth. "The Prodigal." In *New Discovery*, edited by Patrick Murray et al., 19. Dublin: The Educational Company, 2005.
Braithwaite, William Stanley. "It's a Long Way." https://poets.org.
Buber, Martin. "The Education of Character." In *Between Man and Man*, 132–47. London: Collins, Fontana Library, 1973.
———. "Replies to my Critics." In *The Philosophy of Martin Buber,* edited by Paul Arthur Schilpp and Maurice S. Friedman, 693–699. La Salle, Illinois: Open Court, 1967.
———. *Between Man and Man*. London: Collins, Fontana Library, 1973.
———. *I and Thou*. Edinburgh: T. & T. Clark, 1966.
———. *Pointing the Way: Collected Essays*. N.Y.: Harper & Row, 1963.
Camara, Helder. *The Spiral of Violence*. London: Sheed & Ward, 1986.
Campbell, Thomas. "The River of Life." https://www.poetry.com › poem › the-river-of-life.
Cannon, Moya. "Flowers know nothing of our grief." In *Collected Poems*, 82. Manchester, U.K.: Carcanet, 2021.
Carey, C.V. *Mind the Stop: a Brief Guide to Punctuation*. Harmondsworth, U.K.: Penguin Books 1983.
Confucius, *The Analects*. Harmondsworth, U.K.: Penguin Books, 1988.
Dickens, Charles. *A Tale of Two Cities*. N.Y.: Baronet Press, 2008.

Dickinson, Emily. "'Hope' is the thing with feathers." *New Explorations*, edited by John G. Fahy, 49. Dublin: Gill & Macmillan, 2013.

Donne, John. "For Whom the Bell Tolls." https://allpoetry.com › For-whom-the-Bell-Tolls.

Dostoyevsky, Fyodor. *The Brothers Karamazov*. Harmondsworth, U.K.: Penguin 1967.

Eliot, G. *Middlemarch: a Study of Provincial Life*. London: Penguin Books, 1994.

Foley, Thomas. "Drop a Pebble in the Water." https://www.poetrynook.com.

Frankl, Viktor E. *Man's Search for Meaning: the Classic Tribute to Hope from the Holocaust*. London: Rider, 2021.

Frost, Robert. *Robert Frost: Selected Poems*, edited by Ian Hamilton. Harmondswoth, U.K.: Penguin Books, 1973.

Gorman, Amanda. "The Hill We Climb." Presidential Inauguration of Joe Biden. Live broadcast, CNN, Jan. 20, 2021.

Hardy, Thomas. "Nature's Questioning." In *Selected Shorter Poems of Thomas Hardy*, 6–7. London and Basingstoke: Macmillan, 1971.

Harris, Kamala. "Inaugural Concert." Live Broadcast, CNN News, 20 January 2019.

Hartshorne, Charles. *Creative Synthesis and Philosophic Method*. London: SCM Press, 1970.

Heaney, Seamus. *The Cure at Troy*. London: Faber & Faber, 2018.

Hopkins, Gerard Manley. "Thou art indeed just, Lord, if I contend." In *Poems and Prose of Gerard Manley Hopkins*, 67. Harmondsworth, U.K.: Penguin Books, 1971.

Hume, David. *Dialogues Concerning Natural Religion*. Vancouver: Royal Classics, 2021.

Irish News. "RTE Interview with Andrew McGinley." https://www.irishtimes.com › news › ireland › irish-news, 24 Nov. 2021.

Irish Post, "No medal, but Irish gymnast Rhys McClenaghan wins plaudits," https://www.irishpost.com › sport

Ishiguro, Kazuo. "Nobel Lecture." https://www.nobelprize.org>uploads>2018/06.

Kavanagh, Patrick. "Lines Written on a Seat on the Grand Canal, Dublin." In *chief Modern Poets of Britain and America*, Vol. I: Poets of Britain edited by Gerald DeWitt Sanders et al. 332. N.Y. and London: Macmillan, 1970.

———. *The Great Hunger*. 10, Section XII. London: Penguin Modern, 2018.

Kushner, Harold. *When all you have ever wanted is not enough*. N.Y.: Pocket Books, 1987.

———. *When Bad Things Happen to Good People*. London: Pan Books, 2011.

Labaki, Nadine and Khaled Mouzanar. *Capernaum*. Film, 2018.

Lao Tzu *The Tao te Ching*. N.Y.: Paragon House, 1989.

Lewis, C.S. *Mere Christianity*. London: HarperCollins, 1998.

Libera-Going Home-YouTube, https://www.youtube.com.

Longfellow, Henry Wadsworth. "The Arrow and the Song." https://www.poetryfoundation.org

———. "The Secret of the Sea." https://www.hwlongfellow.org>poem.

———. "The Tide Rises, the Tide Falls." https://poets.org.

Marcel, Gabriel. *Homo Viator: an Introduction to the Metaphysic of Hope*. South Bend, Ind.: St. Augustine's, 2010.

McKibben, Candace. "Like islands in the sea, our connections run deep." https://eu.tallahassee.com/story/life/faith/2018/05/11/like-islands-sea-connections-run-deep/602770002/.

Mencius, *Mencius*. London: Penguin Books, 1988.

Milton, John. "Lycidas." In *The English Parnassus: an Anthology Chiefly of Longer Poems*. 132–135. Oxford: Clarendon Press, 1967.

———. "On His Blindness." In *The Penguin Book of English Verse*. 147–148. Harmondsworth: Penguin, 1970.

Murdoch Mysteries (Canadian Television Series).

Niblett, Robin. Webinar: "Global Leadership and International Co-operation in the Context of COVID 19 and Beyond." chaired by Dr. Robin Niblett CHG, Director and Chief Executive Chatham House, July 10, 2020.

Obama, Barrack. "The Inauguration of Joe Biden." Presidential Inauguration. Live broadcast, CNN, Jan. 20, 2021.

Plath, Sylvia. "Crossing the Water." https://www.internal.org › Sylvia_Plath › Crossing the River.

Pope, Alexander. "An Essay on Criticism." In *The English Parnassus: an Anthology Chiefly of Longer Poems*. 199–214. Oxford: Clarendon Press, 1967.

Pope Francis. *Vatican News*. September 5, 2018; December 25, 2020; April 12, 2021.

Rumi, "When I Die." https://allpoetry.com/poem/14327689-When-I-Die-by-Mewlana-Jalaluddin-Rumi.

Saroyan, William. *The Time of Your Life*. 5-act play, 1939 Methuen Drama. London: A & C Black. 2008.

Schrader, Paul. *First Reformed*. Film 2017.

Shakespeare, William. *The Complete Works of William Shakespeare: Comprising His Plays and Poems*. Spring Books, 1968.

Shelley, Percy Bysshe. "Ode to the West Wind." In *The Penguin Book of English Verse* 284–86. Harmondsworth: Penguin Books, 1970.

Sia, M.F. and S.Sia. *That Elusive Fountain of Wisdom: an Enquiry into the Human Thirst for Knowledge*. Newcastle upon Tyne: Cambridge Scholars, 2015.

———. *This Deep Pierian Spring: An Account of the Human Quest for Meaning*. Newcastle upon Tyne: Cambridge Scholars, 2016.

———. *Those Distant Shores: A Narrative of Human Restlessness*. Newcastle upon Tyne: Cambridge Scholars, 2015.

Thackeray, William Makepeace. *Vanity Fair*. London: Penguin Books, 2006.

Tolkien, J.R.R. *The Lord of the Rings*. London: Unwin Paperbacks, 1985.

Tolstoy, Leo. *War and Peace*. N.Y. Schriber's, 1929.

Whitehead, Alfred North. *The Aims of Education and Other Essays*. N.Y.: The Free Press Paperback Edition, 1967.

Wordsworth, Henry. "I Wandered Lonely as a Cloud." In *British and American Poets: Chaucer to the Present* edited by W. Jackson Bate and David Perkins. 401. San Diego: Harcourt Brace Jovanovich, Publishers, 1986.

Wyatt, Thomas. 15: "They fle from me that sometyme did me seke." In *English Sixteenth Century Verse: an Anthology* edited by Richard S. Sylvester, 138–39. N.Y. and London: W.W. Norton & Company, 1984.

Yeats, William Butler. "Sailing to Byzantium." In *The Works of W.B. Yeats*. 163–164. Ware, Hertfordshire: Wordsworth Editions, 1994.

www.ingramcontent.com/pod-product-compliance
Lightning Source LLC
Chambersburg PA
CBHW062024220426
43662CB00010B/1462